THE BUMPER BOOK OF GOVERNMENT WASTE 2008

BROWN'S SQUANDERED BILLIONS

MATTHEW ELLIOTT

AND

LEE ROTHERHAM

Hh

Harriman House Ltd
3A Penns Road
Petersfield
Hampshire
GU32 2EW

Tel. +44 (0)1730 233870
Fax +44(0)1730 233880
Email: enquiries@harriman-house.com
Website: www.harriman-house.com

First published in Great Britain in 2007 by Harriman House Ltd.
Copyright © Harriman House Ltd

The rights of Matthew Elliott and Lee Rotherham to be
identified as the authors have been asserted in accordance with
the Copyright, Design and Patents Act 1988.

ISBN 1-905-64148-6
ISBN13 978-1-905641-48-2

British Library Cataloguing in Publication Data
A CIP catalogue record for this book can be obtained from the
British Library.

Printed and bound by CPI Group, Mackays.

Praise for the first Bumper Book, 2006

The first edition of *The Bumper Book of Government Waste* was published in 2006. It won the 2007 'Sir Antony Fisher International Memorial Award', one of the judges of which commented "You can scarcely write a more congenial book about this subject." It also received widespread coverage in the national press:

"…an amazing new book."

Paul Gilfeather, *Sunday Mirror*

"…one of the publishing success stories of the year."
Patrick O'Flynn, *Daily Express*

"Few books perform a greater public service in exposing the myth that 'government knows best' how to spend taxpayer funds."

Bill Jamieson, *The Business*

"…an extraordinary exposé… fascinating."
Jonathan Isaby, *Daily Telegraph*

"…riveting, and occasionally excruciating."
Alasdair Palmer, *The Sunday Telegraph*

"Never again will I query my wife's shopping bill, having learnt how much the Department for Work and Pensions has spent on office furniture."
Jonathan Maitland, *The Mail on Sunday*

"A well researched new book."
William Rees-Mogg, *The Mail on Sunday*

"…deceptively light-hearted … serves well as both a primer and a wake-up call."
John Massey, *The European Journal*

About the authors

Matthew Elliott was born and brought up in Leeds. In 1997, he moved to London to study at the London School of Economics, where he graduated with a First class B.Sc. in Government. After graduation, he then worked for a number of MPs and MEPs in the House of Commons and the European Parliament.

In 2004, Matthew founded the TaxPayers' Alliance with Andrew Allum and Florence Heath. Under his leadership, the TPA has grown from operating as a band of volunteers meeting in Starbucks, to employing six members of staff working from offices in London and Birmingham, generating more media coverage than any other independent political organisation in the UK.

In 2006, the TPA won the ConservativeHome 'One to Watch' award and in 2007 the first *Bumper Book of Government Waste*, also co-authored with Dr Lee Rotherham, was awarded the Sir Antony Fisher Memorial Award.

Matthew is on the UK Advisory Board of the European Foundation and the Advisory Committee of the New Culture Forum. In 2007, he was elected a Fellow of the RSA.

Dr Lee Rotherham is officially a one-man think tank, according to an old lady he met at a Bruges Group reception once. His life's highlights to date include using Mount Etna to heat up a mortadella ciabatta; getting involved in a gunfight with the future King of England (the Eton Rifles wandered into the wrong bit of the training area); standing on top of the Ziggurat of Ur while serving with HM Forces in Iraq; and making life a misery for numerous Europhile politicians during the drafting of the EU Constitution.

To the 15,976 grassroot supporters of the
TaxPayers' Alliance, especially the 3,267 donors
who have kept the TPA afloat.

Acknowledgements

When Philip Jenks from Harriman House approached the TaxPayers' Alliance in the autumn of 2005 to turn our annual Bumper Book of Government Waste – then a simple PDF – into a commercial book, it must have required a real leap of faith. At the time, the TPA was a small operation, with only one member of staff working out of a dingy office in Victoria. Now, helped in no small part by the success of the first *Bumper Book* published by Harriman House in 2006, we have six members of staff, working from two offices in London and Birmingham, coordinating over 15,000 activists, and generating more media coverage than any other independent political organisation in the UK.

We would like to thank a panoply of people for assorted snippets and tip-offs provided during the research of this book. Some must remain nameless. As warriors on waste in the Mother of all spending battles, Sirs, Ladies, we nevertheless salute your indefatigability. You know who you are.

We would also like to take this opportunity to thank *Florence Heath, Andrew Allum, Tim Aker, Jens-Peter Bonde MEP, Charlotte Bown, Lisi Christofferson, Mike Denham, John Hayes MP, Allister Heath, Chris Heaton-Harris MEP, Mart Laar MEP Simon McGee, Hazel Mowbray, Tim Pollard, Matthew Sinclair, Corin Taylor, Gawain Towler, Sheridan Westlake, Eben Wilson, Mike Wood* and, especially, Philip Jenks, our editor, and the team at Harriman House.

Always remember, fighting waste is a task that all of us can partake in, at every level of government. Smash the System! Well, alright, give it a good flush.

Contents

SECTION 1

An Introduction to Government Waste

Greetings, fellow tax sufferers. Welcome once again to the TaxPayers' Alliance Shangri-La of Government spending, in which mystery land we discover the outlandish and other-worldly manner in which other people take your money and then spend it on things which you don't want, didn't ask for, and don't need.

Unless, of course, you are an artiste with a penchant for videotaping beach scenes of naked people wrapped in light bulbs. But more on that later.

We welcome back readers of the first *Bumper Book of Government Waste* with the promise of a spankingly fresh look at frittering taxes. Sadly, the civil servants have failed to grasp the nettle in so many cases that a veritable wildlife sanctuary remains spread out in a vista before our eyes. Yet this allows us, David Attenborough-like, to descend into new nooks and crannies, to paint you a scene of profligacy that is occasionally obscene, sometimes funny, but all too often simply infuriating.

To our new readers, don't be afraid. This is no arcane tome nor leather-bound codex that spells out, in sorcerous depths and faded ink, the mysteries of accountancy.

Accountancy sucks. If you are an accountant, we apologise. You are doing a great job. Without you, the world would be full of corruption, fraud, mismanagement, and Mafiosi. Just like the European Union. Jam-packed full of imaginary, subsidy-loving goats, with olive groves only marginally less fictitious than Atlantis. But we intend to take you beyond mere number-crunching and show you the real costs of all this waste.

Let's begin with some definitions so we know what we are talking about. For starters, our sources are taken in the main from open reporting. It might be something that has been published by officialdom, for instance the Official Journal of the European Union, or an annual report from a government department. It might be something from one of the watchdogs, such as the National Audit Office, Parliament's Public Accounts Committee, or the Court of Auditors in Luxembourg. It might again be a response to a Parliamentary Question (PQ) in Westminster, Edinburgh, or Brussels. It could be material that has been covered in the national or local media. Or we might just have had a tip-off. There is no shortage of material, unfortunately. But where possible, all sources are attributed on the TaxPayers' Alliance website.

Now let's define Waste. We define it as meaning either money spent that need not have been spent at all, or money spent on a project which yielded a benefit disproportionately low compared with the amount spent. Thus, a million pounds of taxpayers' money spent on creating ten jobs may or may not be considered value for money, depending on whether the jobs:

– were in an area of high unemployment

– were for the long term

– were not a permanent drain on the public purse

– added something to the local economy or demonstrably to the quality of life

– didn't put other people out of a job through direct competition

– encouraged the creation of more private sector jobs

A million pounds spent that did none of these things, that was spent to keep the unemployed off the unemployed statistics list for a year, or which created just the one job, clearly is not. Even if that one job happens to be yours.

You might as well blow the million by handing it over to civil servants to host office parties, drive around in taxis, or buy dandy furnishings for their desk surrounds. But then, that's precisely what they sometimes do.

So join us as we explore the money lines. Some are shocking examples of waste. Others are areas for debate and controversy. Other examples we include as entertaining snippets, so that you're aware of how government works. Just sit back and enjoy the ride.

A Big Hello to the Treasury

At this point, we would like to take the opportunity to welcome some of our book's biggest fans.

The chaps down at 11 Downing Street were very, very interested to hear of the launch of the first edition last year. Just after it was published, Treasury Minister John Healey, accompanied by two of his policy wonks, came out of the Hallowed Sanctum of Whitehall to debate with us on Sky.

Sadly, it was a missed opportunity. Rather than pick up on all the waste that we had helpfully collated, our Treasury friends went all aggressive. They pointed out that they were conducting a series of cutbacks, and even if the targeted savings fell way short of the waste, we in the TaxPayers' Alliance were being beastly for not giving them credit.

Of course, we have been giving them credit. £82 billion last year alone. How much were the Treasury trying to save? A quarter of that. The UK economy grows by that much every year.

They also criticised us for using data that was more than a year old. Well, we use the most up-to-date data they give us. It's not our fault if, for example, the Financial Statements for the Building Research Establishment dating from 1996-97 only got to MPs desks in 2006. Come on Ministers, give us a break!

The Texans have a saying for people who talk big and have nothing to back it up – "all hat and no cattle". Until politicians crack on with serious reform, regardless of which party they belong to, they can expect you, the taxpayer, to rightfully challenge them and hold them to account.

This year, we also dedicate the book to those officials in government departments (and we have met some of them) who recognise the problem and who are trying to do something about it – even if sometimes their ministerial bosses and line manager big cheeses tell them to deposit their comments in the small round metal filing cabinet in the corner of the room, which the PFI contract lady comes in now and again to empty.

The White Elephants' Graveyard

So you've handed over your bag of denarii. The Emperor's tax collectors are not going to chop your head off. This is good. You are relieved. But then later in the day, when you are popping out for an amphora of olive oil, you get some infuriating news. Your hard-earned tax money is being thrown at a whopping pay rise for the public sector so they don't rebel and the soldiers don't come out on the streets. Your hard work as a potter is being taken in order to pay off the gang leaders of a greedy part of government.

Plus ça change. So like 1970s Britain.

It's one thing to fork out huge taxes, but to find they've been squandered by incompetent ministers, injudicious civil servants, or for misplaced party politicking is doubly infuriating. We have had to face them throughout the centuries.

Here are some examples of public spending and state planning that have not gone entirely according to plan. It might make you feel better to know what your ancestors had to put up with too.

415 BC   Athenians equip a grand expedition and attack Syracuse. Their army is captured. Prisoners are forced to work a hellish quarry. Those who could recite from the playwright Euripides were set free – an early demonstration of the value of a classical education. But the Athenian Empire never recovers.

259 BC   Massive work begins on what becomes the four thousand miles of the Great Wall of China. The burdens of forced labour lead to revolution. The purpose of the wall is to keep out foreigners. It has been attracting tourists ever since.

255 BC   Punic Wars. Three quarters of a massive Roman fleet is lost in a storm. The fleet is rebuilt. Two years later, it is lost in a storm. It is rebuilt. Four years later it's lost in a storm.

AD 80   Titus inaugurates the Colosseum with 100 days of gladiators and 11,000 slain animals. These days, doing a computer graphics version with Russell Crowe is a snip at $100 million.

AD 140   Returning to the mural theme, the Antonine Wall is built to keep out the highland barbarians, and give the legionaries something to do. It is a mere stripling of a fortification at 39 miles long. The blueprint dictates that it should have gated forts every two miles, even where the gate opens over a cliff. It is abandoned after forty years as the Romans withdraw back to Hadrian's Wall.

1097   Crusaders visit the Byzantine emperor. They witness his fabulous throne, which flies up and down and has a water organ and singing birds, crafted at opulent cost. A rough and ready Frankish count fails to be impressed by this Blackpoolery and plonks himself down on it.

13th C. Roger Bacon kick-starts the quest to transmute lead into gold. Dante confines alchemists to the Inferno; JK Rowling to Hogwarts.

1570   Work concludes on Berwick ramparts to keep Scots out. This massive, high-tech project is the leading drain on the Treasury for the period. A Scottish monarch succeeds to the English throne 30 years later.

1677   James II builds Charles Fort in south-west Ireland. His soldiers find out twelve years later that though it dominates Kinsale, the neighbouring hill dominates the fort. They surrender.

1698   Scottish settlers found the colony of Darien at Panama. The locals aren't interested in the trinkets; fever wipes out colonists in droves; and the massive debts lead to the Act of Union with England.

1803   Louisiana Purchase. The Senate goes ape when negotiators tell them that instead of getting access to the Mississippi, they have blown $23 million. Only later does it sink in that they've bought the best part of 15 future states, or a quarter of the modern USA, for 3c an acre. Though the land will have to be bought from the native peoples as well, it marks the end to the Cheese Eating Surrender Monkey Empire in North America.

1861   Fortress déjà vu. American Civil War begins in tragi-farce. Fort Sumter surrenders to the Confederates when it finds it has been built in such a way that it can't return fire. The only death comes when the salute is fired during the evacuation.

1932   Forced collectivisation in the Ukraine creates famine, as all the grain is handed over. Peasants who do not look as if they are starving are shot by Stalin for hoarding. As many as 6 million die.

WW2   Germans capture a key laboratory researching armour-cleaving artillery shells made from tungsten. But Occupied Europe has the last laugh. The scientists finish the project just before liberation, and only after using up all the available tungsten.

1958   Great Leap Forward. Mao experiments with collectivisation, reportedly against Kruschev's advice. Crop yields crash while reserves are sat on. Forty million perish. Mao unleashes the Cultural Revolution to reconsolidate his power.

1975   An horrific social experiment in Cambodia means lowlanders freeze to death in the forests, highlanders starve in the paddy fields, and city dwellers are forced on death marches into the countryside. People with glasses are killed, beaten to death to save on bullets. Perhaps a third of the population dies.

1995   Transparency International starts to publish its annual international corruption index. Brits get smug, until they realise where their EU money is going.

2000   Mass panic makes Y2K bigger than U2. Billions of pounds are spent on the Millennium Bug, ensuring that the only piece of equipment that goes offline is the 400-year-old brass Equatorium in Liverpool Museum, which calculates planetary positions, and is a bit outdated anyway.

2001   Foot and Mouth in Britain. Sod the vaccine, let's burn £8 billion.

2006   The Deputy Prime Minister sets up the Decent Places to Live project, then realises that his Office doesn't have the legal power to pay it out. So the money sits around.

2007   Someone looking around the private quarters of former President of Cyprus Archbishop Makarios III, nearly 30 years after his death, opens a storage room. They find two buckets containing gold dust and ancient gold and silver coins that have simply, ahem, been forgotten.

The World's First Tax Cut

"You can have a lord, you can have a king, But the man to fear is the tax collector!"

Ancient Sumerian proverb

It is thanks to the diligent research of an outstanding scholar of ancient Mesopotamia that we have an insight into how old the principle of liberal economics really is. Professor Kramer's deciphering of archaic inscriptions, discovered at the side of a canal in Mesopotamia, show that the tendency of the state to tax and oppress is older than the monuments themselves.

Lagash was a city state in Sumer, modern day Iraq. In previous times it had been a benevolent sort of theocracy, in which the ruling exacted tithes, but not at an oppressive level.

By the twenty-fourth century BC, the scene had changed. The Ur-Nanshe dynasty had ambitions, and it expanded to cover large swathes of the civilised world. For a brief while it ruled supreme, but at a price. That price was paid by the ordinary citizen.

The ancient texts reveal what life was like for the man on the street. In the main, they were farmers and traders, merchants and fishermen, craftsmen and boatsmen of the Tigris. While a proportion of land was owned by the temple, this too was rented out, and much was privately owned. Even the poor owned property and chattels. Enterprise thrived, and trade prospered.

This, of course, made the citizens targets for rulers in need of funds. Personal rights and cherished freedoms were quashed as the rulers gobbled up private wealth to support their armies and administration. But the successes proved ephemeral, and the burdens became even more oppressive to prop up the decaying state. Even in years of peace, the wealth that was brought into the hands of the powerful meant that the wartime taxes were maintained, while the weak were abused and dispossessed.

The inscriptions tell a sorry tale. The inspector of the boatmen seized the boats. The inspector of the cattle seized the large cattle, then the small cattle. The fisheries inspector seized the fisheries. Sheep were taxed when they were sheared. The divorcing man paid a tax. The perfumer preparing unguents paid a tax. The temple property was confiscated, so that the oxen of the Gods ploughed the onion and cucumber patches of the monarch in the Gods' best fields. Everyone got in on the act, the vizier and the palace doorkeeper taking their cut.

As Professor Kramer observes:

> *"Even death brought no relief from levies and taxes. When a dead man was brought to the cemetery for burial, a number of officials and parasites made it their business to be on hand to relieve the bereaved family of quantities of barley, bread, and beer, and various furnishings. From one end of the state to the other, our historian observes bitterly, 'There were the tax collectors.' No wonder the palace waxed fat and prosperous."*

And you thought inheritance tax was a modern invention.

However, a hero stepped to the fore. Urukagina became ruler, and instigated a financial revolution. He removed the inspector of the boatmen from the boats. He removed the cattle inspector from the cattle. He removed the fisheries inspector from the fisheries. He removed the collector of the sheep shearing tax. He ended the divorce tax. He stopped collecting tax when perfume was prepared. On burial, the revenue take was greatly reduced. At the same time, the injustices in the land that had been perpetrated against the weaker citizens were ended, and justice was restored.

Sadly, these reforms came too late for Lagash. Its strength and power had been sapped by decades of abuse. The golden age of Urukagina lasted only ten years, and his reforms were thereafter "gone with the wind". The neighbouring city of Umma eclipsed the old power, and its ruler Lugalzaggisi swept into Lagash in his chariots.

A harsh lesson lies there for all of us who seek to defer hard decisions on tax and waste.

The Price of Government

This year, the British Government is spending a lot of money on your behalf.

It is so big, we don't think it lies within human knowledge to properly picture it. But let's try.

The total amount of money constructively flowing around the UK economy is about £1.2 trillion. That sounds a lot, but it works out at enough to give £1,000 to everyone in India and Pakistan. Incidentally, it's in the order of magnitude of the total mortgage debt of UK homeowners, just to give you something else to panic about.

The government's take of that has increased over the last few years. According to the OECD, it was 37.5% in 2000. In 2007, it is estimated to be 45.3%. This means we are now way behind the United States (36.9%) and Japan (36.2%) in having a competitive economy, and about to fall behind Germany, whose tax take is high but falling.

In practical terms, consider this: if we were paying the tax rate we were paying in 2000 instead of the one we will be paying in 2007-08, the country would be paying £93.6 billion less.

On an individual scale, that translates as a tax hike of £1,545 for each person in the country. That's how much extra is being drained from the economy to fund central government schemes.

It gets worse. The latest figures show that the government ran a deficit in 2006 of approaching £30 billion. This is the amount it spent more than it collected through taxes.

As a comparison, the Bank of England has gold and foreign currency reserves, in total, of around two thirds of that overspend.

Not only, therefore, is it taking more money from the taxpayer, and crucially taking more money from the people who generate wealth to provide the taxes, but it even has to take out loans and indebt us in the process.

This is, frankly, incompetent financial management.

Where is all this money spent? Here are the big takers:

- £121 billion goes on social security spending. The concept is fine, until you look at the levels of fraud and the disincentives in the system that stop people going back to work.

- £30 billion goes on debt interest – simply paying the creditors for money loaned to the government.

- £104 billion goes into the NHS, including administration (the pensions scheme alone absorbs £10 billion and is going up by a billion a year).

By comparison, the Department of Transport has a budget of £20 billion to keep Britain moving.

Government spending 2007-08

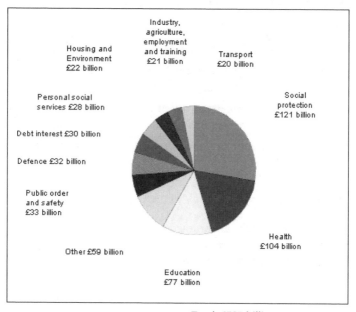

Total: £587 billion

Source: Chart 1.1, Budget 2007, HM Treasury

It doesn't take a rocket scientist to realise that with such massive budgets, there might be room for some savings. But when you learn that some departmental budgets have tripled in a handful of years; that money has flowed into public sector coffers faster than management have shown themselves capable of (sensibly) spending it; and that government itself has said that there is scope for £21.5 billion of cutbacks; well, then you know something has gone horribly wrong.

That £21.5 billion sum is what the government came up with in the review it commissioned, undertaken by Sir Peter Gershon. Those Gershon savings could have been spotted and put into place back in 2000, when the public sector spending started to really take off. How much has that failure cost us? Even allowing for gradiated growth over the years – in other words that the costs snuck up on government bit by bit – it suggests that the government admits having wasted £65 billion of our money since the report was published.

That's enough from our pay packets to buy everyone in the country a 250-year subscription to *Readers' Digest*; or around 15 years of free sports cable for every household in the country.

If concentrated in one place, it's enough to make everyone in a town the size of Gosport or Inverness a millionaire overnight.

Did anyone get fired for this waste? Answers on a postcard please to Number 10 Downing Street.

£101 Billion of Waste

But how much of the government's current £587 billion budget – funded from taxes we could otherwise choose to spend or save ourselves – is being wasted?

We've done some sums. Obviously, we don't have an army of accountants or civil servants at our beck and call. Nor do we have free and easy access to all the tomes and ledgers that would reveal the hidden costs and arcane tax pitfalls. But we believe the ballpark figure to be basically right.

We estimate that the government is currently wasting £101 billion of our hard-earned money.

Item	Waste	Explanation
Road building overruns	£36,826,087	According to the National Audit Office (NAO), overruns in road building by local authorities and the Department of Transport cost nearly £37 million.
Abolish the Common Fisheries Policy	£46,890,232	Abolishing the Common Fisheries Policy, which has failed to protect fish stocks and hurts the interests of British fishermen, would save British taxpayers nearly £47 million, as well as helping the British fishing industry.
CAP late payment fine	£65,500,000	There is a strong possibility that the UK government will be fined for its failure to make CAP payments on time. We're assuming that there is a roughly 50% chance that DEFRA will have to use the money they've set aside to pay the fine. If they use half of their contingency fund, taxpayers will be worse off by over £65 million.
Better management of NHS staff costs	£78,000,000	The Department of Health estimate that the NHS could save £78 million by improving productivity and managing agency staff costs more effectively.
Public sector fraud	£111,000,000	The National Fraud Initiative estimates that the total cost of fraud to the public sector was £111 million in 2004. It has probably risen since then.

Legal Aid overspend	£130,000,000	If the Legal Aid budget were more tightly controlled, £130 million could be saved for taxpayers.
Failed CSA reform	£200,000,000	Since 2003, over £1 billion has been spent attempting to reform the CSA. The Agency has now been abolished and its functions reassigned, but we still have to cover a fifth of this bill – £200 million – this year.
Government advertising, marketing and PR increase	£211,000,000	Reversing the increase in spending on government advertising, marketing and PR since 1997 would save taxpayers £211 million.
More efficient food procurement	£220,000,000	The National Audit Office has identified potential savings in food procurement of £220 million across the public sector.
Reduce unused prescriptions	£300,000,000	Every year £300 million could be saved by reducing the amount of drugs dispensed by the NHS but never used by patients.
Missed hospital appointments	£307,000,000	If the NHS cut the number of missed appointments in half it could save £307 million.
Supporting failed asylum seekers	£308,000,000	Britain spends £308 million every year supporting failed asylum seekers.
Tax Credit fraud and overpayment written off	£380,000,000	Over the last five years £1.9 billion has been written off in Tax Credit fraud and overpayment. £380 million is a fifth of that figure.

New consultants contract	£572,000,000	Only 19% of NHS trusts and 12% of consultants think the new consultants' contract has improved patient care. So approximately 80% of the cost of the new contract has been spent by trusts who believe the money has been wasted.
Selling government assets	£708,000,000	Selling government assets such as Channel 4, the Royal Mint, Bisham Abbey would produce a one-off windfall of £708 million for taxpayers.
Hospital infection	£1,000,000,000	Infections caught in NHS hospitals cost taxpayers £1 billion every year.
Sure Start	£1,000,000,000	According to research for the British Medical Journal, the government is spending £1 billion a year on a Sure Start Scheme that "may make crime worse".
Public sector sick leave	£1,100,000,000	If levels of sick leave in the public sector were reduced to those in the private sector £1.1 billion could be saved.
Halve public sector use of consultants	£1,400,000,000	According to the National Audit Office, "there is some way to go before central government overall is achieving good value for money from its use of consultants". If the use of consultants was halved, £1.4 billion of taxpayers' money would be saved.

Public sector IT waste	£1,590,000,000	It is estimated that the public sector spends £15.7 billion each year (and rising) on information technology. According to the Work and Pensions Committee there is "a significant proportion at risk of being wasted". Assuming that just 10% is wasted, that amounts to nearly £1.6 billion.
Get a third of claimants off Incapacity Benefit	£2,197,000,000	Frank Field MP estimates it should be possible to get a third of Incapacity Benefit claimants into work. Doing so would create nearly £2.2 billion in savings for taxpayers.
End unfair Barnett Formula	£2,282,137,400	If Scottish public spending were restricted to the same level as that of the North East – a much poorer region – nearly £2.3 billion could be saved.
NHS NPfIT overspend	£2,380,000,000	The NHS National Programme for IT (NPfIT) will cost up to five times the previously stated cost of £6.2 billion over 10 years, meaning that the total bill could be as high as £30 billion, representing an overspend of nearly £2.4 billion a year for ten years.
Subsidising foreign farmers	£2,580,000,000	Britain's net contribution to the EU budget is £6 billion a year. About 43% of the EU budget is allocated to the CAP, which means that £2.58 billion of our net contribution goes to subsidising farmers in other European countries.

Fraud and mistakes in the benefit system	£2,600,000,000	According to a recent National Audit Office report, fraud and mistakes in the benefits system cost taxpayers £2.6 billion a year. Labour MP Frank Field believes that the real figure could be as high as £7 billion.
Major defence projects overrun	£2,700,000,000	This is the amount that could be saved if defence projects kept to budget. We have ignored the reductions the MoD claimed since last year as, according to the NAO, "these re-allocations do not represent a saving to the Department as a whole. By transferring the costs elsewhere the Department potentially may have to forgo other activities, which could previously have been provided, or make corresponding efficiency gains to accommodate the expenditure."
Local Government procurement savings	£3,000,000,000	The CBI says that huge savings can be made by making local government procurement more efficient.
Rise in cost of central government administration	£5,322,619,149	The inflation-busting rise in the cost of central government since 1997 has cost taxpayers over £5.3 billion.
Public-private sector pensions gap	£6,000,000,000	The Institute of Economic Affairs estimates that the direct cost to taxpayers of the government's u-turn on public sector pensions in response to union pressure is at least £6 billion a year.
Scrap the DTI	£6,899,000,000	If we scrapped the Department for Trade and Industry (or the Department for Business, Enterprise and Regulatory Reform, as it's now called) as the Liberal Democrats promised to at the last election, we could save almost £7 billion a year.

| Departmental overspend | £14,354,000,000 | If government departments stuck to their budgets it would save the taxpayer over £14.3 billion a year. |
| Rise in cost of quangos over last two years | £41,333,333,333 | Over the last two years, the cost of quangos has risen 50% to over £123 billion. Reversing this increase would save taxpayers over £41 billion a year. |

TOTAL   **£101,412,206,201**

£101 billion is an awful lot of money. Is this figure backed up by any economists of even greater eminence than those at the TaxPayers' Alliance? Indeed it is:

The European Central Bank found that if the UK's public spending were as efficient as that of the US, or Japan, the Government could spend 16% less than it currently does, while still producing the same level of public services.

The table overleaf shows the comparative performance of different countries, with the UK ranking well down the league. Our score of 0.84 compared to the US, Japan and Luxembourg's 1.00 gives rise to the 16% deficit.

Country	Efficiency
United States	1.00
Japan	1.00
Luxembourg	1.00
Switzerland	1.00
Norway	0.73
Ireland	0.96
Australia	0.99
Austria	0.67
Netherlands	0.72
Iceland	0.87
Denmark	0.62
Sweden	0.57
Canada	0.75
Finland	0.61
New Zealand	0.83
United Kingdom	0.84
Germany	0.72
Belgium	0.66
Spain	0.80
France	0.64

Source: 'Public sector efficiency: an international comparison' - Antonio Afonso, Ludger Schuknecht and Vito Tanzi - European Central Bank working paper 242, 2003

Given that government spending is expected to have reached over £587 billion in the current 2007-08 fiscal year, this suggests that public spending and hence taxes could be slashed by about £94 billion without any deterioration in service quality – an estimate just below the £101 billion reached in this latest edition of the *Bumper Book,* taking into account one off examples of waste.

What could be done with £101 billion?

The government could:

- Fill to the brim two of the very largest freight ships in the world – the 400,000 dead weight ton vessels that are too big to fit through the Panama or Suez canals – with pound coins in order to transport the money to a private island bought with the remaining £13 billion. Vatu Vara in Fiji is the most expensive private island in the world at £40 million so the government should be able to buy over three hundred islands. Of course, this idea might cause something of an economic crisis as there are only 1.4 billion pound coins in circulation.

- Build a six foot high wall made out of gold bricks around the entire special designated security zone of Parliament. The zone has a 6 kilometre perimeter. That should be sufficient to keep the terrorists out… and the politicians in.

- Buy enough Old Masters such as Rembrandt's 'Portrait of a Young Woman' to paper the entire frontage of the Treasury's headquarters.

- Paper the entire East Midlands and London with £5 notes, and still have a few billion left over to build a solid silver crane from which to admire your handiwork.

- Convert the £101 billion into one penny coins, pile them on top of each other, and reach the moon and back five times.

- Cut the tax burden for each household by £4,009.97 a year.

"A taxpayer is someone who works for the federal government but who doesn't have to take a civil service examination."

Ronald Reagan

SECTION 2

Departmental Waste

The government gets very tetchy when charged with wasting taxpayers' money. One symptom of this is the way, every four or five years, ministers start pointing the finger at MPs who they think are asking too many questions.

The average cost of answering a written parliamentary question (PQ) is £134. This rises to £369 for an oral question, because extra work has to be done in case the minister gets ambushed by the supplementary question, which would probably begin with *"If that's the case, then why on earth..."*

Obviously, the Leader of the Commons can't protect fellow ministers by banning oral questions, because that would mean the suspension of Parliament, as famously attempted in 1642. That particular spat led to a Civil War. What he does instead is to try to lean on the Speaker and relevant procedural groups in the House to squish MPs who have a habit of asking awkward written questions. They also happen to be the ones who ask the questions taxpayers want answers to.

One of the tactics used to discourage these MPs is to try to smear their reputations by turning the 'waste' argument back on them. PQs, so the argument goes, are themselves a waste of taxpayers' money because civil servants have to spend time preparing answers to them. It is a specious argument, for many reasons.

Firstly, it deliberately overlooks the fact that civil servants are being paid anyway, so there is no extra cost incurred.

Secondly, the amount of time they spend is rarely as long as claimed. One of the authors of this book has been on the providing end of the PQ procedure, and it took ten minutes to draft a reply to two PQs.

Thirdly, even if the cost of each PQ is £134, that is a modest sum compared to the potential savings from a well-targeted question that shames the government into action. One might even argue that there is a net benefit in having civil servants spend time answering questions as it is time they cannot spend drafting new laws and regulations to burden us.

The second tactic used to smear MPs is to depict particular questions as frivolous or vexatious. In 1998, John Redwood asked a number of questions about the predilection ministers had shown for spending public money on household items like washing machines in their official homes. An enquiry into £52,000 spent on Margaret Beckett's kitchen units seems fair enough to us. But the spin doctors tried to trivialise it as a wasteful question on ministers' vacuum cleaners.

There was another attempt at smearing last year. An MP asked how the authorities dealt with the thousands of pounds of lost property found every year in the Royal Parks. The spin doctors denigrated the question (and by implication, the questioner) as a frivolous waste of time not worthy of anyone's attention. In fact, it revealed that the lost goods are auctioned and the proceeds given to charity – entirely laudable, and good to know.

The fact of the matter is that written PQs keep the government of the day accountable. That's why the system is so favoured in English-speaking and Northern European parliaments in particular, and has been introduced by MEPs to inject some element of transparency in Brussels.

So we in the TaxPayers' Alliance pay tribute to the masters of the parliamentary written question, people like Lib Dems Norman Baker and Vince Cable, and Labour's Frank Field and Kate Hoey, as watchdogs of democracy. The next time you see a 'leaked' comment on the supposed cost of a question, attacking a parliamentarian for wasting taxpayers' money, consider instead the cost of not asking one.

Department for Education and Skills (DfES)

Now split into the Department for Children, Schools and Families and the Department for Innovation, Universities and Skill ... but that's too long for a title.

Factoids

- Since May 1997, 1,356 schools have been put on special measures and turned around, and 228 schools have been closed as irredeemable.

- The Department doesn't know how many schools were put on the failing list because they had taken on students from a neighbouring school that had shut down.

- Nearly a quarter of a million pupils have statements of Special Educational Needs (SENs).

- The number of pupils the government believes has Special Needs *without* such a statement is a staggering 1.25 million – or one pupil in seven – up by 40,000 from the previous year.

- Since 2004, the Department has spent £669,000 on equality and diversity programmes.

- The Department's 'Sure Start' programme, designed to help deprived children, has been criticised by academics for making things worse. Parents found the scheme "stressful and intrusive".

- One in five teachers (about 5,000 per year) leaves teacher training and doesn't start teaching. Half of them never will.

- According to official statistics, an impressive 102% of all 3 year olds are in nursery school.

- The central department employs an average of 48 temps a month, on a generous average salary of over £46,000.

- The Department spent £75 million writing off student loans for new teachers in key areas.

- The male:female ratio for students taking a degree in Mechanical Engineering runs at 13:1, Computer Science runs at 5:1, and Economics 2:1. On the other hand, for Nursing it's 1:10, English Studies it's 1:4, for Psychology and for Sociology 1:3, and Drama 2:5. On average, 15% of students drop out of their courses.

Let's now turn to the Department for Education and Skills – the one that looks like it has a fake jungle in its reception.

Publishing

The DfES has had to pulp a rather large quantity of its publications which it had printed in excessive numbers. Some idea of the scale of the problem is given by the fact that it cost £9,000 simply to dispose of them, and that this expenditure was recouped in just two months by the savings made in storage.

The obsolete stock included a number of books for years 7, 8 and 9, and (rather appropriately) two lots of books dealing with numeracy. Totting them up, we count 368,836 books pulped. Some of these had cost over £3 each to publish. Just to print them in the first place had cost the taxpayer £569,690. Let's hope that as they went through the shredder, copies of 'The Learning Challenge' made an impact upon the publication's planners.

Truancy initiatives

In last year's *Bumper Book*, we highlighted how truancy in state schools had massively increased, despite millions upon millions of pounds being pumped into anti-school dodging schemes. A target of a one third cut was made. It wasn't met, so a new target of a one tenth cut was set. This wasn't met either.

The government has clearly taken note, beefing up its 'Schools Absence Strategy'. About 13,000 of what are styled "persistent truants" in around 200 schools are being given special treatment. The help consists of an individual twelve week action plan, a dedicated field officer, regular monitoring against parentally-agreed goals, and "co-ordinated multi-agency support".

To keep the civil servants in Whitehall happy, each local authority which has any of these schools in its patch must provide half-termly data to the DfES, and has to demonstrate agreed "actions and per-school targets". To say the least, this seems a trifle overblown and nannyish. And it will of course be ineffective.

Absenteeism in fact has become so bad that when the government set itself targets to fix the problem, it set the date ahead at 2008, and the comparison date at 2003. That's a little bit like a hospital comparing a patient's condition not with how he normally is, but with how he was five minutes after he fell down the stairs. And then using his condition in a month's time to draw conclusions about the efficacy of his treatment. This is officially known as 'tweaking the stats'.

It's not altogether surprising that the Department is up to these tricks when you consider some of the daft things it has been spending money on to combat truancy: £11.25 million to buy electronic registration systems for 530 secondary schools (in our day, it was a piece of paper); £14 million for local authority behaviour and attendance consultants; £800,000 on advisers "to provide support to local authorities on their attendance strategies"; £300,000 on just eight advisors seconded from local authorities back to the government; and £200,000 for events for local authorities "to share effective practise on attendance management".

Sadly, we don't know if these events were well attended.

School playing fields

Since 1997, the Department has approved the sale or otherwise disposal of 174 school playing fields, counting only those large enough to play a decent game of football on, i.e. those which are at least two thousand square metres and not shaped like a golf course. This adds up to 273 hectares of turf, almost half of which came from closing schools.

The land is valued at an estimated £273 million, money which was earmarked to be re-spent by the Department.

To its credit, the Department has instigated a School Playing Field Advisory Panel to vet the sales (though local councillors might do the job more democratically than a quango). One or two concerns still linger, however. The Department has no idea how much of the money was siphoned off through PFI and PPP deals into the private sector. Also, it transpires that thirteen of these schools were in London, an area where there is obvious public interest in maintaining green spaces rather than building over them. And then there's the 1997 election manifesto, which explicitly made a pledge on the issue. It said:

> *"School sports must be the foundation. We will bring the government's policy of forcing schools to sell off playing fields to an end."*

Oops. Wrong sort of foundation.

Skills training

Gaffes like those cited above might explain why the DfES has realised it has a skills deficit. Over a 12 month period, 14 members of staff were assessed as requiring a 'Skills for Life' course, and attended one through the Department's learning and development unit. Worryingly, the course is designed for people lacking basic reading or maths ability.

Foreign students in Britain

One little-known entity, shared with the Department for Work and Pensions, is the Joint International Unit, whose overriding function is to "promote internationally the government's policies". Key to this is a proactive role in recruiting foreign students. It has been particularly successful of late, exceeding its 2005 target of recruiting an extra 25,000 non-EU students to study A levels and similar in Britain (presumably to fill the gaps of all the schoolchildren playing truant), and an extra 50,000 university students as well. It cost £35 million to run last year, going up to £44 million this year, not counting a Prescott recruitment campaign of another £1.2 million.

Perhaps having all these fee-paying foreign students is a good thing. Around one in eight students simply drops out of university without either transferring or obtaining an award. There are currently almost exactly one million full-time domiciled students in the UK (excluding another 727,000 part-timers). That means around 140,000 of them will have dropped out with nothing to show for it, except for some debt, a clanky Renault 5, and a collection of assorted saucepans and tea-stained mugs. The stats are just as bad in the Further Education Colleges, with one in five dropping out but only one third of these actually transferring to a course they want to do.

We are delighted to learn that our educational establishments have such high international esteem that they attract foreign students. We are a little worried at what some of them are researching as postgraduates. The following figures were provided as rounded to the nearest five.

Biology: 15 students from Iran, 55 from China, a couple from the Sudan, and 5 from Syria.

Chemistry: 15 postgrads from Iran, a couple from Burma, 200 from China, a couple from the Sudan, and 5 from Syria.

Physics, including Nuclear and Particle Physics: 15 Iranians, 80 from China, 5 Sudanese and 5 Syrians.

Studying Chemical Process and Energy Engineering, which includes the categories of Atomic Engineering and Nuclear Engineering: 30 Iranians, 85 Chinese, a couple of Sudanese, and 5 Syrians.

Oh, and there were apparently also a couple of North Koreans doing postgrad research on Chemistry. Presumably the media studies specialists stayed at home.

We do not invite the reader for one moment to leap to any conclusion about whether any of this could involve technology transfer about weapons of mass destruction to potentially less than friendly states. Any given student's work might be about life-saving drugs, or how to use super zappy lasers for keyhole surgery. The Chinese students could indeed mostly prove to be from Hong Kong, and have strong cultural ties with Blighty. Again, it is not clear how much the taxpayer is contributing, though we are aware of seven of the Chinese nationals receiving Chevening scholarships from the Foreign Office to support their work. Nevertheless, the country is subject to an EU arms embargo, and has recently demonstrated a willingness to throw rockets into space to whack satellites. Do you really want to subsidise that?

It is unnerving, too, that the Voluntary Vetting Scheme, which has been running since 1994, does not cover Burma and Sudan, especially given that the latter was the home of Bobby bin Laden for a while. And we also remember a few years back being told by a professor about an Iraqi who had been studying how the wind dispersed gases from chimneys – knowledge which is equally applicable to gas coming out of a canister.

What of other education initiatives? How do they stand up to scrutiny?

School for socialism

The government has been generous with one set of educators – the Trade Unions – supporting the TUC in setting up a Union Academy, which in turn spent £4.4 million of public money on 'Unionlearn' in May 2006, and £12.5 million on the Union Learning Fund. Moves to increase the skills base of the workforce, and to improve our national competitiveness are, of course, important, but one has to ask whether the unions, with their strong party political links, are the right channel for funds. Unionlearn's own website carries material that any state teaching establishment would be forbidden from using because it is so clearly partisan. The courses give a flavour of the bias:

- *Union Reps Stage 1*
  The job of the union rep; Building union membership; Making the union work; Using and making agreements; Representing members; Grievance and discipline; Your rights and negotiating at work; The rep within the wider union; Looking forward and making plans.

- *Health and Safety Stage 2*
  Building a safe and healthy workplace; Building health and safety organisation; Keeping up-to-date on health and safety; Effecting Change in health and safety; Planning for the future.

- *Equality Rep Courses*
  Women's Programmes; Tackling Racism & Discrimination; Equal Opportunities; Lesbian & Gay Issues; Disability Champions@Work; Equal Pay; Countering the Far Right.

So on examination, it's not all quite the "basic skills to MBAs" that the Department pretends it is. The Labour government appears to be supporting its own party funders and political allies in a School for Socialism.

This is par for the course. The Treasury is reported to have funded unions to the tune of £10 million. The Union Modernisation Fund is said to have paid out for a website for one union, and items like a Migrant Workers Support Unit for another. Thirty unions are reportedly getting this assistance.

Some of the programmes are either ambiguous and raise questions, or stand out in particular as having a political tinge:

- £60,000 to the Retained Firefighters' Union for a 'Local Representatives Empowerment Strategy' and £5,875 for 'Using the Internet to Activate and Empower Members'.

- £198,324 to the GMB on 'Race and Diversity'.

- £33,405 to the Bakers, Food and Allied Workers Union on 'Membership Diversity' and £17,241 for 'Membership and Communication Systems'.

- £52,400 to the Society of Chiropodists and Podiatrists for 'Shaping the Future (Phase 2)'.

- £172,870 to Wales TUC for 'Equality at Work'.

- £66,260 for Connect's Knowledge Management System.

- £195,550 to USDAW for it to develop a Management Model.

- £150,000 to the Transport and General Workers Union for 'Developing and Supporting Workplace Union Equality Representatives' and £48,150 for 'Preparing Opinion-Formers for Information and Consultation' (which sounds suspiciously like lobbying).

- £4,546.80 to the WBBS Staff Union for 'ICE – Integrate, Communicate and Embrace'.

- £69,500 for the ASLEF 'Membership and Communications Modernisation Project'.

- £83,960 for the General Federation of Trade Unions for 'Foundations for Success'.

Section 72 of the Trade Union and Labour Relations (Consolidation) Act 1992 precludes spending on political objects from union modernisation fund support. We think some of these might well infringe that rule. It is, of course, a complete coincidence that the unions fund the Labour Party and dozens of Labour MPs.

DfES quangos

The DfES, like other departments, is also responsible for a set of quangos. These include:

Investors in People (UK)

Investors in People is charged with maintaining quality control on the Investors In People stamp, which for some obsessives is a mark of a caring company. An Investors in People adviser will cost your company upwards of £550 per day, an amount which varies according to whether your company is humongous or is in Nowheresville.

If your company is large, it is a racing certainty that you already invest in people, otherwise you would be a small one. But no, that is not how the Department thinks. Large companies need Investors in People Corporate Solutions. You can already deduce from the word 'Solutions' that these advisers are hired from the private sector where they work as business advisers.

Investors in People, by the way, employs 52 staff and costs £5.5 million a year to run. On the plus side, since 1997 it has been regularly awarding itself the Investors in People award, which is a bit like Stalin making himself a Hero of the Soviet Union.

But this rather misses the whole point. The government's own figures acknowledge that England ranks 27th out of 30 industrialised countries for participation in education or training at the age of 17, and that some elements of society fare even worse than that. One such group, identified in the Department's own annual report, is "white working class boys", yet political correctness seems to preclude targeting this group with the specific aid that would give them the skills they need at school-leaving age; instead, the government makes a lot of noise about fixing quotas for them at Oxbridge.

The National College of School Leadership (NCSL)

The NCSL has its own £26 million campus, recently purchased in Nottingham. This body "offers head teachers, deputy heads and other school leaders the professional support and recognition they deserve and which other professions take for granted." It also intends to "identify and grow tomorrow's leaders", as if such state-directed control-mongery can operate like a Fison's compost bag. In one sense, it's a state-funded professional association that employees in the private sector would set up by themselves and subscribe to. Last year, this cost the taxpayer £95 million. At any one time, there was an average of 247 people working there.

The Learning and Skills Council

The Learning and Skills Council has an annual budget of £10.4 billion putting it in an altogether different league. £371 million of this is for "world class buildings" in which to teach Further Education. Presumably this is to avoid celebrated historic cases such as the university car park top floor which was redeployed as a tennis court because the architects hadn't factored in the weight of the cars; the first floor swimming pool that for similar reasons could never be filled with water; and the university telescope that was too heavy for its mountings. But then, if you do involve the students in the design stage...

The Office for Fair Access (OFFA)

This is nothing to do with big ditches on the Welsh border. It is "an independent, non departmental public body which aims to promote and safeguard fair access to higher education for under-represented groups in light of the introduction of variable tuition fees in 2006-7." In other words, the government figured out that if it costs more for students to go to university because of high tuition fees, people from poor families won't go. This quango 'reminds' those high cost institutions to bear these kids in mind.

General Teaching Council

A similar sum of around half a million pounds a year goes into the General Teaching Council, which is a peculiar round table for teachers that mimics the unions and any professional voluntary organisation already going.

Adult Learning Inspectorate

We're not altogether sure for that matter what the Adult Learning Inspectorate brings to the table. For £27 million a year it should be something magical. How businesses benefit from having ALI delegations troop in to assess their staff training, other than saving money they might have spent on private consultants to do the same thing, is anybody's guess. Nor are we sure what the Inspectors get out of knocking around South Africa and Oman, bar a suntan. We've read the corporate plan and it's consultancy gibberish.

School Food Trust

Then there is the School Food Trust (SFT). This provides "support and advice" to schools, presumably encouraging them to narrow the gaps of the playground railings so mothers can't pass burgers and shakes through them at lunch time. It also "ensures that the issue of school food remains high on the agenda". In political circles, this is known as "lobbying". When £15 million quangos lobby, you know you are onto a loser. But then, look at its broader agenda, which includes "reducing diet-related inequalities in childhood through food education and school based initiatives". You would think that dinner ladies have to achieve some notional standard of ability in order to be employed in the first place. It should not be beyond them to acknowledge that Jamie Oliver has a point about turkey twizzlers and the like. But we are now at a stage where, driven by this interventionism, some schools are even introducing their own rules on the contents of packed lunches brought from home, and have lunchbox police monitoring them. There is a limit to what is reasonable in a free society.

In English schools over 2004-05, 19,750 pupils were suspended or expelled for attacking a teacher, 90,670 for threatening or verbally abusing a teacher, 3,640 for sexual misconduct, 11,570 for drugs or alcohol, and 106,500 for persistent disruptive behaviour. We tactfully suggest this is where the department's focus of effort should properly lie.

As a final observation, last year we created a sin bin of MPs who were asking ministers questions purely so that they could use the material in their local campaign literature. You may remember the format – something not a million miles away from: "Could the Minister supply some stats on policing or schools that show how wonderful the Government has been in my patch?" Ministers would reply in uncharacteristic depth and detail. Well, that tradition continues. Worse, ministers have indicated that they are "investigating ways in which we can disseminate more information about the effects of our policies at a local level." The DfES appears to be at the forefront of this campaign to get ministry employees drawing up pie charts for government backbenchers. Let's hope that civil servants see sense and pull the plug on it.

And then there was …

☹ Departmental staff spent £6.2 million on travel expenses last year.

☹ The Department estimates that £124 million of student loans handed out in 2004 will never be repaid.

☹ Over a nine year period, the Department spent £112 million on centrally-run advertising and promotional work.

☹ £50 million will be spent on giving disadvantaged pupils home access to computers. No provision has been made to stop them being used just for games.

☹ The School Food Trust has a budget of £7 million, employs 33 staff to make our kiddies love lettuce, and hired 16 consultants for one-off tasks in 2006.

Department of Health (DH)*

Factoids

- The NHS remains the third largest employer in the world. If it were a country, it would be the 33rd largest economy on the planet.

- The Department's board member bigwigs are individually responsible for items on a 'High-Level Risk Register', listing budget areas that are in danger of crashing, though we have yet to find anyone who has been fired for any failures. This might help explain why even the list itself is secret.

- Around 50,000 people a year get home visits from 'Crisis Resolution Teams' on NHS mental services. This £155 million service treats people with acute psychiatric cases away from the wards.

- The DH runs an NHS Bank to manage the cash flow to 28 Strategic Health Authorities.

- The Department invented CALM to target suicides amongst young males. It is an acronym for the Campaign Against Living Miserably.

- The Department of Health reported 43 incidents to its Health and Safety Incident Centre in 2005-06. This probably accounts for the £80,000 compensation handed over to civil service staff.

- Around £6,000 was reportedly blown – literally – on recruiting Colombian Mauricio Velez to play pan pipes in doctors' surgeries. We object. Ever since we got a bargain bucket CD from Woolworths, we prefer the haunting tones of Tito Rodriguez.

- 12 civil servants in the Department are on over £150k a year, and 286 are on over £55k.

---

* We prefer 'DoH'

- For over 70 years, hospitals have been able to reclaim costs of treating patients from the person who caused their injury. In 2004-05, £117 million of NHS costs were recovered this way.

- The NHS email system handles 700,000 pings a day.

- Spending on the NHS IT programme by October 2006 had reached £918 million.

- The Care Standards Tribunal was established in 1999 for appeals for those banned from working with children. It costs £1.2 million a year, and has dealt with 71 cases so far. Seventeen appeals have been allowed.

In 1997, the Labour Party manifesto said:

> *"The Conservatives have wasted spending on the NHS. We will do better."*

Full marks so far.

For some years, though, critics of the government have been saying that *Yes*, there has been a lot of money thrown into the NHS with the intention to improve services, but *No*, it hasn't produced the expected improvements because that shovelling of tax loot has been done without any serious planning.

According to the government, expenditure on the NHS has gone up (ignoring inflation) from £54 billion in 2002-03 to £92 billion by 2007-08. This is officially known as An Awful Lot of Taxpayers' Money Delivering What Exactly? Consultants to the industry know it by a different expression: Bonzo Vegas Time.

One simple yardstick is the number of nurses. In 1997, there were 318,856 nurses out of a total 1,058,686 NHS staff. This had increased in 2005 to 404,161 nurses. But the overall number of NHS personnel had also gone up, to 1,365,388. While the government had delivered more nurses, it had also created more jobs for people who weren't on the front line (and by definition, at disproportionate cost), which meant that the actual proportion of NHS staff that nurses made up hadn't changed from 30%. We have the extra carers, but with them came a larger number of administrators.

This might explain why no less than 61 NHS Trusts have had to set up 'Turnaround Teams' to rescue themselves from debt. In many cases this will mean ward closures. What is particularly irksome is that costly consultants are reportedly being hired to advise on this.

So it was with interest that we read the former Secretary of State for Health Patricia Hewitt make this admission in the DH's annual report:

> *"Investment alone cannot deliver the improvements*
> *we want to see. For the extra money to work for*
> *patients, we must step up our reforms."*

Fine words, if many billions of pounds of waste too late.

But even now there is a failure to deliver on promises. For example, two benchmarks – the rate of deaths and of hospitalisation through accidents – have actually gone up. Perhaps we shouldn't be surprised. The Department's own civil servants had 52 reported accidents in 2005, seven leading to absences, two of which were RIDDORS – Reports of Injuries, Disease and Dangerous Occurrence Regulations whose paperwork gets sent to the 'Health and Safety Incident Centre'. Eleven, incidentally, were "near misses", which are defined as "any unplanned occurrence that does not lead to injury of personnel or damage to property, plant or equipment, but may have done in different circumstances". As in, "You imbecile, an inch lower and you would have chopped my John Thomas off!" Always nice to know someone is collating these things.

The Department has helpfully published documents to help staff cut waste, thanks to its in-house Institute for Innovation and Improvement. Its 'Delivering Quality and Value' series suggests:

> *"Improvement of assessment processes, e.g. move from an 'admit to decide' system to one that facilitates 'decide to admit'.*

> *"Using practice-based commissioning to incentivise the proactive management of potential high impact users."*

> *"Identification of ambulatory care sensitive conditions accounting for disproportionate hospital admissions and resources."*

Stick with it, because behind the management-speak rubbish is a useful insight into the areas where the NHS is seen by the Department's own advisors as wasting money.

To start with, it believes that a lot of money could be saved by treating more patients in the community. The report suggests a saving of £437 million if 30% of people who walk in with the 19 most common conditions were dealt with outside of the wards.

Then there is that strange phrase "ambulatory care sensitive". Opposite is a list of such cases for which it believes community nursing would free up hospital beds.

Emergency admissions by ACS condition 2003-04

ACS condition name	No. of Spells	Cost in £m
COPD	106,517	253
Angina (without major procedure)	79,228	134
Ear, nose and throat infections	72,831	52
Convulsions and epilepsy	64,664	77
Congestive heart failure	62,592	211
Asthma	61,624	64
Flu and pneumonia (>2 months old)	56,616	158
Dehydration and gastroenteritis	54,402	96
Cellulitis (without major procedure)	45,522	97
Diabetes with complications	17,695	42
Pyelonephritis	8,469	13
Iron-deficiency anaemia	8,268	20
Perforated/bleeding ulcer	7,327	26
Dental conditions	6,207	8
Hypertension	5,379	9
Gangrene	5,309	32
Pelvic inflammatory disease	5,070	9
Vaccine preventable conditions	2,326	5
Nutritional deficiencies	53	3
Grand total	669,720	1,301

The report also recommends recognising that between a tenth and a quarter of hospital expenditure is taken up by a small number of 'high intensity users' who were admitted to the hospital three or more times a year. It suggests that some form of improved management could save money here too.

We assume by this they mean sorting out cases where patients are kept in wards despite being fit to leave. One patient cost a hospital an estimated £300,000 by being kept in a ward for four years after being judged fit to leave. Ten patients were found to have been kept in wards at an estimated cost of £1.4

million, despite being medically dischargeable.

The report goes on to suggest that £141 million could be saved by having a standard rate of referrals across the country; another £80 million could be saved by cutting the numbers of those who don't attend or who don't need to attend acute trusts, and £10 million could also be saved in the same way in dermatology.

It transpires that there is massive variation in the way Trusts deal with elective surgery, ranging from tonsillectomy to dilatation, and curettage to dealing with grommets. If you have grommets, you have our deepest sympathy. Try at least to have a grand day out.

Another 390,000 bed days, says the report, could be saved by improving day case rates, saving £88 million. Nineteen thousand bed days, or £4 million, could be saved by sending more people home on weekends, as it seems for some reason fewer people are discharged then than during the week (this may involve the in-laws visiting).

Twelve Acute Hospital Trusts lose over 9% of nurse time due to sickness. Another 58 lose over 7.5%. This too is identified as an area for improvement. Electronic recruitment of nurses via NHS Jobs might save £80 million. More esoterically, miscategorising bladder ops are assessed to waste £2,400 every time they happen.

Some savings have been made. The Department lost 1,400 civil servants, though a look at the small print shows that half of them were simply moved into NHS bodies as administrators. £20 million has been saved by stopping some patients staying in overnight. Another £65 million has been saved by the workforce somehow being sick less often, though no miracle cures have been patented so that saving remains a mystery.

Meanwhile, large amounts of money have been spent tackling the genuine issue of attacks on hospital staff. How? By sending over 40% of frontline NHS staff on the 'Conflict Resolution Training syllabus'. A better solution than sending hundreds of thousands of staff on negotiating courses more suited to hostage situations would be to increase the rate of conviction for people who carry out these attacks, which even on the latest figures stands at a paltry 6%. The small increase in convictions that occurred over previous years seems to have cut figures drastically according to the government's own stats. More could be done.

We are not entirely convinced the Department has been spending your Lottery money wisely either. The Healthy Living Centre (HLC) project was set up with £300 million to create a national network of these bastions of righteous living – 352 across the UK. But this appears to have been a fad policy.

The Department's review of the HLC programme, drawn up by the Tavistock Institute, expresses reservations about the future funding of the programme, based on the fact that it crosses a number of policy agendas, and says that there is a "considerable question mark" over its sustainability.

The £300 million doesn't appear in retrospect to have been "invested" in much. The single largest element was spent on the 'Action to Promote Good Mental Health' programme, justified by the claim that depression costs the economy £9 billion a year. That means on average you, reader, waste the economy £1,500 from being depressed. So you'd better shut this book right now, before the economy crashes.

We also learn that centres have supported physical exercise by providing lessons in gardening, 'green gyms' or outdoor environmental work, armchair exercise, street dancing and line dancing.

Healthy eating has been supported by cookery classes. This, you might think, is less controversial, until you read the anecdote provided by the report about the National Chinese Healthy Cooking Competition that the funding sponsored:

> *"The nine dishes are lined up along the judges' table behind signs declaring the name of the team and the name of the dish. As all the dishes are there the audience lines up to have a look. A shudder goes through the audience as it realises that the bean curd*

in one of the dishes has gone off. One of the judges says that bean curd is very sensitive and may simply have gone off because of the heat on this particular day and says he has not subtracted any points for this."

Fantastic. Never mind that a hundred primary school children were poisoned by dodgy bean curd in Wuhan, China in 1999. Healthy eating must take a back place in the new age healthy eating competition. All must win prizes.

Elsewhere, an anger management team was set up. Though only half a dozen bothered to attend, the organisers were upbeat. As they explain:

"The consensus was that if the group did not exist they would not be accessing any help at all. The consequences of this ranged from 'just sitting at home' to being dead."

The NHS also seems to have questionable priorities with some of its other programmes. In October 2005, the DH celebrated Black History Month at two sites joined by video link. If they had stuck to the real health issues concerned – the shortage of blood and marrow donors from the black community – this would have been highly laudable. But was it really beneficial to the black community for the Department to organise a panel debate and buffet lunch with 140 DH and NHS staff in attendance? We also wonder if it is appropriate to spend public money on an awards scheme run by the Department's Equality and Human Rights Group that is specifically directed at ethnic minorities within the NHS, rather than at the entire workforce regardless of race, creed or colour.

Then there is the Mosaic project, which "seeks to promote race equality through procurement". Quite how varying your methods of buying your office furniture can foster racial equality remains a mystery (a £60,000 conundrum in fact), though no doubt the Department's Ethnic Minorities Working Group can advise.

New initiatives are being developed all the time, even as the benefit of the old ones remains unevaluated. The Pacesetters Programme, launched this year, aims "to work on innovations across all strands of equality – age, disability, ethnicity, gender, religion or belief, sexual orientation and gender identity". The programme is supposed to focus on both "public health/patient care" and "the NHS workforce". Quite how much public money it will consume is at present unclear.

Make no mistake, the TaxPayers' Alliance supports equality for all people as individuals. We passionately believe that people should be treated for who they are and not what they are. What we question is the use of public money to support minority campaigning groups, and particularly if their campaigns carry a political agenda. The country has come a long way, after all, from the society we look back on in the outstanding 'Life on Mars'.

The same criticisms can be levelled at the Department's apparent obsession with improving its position in the annual Stonewall Corporate Equality Index. In June 2005, the Department – i.e. the taxpayer – for the first time sponsored a float for the annual 'Pride London' parade for DH and NHS Lesbian, Gay, Bisexual and Transgender (LGBT) staff, costing several thousand pounds.

The Department is also supporting the second 'LGBT history month', spending around £2,200 a year. Given that LGBT is a campaigning organisation rather than a simple social one, this is questionable. We know the Home Office did likewise, but it cost taxpayers only £50 of light refreshment as moral support.

A key ongoing campaign is 'Schools Out' – a campaign on lesbian, gay, bisexual and transsexual issues in schools. If School Parent Associations are happy with this campaign group's material, all well and good. But we are concerned that many parents would view it as state support for a controversial and politically-charged campaign.

Needless to say, the Department has its own Sexual Orientation and Gender Identity Advisory Group that works on the issues of 'better employment', 'inclusive services', 'transgender issues' and 'reducing health equalities' for its members.

If we knew that similar groups existed representing retiring staff, pregnant employees, single parents, Fathers for Justice, shy people, and new arrivals, and received equal support, we would be less suspicious of the motives of management. But when the civil service is supposed to be politically neutral and members cannot affiliate to any political party, then it is reasonable to raise an eyebrow at financial support by the government for organisations with overt political or campaigning interests.

Similarly, if it was a matter of providing after hours office space for meetings, that's one thing. But the Department of Health funded its Sexual Orientation and Gender Identity Advisory Group to the tune of £102,000 in 2005-06. And the group is getting the same amount this year.

The attitude of the Department heads increases our suspicions further. In 2004, they hired an external consultant to undertake an 'equality impact assessment' as part of a restructuring package (the consultant's conclusion was there was no impact on equality). In 2002 and 2003, all staff were required to take part in diversity training. The costs of what for most people would have been a politically correct waste of time are unknown. [*Memo to Secretary of State:* your job is to treat ill patients.]

Another example of a diverted policy agenda has been the Department's fixation on patient feedback. The DH has blown wads of money on mechanisms to gauge how patients feel, rather than spend the money on the patients themselves. It wasted £32 million on a survey of patients "to explore their choice preferences around GP services", and another £40 million on a survey "to conduct surveys of patients' experience to support the quality and outcomes framework". GPs we have spoken to say this was nothing but a nuisance for patients and doctors alike. £179,500 also went on a patient opinion website.

In parallel to the Department's patient feedback programme,

the Healthcare Commission quango spent £475,000 on an NHS patient survey advice centre, and estimates that each time it conducts a survey it costs the public £4,000 for each NHS Trust and £3,500 for each mental health trust. As in other sectors of government, the trend appears to be to *seen* rather than to *act*.

The Minister could start by applying some joined-up government. Narcotics addiction is patently a major source of crime, particularly street robberies and burglaries. It destroys lives as well as homes. It supports organised crime in this country, and international terror and insurgency abroad. It is also big business.

But there is no coherent attempt by government to tackle a problem which stretches from the hospital bed to our soldiers patrolling the Afghan opium fields of Lashkar Gah. The Department's ministers acknowledge this problem. According to their annual report:

> "*In-patient and residential facilities are under-provided for* [note the euphemism] *within drug treatment pathways and unlike other types of drug treatment have not grown in recent years. A shortage of these facilities reduces patient choice and the proportion of patients who become drug-free.*"

Their solution? An additional £38 million. The National Treatment Agency which sits on top of the pyramid overseeing government strategy employs a staggering 146 staff. That can't be cheap. How many of these posts would better be employed on the front line?

Let's reflect for a moment on the scale of the problem. The estimated UK market for crack in 2003-04 was £1.48 billion, but with a colossal plus or minus error margin of 394%. The official estimate for trade in heroin was £1.2 billion, with an error margin of 228%. For powder cocaine, it was £973 million, allowing for an error of 267%. All told, the total drugs trade was estimated at £5.27 billion in value, but with an astronomical error margin of 1,310%.

The cost to society, however, is much higher, at perhaps £12 billion once you add in fraud, burglaries, robberies and shoplifting.

There's another alarming trait. Since 2001, the price of a gram of cocaine has dropped from £60 to £49; a 0.2g rock of crack is down from £21 to £19; a gram of heroin is down from £63 to £54; and ecstasy is down from £7 to £4. What does this mean? Simply, that however fast the demand for drugs is growing, the supply is growing even faster. Drugs are easy to get hold of.

According to government estimates, there are about one third of a million people who use heroin, or crack, or in the vast majority of cases, a combination. But this only lists the hardcore users. It is an astounding figure. No one can say how many use cocaine on top of this.

The Department recognises that two in three of those who inject drugs have spent time in prison, and that half of them take up the habit when they are inside. Is the Department's solution to try to stem the flow of drugs into this supposedly closed community? No. It's to spend £114,000 on producing 40,000 copies of a rap CD, 'Music 4 Messages', telling inmates how to avoid Hepatitis C. Staggeringly, a minister explained that the Department was targeting people in custody who were *not yet* injecting with the message of how to stay safe during drug use. It might be vaguely innovative, it might even be an important issue, but isn't it also a massive missed opportunity?

Even the Home Office realises that "treatment works and is highly cost-effective". It estimates that for every £1 spent, at least £9.50 is saved in crime and health costs. Where then, is the sense in spending a reported £200,000 on an eight month investigation of alleged cocaine abuse by famous supermodels that never results in charges?

Sometimes, the Department gets the theory right but the practice wrong. A good example is the National Patient Safety Agency (NPSA), whose job since 2001 has been to spot common failings to save lives and/or save money, and to send out memos to DH staff urging a change of practice. A fine idea.

As part of its work, the Agency spotted 321 safety incidents relating to medical infusion devices over a six month period and concluded that this was somewhat high. So it sent out a note saying that the way the pumps were being used meant that patients were more at risk than they need be, and when that advice was followed, millions of pounds and possibly lives were saved.

All pretty encouraging – until you consider that it took well over 18 months to get from the 'identification of dangerous practices' stage to the 'let's do something about it' stage.

One more example: in 2002, the Medicines and Healthcare Products Regulatory Agency identified a number of incidents of concern. The NPSA decided that this was a priority area, and conducted its survey over the latter part of 2003. On the basis of the pilot study, the NPSA decided the NHS needed more advice, which was put out in May 2004. Well done, NHS. It took you two years but you got there in the end.

No wonder last year that the National Audit Office revealed that half of all incidents in which hospital patients had been harmed could have been avoided if lessons had been learned from previous incidents. Two top officials in the NPSA were sent on gardening leave after the Commons' Public Accounts Committee described it as dysfunctional. They are said to still be receiving £95,000 a year each for their part-time jobs.

No discussion of waste is complete without a discussion of quangos, and in this particular area, the Department of Health has few peers. Overall, it 'sponsors' 601 quangos to look after its various institutions, with 4,387 members belonging to them. Most of these quangos look after hospitals and the like.

One of our particular favourites as far as the 'Other NHS Bodies' list is concerned is the NHS Litigation Authority. Intriguingly, it was authorised in an Act of Parliament dating from 1977, but was only actually established in 1995. It covers clinical negligence, but also the Property Expenses Scheme, presumably lawsuits that result when an ambulance clips a parked Bentley. A secondary role is that it is supposed to "promote the highest possible standards of patient care and to minimize suffering resulting from those adverse incidents that do nevertheless occur." As an agency of the NHS, this Mother Theresa approach appears to give its 155 full-time staff quite a schizophrenic responsibility. They have to represent both the interests of the sued or sue-able NHS and the 'well-being' of the patient. It is estimated that claims not yet made but in the pipeline amount to liabilities of £8.2 billion for clinical and £0.13 billion for non-clinical faults.

As for the quangos, one might possibly include the Healthcare Commission. Its job is to award stars to NHS organisations, register its private competitors, and carry out healthcare reviews. It gets £70 million from the State, but shockingly also derives income from the registration and inspection fees it charges private and voluntary healthcare providers – presumably including charities and hospices and perhaps many small nursing homes – averaging out at a charge of about £5,400 each. Last year, this brought in £7.4 million, up from £4.7 million the year before. We fear that much of this is akin to a surcharge on public spirit. Let's hope that the consultation that the Commission has just been undertaking sorts out the anomalies.

The Pharmaceutical Price Control Tribunal wins the award for value for money. It has one permanent employee, its Clerk, who is paid an annual retainer of £3,700. Last year there were no appeals to the Tribunal. We assume he spent a lot of time just waiting by the phone.

At the end of the day, though, the Department is so massive and fragmented that the centre doesn't seem to have any idea what is going on in its provinces. Here's where you come in locally. If you get a spare moment, why not check out your own NHS Trust? It is required by law to report any project it cancels or scales down that costs over £250,000, and you should be able to find a list of them in its annual report of accounts. Keep your ear to the ground too if you come across any items that for some strange reason have been budgeted at just under a quarter of a million pounds.

In sum, the Department of Health is a behemoth with a life of its own. That's why the top dogs in the Department maintain a high-level risk register. Each identified danger is assigned a board member to keep tabs on it. Perhaps it is a sign of the times that the register currently contains 20 risks.

And then there was ...

- ☹ An estimated £600 million is wasted every year by patients who don't turn up for appointments.

- ☹ An estimated £40 million is spent every year on paying for and replacing temporarily suspended staff in the NHS.

- ☹ It has reportedly cost the NHS £1.4 million to replace a surgeon who has been suspended on full pay for four years. The cardiologist's crime was to blow the whistle on dangerous overcrowding – which ended when he went public.

- ☹ Hospital 'HQ Admin' costs £564 million a year.

- ☹ 37,000 hospital meals are wasted every day, costing £36 million a year.

- ☹ £400,000 was reportedly spent on modern art for seven mental hospitals, and another £100,000 on assessing whether it was money well spent.

- ☹ £1.39 million was blown by the Department (excluding local costs) on the 'Your Health, Your Care, Your Say' consultation programme. £1.05 million went on badgering people, including "a series of regional deliberative events" and "a national citizens' summit".

- ☹ The Department spent £3,001.92 on Christmas cards last year. That included VAT. To make ministers feel better, each card included a 25p donation to charity. But that was divided equally between 69 charities. We reckon that at absolute best the Department handed over £30 to each charity.

Department for Transport

Factoids

- The government's fleet of internal mail vans and chauffeurs costs £19 million a year to run, and employs around 300 people.

- The government car pool consists of 843 cars, of which 134 were made in the UK.

- On top of its car pool, the Department and its agencies spent over a quarter of a million pounds on taxis over a nine month period.

- The Mobility and Inclusion Unit has a budget of around £1.8 million a year.

- We were going to applaud Peter Hendy, Chair of the Commission for Integrated Transport, for taking a pay cut so as to only receive what ordinary members of the board get. But then we found a report in the *Guardian* saying he gets £320,000 a year from Transport for London as well, so the paean will have to wait.

- £18 million is being spent over two years to support projects to cut congestion, some of which almost certainly involve setting up local congestion charging schemes – in other words, road tax.

- The Office of Rail Regulation is owed £55,000 for season ticket loans provided to staff.

- The ORR is also spending £375,000 to restore rented office space to what it looked like 15 years ago.

- When Tony Blair was PM, his office floated the idea of a 'Blair Force One' (cost: £12 million a year) but scrapped the Royal Yacht Britannia (cost: around £8 million a year).

The privilege of owning a vehicle is one of the most highly taxed honours in the country. First, you need to pay tax for a paper disk giving you the right to drive it on a public highway.

This excludes certain bridges and highways for which you have to pay an additional toll. Then you pay a tax to your local council for the right to keep the car stationary in the street. If you want to move it, you need petrol, which is extremely heavily taxed. Of course, you need your car insured, which is taxed. You need it certified fit to drive, which you do by paying for an MOT examination every year – taxable, naturally. If something breaks, of course you pay tax on the repairs. If you live in central London, you also fork out the Congestion Charge, or as it should more properly be known, the Congestion Tax. It applies even if your local council removes your right to park in a given spot, and you have to move your car round the corner to a new location.

Hardly surprising, then, that the government needs a department to manage all this.

Especially when you realise that the taxation is going to get even worse.

The Transport Innovation Fund (TIF) is a £10 billion government project to provide "pump-priming support" to cut congestion and increase productivity, starting from 2008-09. *How* is anyone's guess, though latest intelligence suggests by adding toll booths to everything.

Even the government recognised that "road pricing could not be implemented in a single, national 'big bang'". Its solution is to "demonstrate" in various cities and regions how yet more taxation of motorists carries "benefits". This is where the TIF comes in, by using pump-priming funding in ways that will "complement and support the wider packages of transport measures that authorities are developing" and "exploring the potential synergies with market-led services".

There are 33 million vehicles on Britain's roads. Picture the amount of money we are talking about here; £10 billion of taxpayers' money would be enough to buy each car owner a top-of-the-range sat nav system with the latest traffic updates, which we suspect would be as effective a long-term solution as anything the Department will come up with.

This being so, it comes as no surprise to learn that the Department has around 70 staff who deal with "communication", including 14 press officers, 22 in marketing, 15 in internal and electronic communications, and 4 to administer them. The pay bill comes in at around £3 million.

Some of the Department's agencies have intriguing second jobs. The Vehicle Certification Agency (VCA) tests cars and bits of traffic in ways that would make Jeremy Clarkson green with envy. It employs 140 staff, mostly in Bristol and Nuneaton. For reasons unclear, it is also operating as a competitive agency in Detroit, Kelena Jaya in Malaysia, Peking, Seoul, and Nagoya in Japan. While potentially providing marvellous postings for UK civil servants, it's an unusual interpretation of the role of the public sector.

The Government Car and Despatch Agency (GCDA) continues to fascinate. It runs a fleet of around 160 cars, which are designated for use by 'Ministers, Senior Civil Servants and others in government and the wider public sector', a conveniently vague mandate. According to the official guidance document Travel by Ministers:

> *"Cabinet Ministers will be provided by the GCS with an appropriate car, at present the Vauxhall Omega Elite or the Rover 75 Connoisseur. Ministers of State and Parliamentary Under Secretaries of State will be given by the GCS the choice of a Rover 45, Ford Mondeo, Vauxhall Vectra or Nissan Primera with an engine capacity in the 1.8 to 2.0 litre category, with a comfortable but not extravagant level of fit, for their allocated use."*

Senior civil servants and the major chief executives get to travel in the same style as junior ministers. The three big league civil servants on the other hand travel in the grander vehicles.

Ministers can use the vehicle during the week, and for travel to and from their constituency if they are carrying a red box (which it would be embarrassing to lose on the train). Spouses and partners can use a vehicle for an official public function, like having canapés with the Chilean trade delegation, or presumably attending the 2012 Olympics. If a trip combines party political with government business, then the minister has to cadge a lift locally to get to his next podium and then be picked up from there.

Of course, ministers can't be driven around in a hulk. So a number of replacements are bought every year. In 2005-06, 64 new cars were bought, at a cost of £977,000.

The Department also runs a lesser-known short-term hire and green car service, which can be used for the broader civil service and also the wider public sector.

For the record, ministers otherwise qualify for first class rail travel. They can fly if it makes sense, preferably by a British carrier (as the French would spy on you if you flew theirs, it was revealed of Air France). Senior ministers are entitled to use the best available class of air travel for all journeys by air. Junior ministers may travel by the best available class for flights lasting longer than 2.5 hours but should normally travel by Club or equivalent class, or economy class when an intermediate class is not available, on flights of less than 2.5 hours. Non-scheduled special flights have to be authorised by the minister who runs the department, so there's no bagging a 747 just for you.

This all becomes an environmental issue when the Deputy Prime Minister is accused of taking a helicopter one way while his car is driving up to collect him afterwards.

But there's more to the Department than wheeled transport. It was the Maritime and Coastguard Agency, for example, to whose lot it fell to issue a Schedule to Prohibition Notice forbidding the SV Grand Turk in Southampton harbour from firing off broadsides. According to the Marine Accident Investigation Branch back in 2001, a premature ignition of black powder on a nine pounder piece caused an injury to a crew member as the cannon fired off unexpectedly. So very Wile E. Coyote.

Home Office

Factoids

- The Department spent £288 million in 2005-06 detaining and removing illegal immigrants. 3,800 left under the Assisted Voluntary Return Scheme.

- The Department runs the 'Life in the UK' test for citizen applicants. At the end of February 2006, 25,000 had taken the test with a pass rate of 70%. The Home Office doesn't know how many exemptions it has granted.

- The Home Office employs over 73,000 staff. 904 of them had accidents at work in 2005.

- An assistant immigration officer working in Heathrow between 2000-04 was himself an illegal immigrant; as was a prison officer working at Holme House, a Cat B prison that incarcerates illegal immigrants; and a further 12 were found to have been working on Home Office premises right under staff noses at various times between 2002-06.

- In 2006, the Department commissioned reports on 38 topics, including: Drivers of Perception of Race Discrimination; looking at how people understood Confidence Questions in the British Crime Survey; a Competence Assessment Project for Prisons; Checking over Quality of Prison Life Research; assessing at what age males and females reach emotional maturity; and the development of an Offender Feedback Questionnaire.

- The maximum fine for a Penalty Notice for Disorder that can be handed out on the street is £80. Each costs £91 to administer. Half of them go unpaid.

- The Home Office has unknown liabilities towards victims of foreign nationals whom it failed to deport, and who then committed further crimes.

- The Home Office is just about the worst offender on late payments for work done, with 13.14% of bills unpaid within 30 days. This is slightly better than the NI Office and Constitutional Affairs, while the Treasury fails for 5.3%.

And so now we turn to the department which, according to former Home Secretary John Reid, is not "fit for purpose". Not that its job is always straightforward. It includes keeping a look out for members of the 14th Waffen SS Division who are still knocking around, sixty years after the end of World War 2. Apparently, there are 1,450 former storm troopers on our streets. As a Home Office Minister explained, "The Metropolitan Police visited a sample of 13 former members in 2005 to ascertain any information about crimes against humanity but no such crimes were disclosed." You don't say.

The Home Office is also, we understand, the lead department for tackling a number of designated gang units. However, due to Health and Safety risk assessments, members aren't allowed to actually go out and meet the gangs. They leave this to unpaid volunteers, who are deemed expendable.

That's not to say that someone doesn't think there is merit in the Department. Over the last two years, 20,000 non-pensionable special bonuses worth £15 million were handed out to staff as "prompt and tangible recognition for outstanding achievement in particularly demanding tasks or situations". We would love to know how many of these were in offices that covered foreign prisoner release, prison building plans, updating data from foreign police records, ID card assessments, the school sex offenders' register, police force mergers...

We'd also like to be able to scrutinize bonuses from a couple of years earlier. Only now are the true costs of the Pinochet fiasco beginning to emerge.

Costs of the Pinochet fiasco

The Treasury Solicitors office cost us £670,588.82, paying £63,000 to its own solicitors, £292,000 for outside solicitors, £155,000 for the solicitors representing Belgium and Amnesty International, £12,000 for the cost of Pinochet's medical examination on 5th January 2000, £11,000 answering letters from the public, and £166,000 on staff costs. £28,500 was reclaimed from Senator Pinochet.

Meanwhile, the Crown Prosecution Service bill came to £676,691. One sixth of this was the cost of interpreters, travel, subsistence and photocopying. Staff costs for the legal secretariat of the law officers came to £60,000. The bill for the Chancellor's Department came to £1,209,775.05. This included the sets of bills for Pinochet's first two hearings before the Lords, costing £420,000. The remainder covered the costs from lower level hearings which Pinochet had won, so his lawyers had to be paid for.

Treasury Solicitor's fees came to a further £100,053.76. On top of all that is the cost to Surrey Police to cover the Wentworth home, at £1.2 million, and an unknown figure covering the Met's costs in London.

So all told, the known Pinochet bill came to £3,857,108.58. Not bad when you consider you get a diplomatic incident thrown in for good measure.

All par for the course, really.

Stansted hijack

Remember the Afghans who hijacked a plane and flew to Stansted? Two Home Secretaries tried to deport them, and a third of the plane's passengers seized the opportunity to claim asylum with them. The Home Office is estimated to have forked out £500,000 to the gang in benefits payments and £3 million to the passengers, to add to the millions spent when the plane was on the tarmac. Ministers lost the case to deport them. They didn't even manage to bang anyone up for the hijacking, which cost £5 million in two Old Bailey trials.

The total bill came to £15 million for the whole sorry saga. Ministers were patently hoisted on their own petard in the shape of the Human Rights Act which they themselves had introduced, and which critics at the time warned was ill-considered.

Nevertheless, they are a caring crew in the Department. Almost 3,000 members of staff were given flu vaccinations as part of the Home Office's internal flu campaign, despite not being in the at-risk age bracket. A smoking ban was also introduced early across all its offices, with support given to all staff who want to give up (though the take-up rate seems to have been minuscule, despite famously having a role model in the former Home Secretary John Reid).

The Department is currently undergoing "a transformation that seeks to put staff well-being at the heart of our business". Health and Safety priorities for 2006 have been:

> *"to reduce the risk of slips and trips as they continue to be a primary cause of accidents, the introduction of stress management standards and the provision of new training and support arrangements."*

The total cost of this is unknown, but we do know that the personal development scheme includes:

> *"one-to-one coaching for directors, including 360 degree feedback to improve senior leadership, new mentor training and a programme of leadership master classes"*

The cost of this alone came to £44,500 (excluding internal staff costs).

And then there was …

⊗ The Department spent £55,260 (including installation costs, and VAT to the Treasury) on its Interior Art Strategy for its new premises at Marsham Street.

⊗ In 2004, the Department paid for 1,047,330 working lunches by staff and visitors.

- ☹ In 2006, it spent £800,000 on taxis for Home Office staff – up by half a million pounds in five years.

- ☹ The Home Office spent over four times the amount on an agency that recovers criminal assets than the agency actually recovered.

- ☹ It also spent £4 million on detectors at ports to discover illegal immigrants, to great fanfare. It transpires that these devices are readily triggered by the sorts of vibrations generated by ferries, lorries and cars, all of which are quite common at ports.

- ☹ Some bright spark blew £164,000 on a new logo for the Serious Organised Crime Agency. It has some sort of panther on it.

Dept. for Communities and Local Government

Factoids

- £196 million is spent on central administration of the regions.

- £101 million is spent on the actual government offices locally.

- In 2004-05, English regions had a dedicated departmental budget of £1.8 billion. About two thirds went to the regional development agencies.

- The USA has Hangar 18 in Area 51. We have Hangar 97 in Little Rissington. Ours doesn't have flying saucers. It tests fires.

- 247 people work at the Department's Fire Service College. One is a "casual civil servant" – presumably he wears slacks. It has a fake shopping complex, a physics lab, TV studios, 4 squash courts, a conditioning room, a chapel, and 300 acres of training area.

- The Department is the home of the Women and Equality Unit, transferred from the DTI in 2006, which gives some clue to its overall priorities.

- The Department is spending £76 million on the New Dimension programme: training for mega disasters.

- £2.9 million is being spent on a Client Record form.

- One of the Department's strategic priority targets is "liveability", for which the Department has a "suite of indicators".

- The Department launched a competition for a £60,000 affordable home, then revealed it to be the build cost, not the development or sale cost.

- The Department's accounts also reveal £30 million listed under the civil defence budget, but mysteriously it is "Not Identifiable".

- 16 areas receiving Local Strategic Partnership funding in 2005, one in five of the total, were assessed as amber/red for their poor management of the neighbourhood renewal fund. One was Tony Blair's former seat of Sedgefield.

You may remember this department better as part of the great empire of the late Khan of regional government, former Deputy PM John Prescott. He went one cowboy suit too far, and was hived off to manage a couple of mahogany tables round the back of Whitehall somewhere.

Homelessness

One of the policy leftovers concerns homelessness. This is a real human issue, one that touches real lives. There are people on the streets who don't want to be there. There are also people on the streets who are indifferent and don't want to help themselves. The challenge is to give them a chance and encourage them to take the proffered helping hand.

So let's take a look at some of the costs involved in what was briefly a high profile issue. The Rough Sleepers Unit, for instance, which was set up in 1999, had a £200 million award for a three year lifetime. £80 million was administered by the Housing Association for permanent accommodation. £90 million has gone into improving hostels. And over three years, £44 million was spent through the Supporting People budget. Meanwhile, local authorities get around £45 million a year.

The net result is that there were 1850 rough sleepers in England on any given night, and tonight there are estimated to be 500.

Has this reduction been achieved cost-effectively? Perhaps not. Last year, 36 LEAs had cuts in their government grant, while only 18 had increases to prioritise and to "better reward performance". So the real unsung heroes remain the volunteers and the charities which continue to do the donkey work away from the spotlight.

The Millenium Dome

The Department has also inherited the legacy of the Millennium Dome from those troubled days of yore. It is still coming to terms with its botched efforts to sell off the Dome – potential bidders had been left confused about how much land was actually on offer, information was not shared equally amongst the bidders, and, as one report put it: "It is difficult to be confident that the deal finally secured offered the best value for money that could have been achieved."

Surprisingly, a government agency will continue to be directly involved in the site – now called O2 – despite it having a 999 year lease. English Partnerships will supply "a dedicated EP team" to monitor development of the site and ensure the promised housing developments are built. It employs eleven people on site. Even in private hands, the public are still paying out for the folly.

English Partnerships grew in 1998 through a merger with the old Commission for the New Towns. This latter body employed around 300 people whose task it was to make the Hemel Hempsteads and Milton Keyneses of the world grow. An unknown proportion of English Partnerships personnel is still occupied on that immediate post-war task.

Neighbourhood renewal

Prepare for some jargon.

> "During 2005, all 87 NRF LSPs that relate to the 88 local authority areas in receipt of NRF covered their PMF self-assessments and annual reviews with GOs as part of the 2005/06 performance management framework."

If, like us, you didn't get that first time round, this means that the people in run-down local authorities who spend money on Neighbourhood Renewal conducted a self-assessment. 35% were identified as "green overall", 47% as "amber/green", and 18% "amber/red". In other words, one in two was a bit dodgy, and one in five was well dodgy. Given that Neighbourhood

Renewal involves an annual budget of over half a billion pounds, this is rather worrying. In three cities it was even decided to withhold 10% of the grant unless they pulled their socks up.

Support for Inward Investment

We go further and question the overall value of this Department. It spends £2.89 billion a year on capital projects in the English regions, part of which includes support for what it styles "regional inward investment". A review of its publications does not reveal if it has carried out any study of where the inward investment is coming from. If it turns out that the regional support is merely subsidising investment that would have gone to another part of the country anyhow, then it is clearly a waste of taxpayers' money to fuel the battle between agencies as they attempt to lure businesses to their patch.

These agencies are big players. Take the South West's. It has a staff of over 280. The South East Development Agency covers an area with an economy larger than South Africa's. A fair amount of its effort if not its purpose seems to be spent on managing EU grants, themselves not always of crystal clear benefit. At the very least, central government should commit itself to an honest cost-benefit audit of these institutions, and assess how many lasting private sector jobs they have created.

And then there was ...

☹ One quarter of all homes built under the Key Worker Schemes are lying empty. The figure is approaching half in London.

☹ John Prescott's Homeless and Housing Support Directorate reportedly spent £5,731 hiring Hampton Court Palace for an internal conference on homelessness.

☹ £5.8 million is being spent on a National Coordinating Body for Home Improvement Agencies, and £4.75 million on a National Evaluation of Neighbourhood Management Pathfinders.

- ☹ Hampshire Council spent £250,000 fixing kerbs that are 2mm too high. Engineers were despatched to 374 crossings where the kerbs were believed to be excessive.

- ☹ Hull City Council spent £300,000 on the design of a new logo that looks like a cog, then decided that the old logo was in fact better so continued to use the 3 crowns logo.

- ☹ Monmouthshire City Council plan to spend £18 million on bizarre modern art to mark the boundaries of Wales. These plans are to go ahead despite one of its constituents being denied a life saving cancer drug costing £15,000.

- ☹ Bolton City Council wasted £75,000 on elephant statues. The elephants cost £30,000 to buy, but after attempts of vandalism and robbery, £13,000 was spent on their restoration, followed by the installation of CCTV at a cost of £33,000 to prevent further attack.

- ☹ Bournemouth City Council spent £6 million on a coastal erosion prevention scheme, which involved the placement of stones onto the beach. They have since removed them at the cost of £165,000 in order to gain back the lost tourism.

Department for Constitutional Affairs (DCA)

Now part of the Orwellian-sounding Ministry of Justice

Factoids

- 36% of asylum cases take longer than six months to legally resolve.

- The Department runs a special budget called 'Very High Cost Civil Cases'. This is where solicitor's fees are expected to run to over £25,000 or a QC is involved.

- Per head, the DCA spends nearly three times as much on people in the North East as in the South East, nearly twice as much on the Welsh as on people from Birmingham, and twice as much on Londoners as on people from Yorkshire.

- The DCA currently has 100-120 procurement projects ongoing, but can't say which are the biggest.

- Since the European Legal Aid Directive for cross-border cases came in, there have been 11 applications for aid in England and Wales and 27 applications transmitted overseas.

- The cost of people not bothering to turn up to Crown Court is estimated to run at £5.4 million a year, before taking into account the lawyers' bills.

- In 2005-05, 61,616 court cases were dropped by the Prosecution, despite an initial assessment that a conviction was possible and in the public interest.

- The total liabilities of the Judicial Pensions Scheme – pensions for retiring judges – run to £1.4 billion.

- The Department is responsible for £1.6 billion's worth of Crown Courts and £15 million of Judges' Lodgings.

The DCA is the fiefdom of the Lord Chancellor.

We are concerned to learn that an unknown amount of money

has been assigned for PR purposes. The DCA's press office has been beefed up to cover the whole spread of the Criminal Justice System. This includes "an electronic briefing system, based on the Number 10 system". Its aim? "To help respond to misinformation and brief the media." That will be a non-partisan use of public funds then, won't it?

The Department has nonetheless saved some money – £60,000 in fact – by hiring out its buildings for television filming (presumably not Big Brother) and for celebratory events. However, some of that money is from events held by other government agencies, which hardly counts as an overall saving for the taxpayer. Nevertheless, it has through this and other means raised money from outside the department by its Wider Markets Initiative – £2.3 million since April 2004.

Separate, but also connected with the courts, are the Law Officers' Departments. 2005 was not a happy year for them. For the first time, some self-employed barristers decided not to accept defence or prosecution work in a month-long dispute over the level of legal aid fees. This can't have been good. Many of the Law Officers' departments are overwhelmingly reliant on buying in legal beavers. The Crown Prosecution Service, for instance, in 2005-06 spent £140 million on advocacy services from private sector barristers and only £3.3 million in-house; the Revenue and Customs Prosecution Service spent £15.7 million as opposed to £380,000 in-house; and the Serious Fraud Office spent £2 million in the private sector because it doesn't have in-house barristers at all.

Meanwhile, the latest 2005-06 figures for the Serious Fraud Office show that £3.9 million of legal costs have been awarded against the organisation through botched cases, along with £822,000 in damages. Perhaps this could be an early subject for study by the Department's new hirelings. The SFO has responded to requirements to cut expenditure under the Gershon plans by tripling its consultancy budget to £150,000.

The Treasury Solicitors (TSol) Department is a less celebrated body, but some of its units merit close review. One is the

Litigation Group, whose job it is to defend departments from being sued. It is one of the largest civil litigation practices in the country, handling 11,000 new cases every year. This tells you a lot about how much money taxpayers are forking out in damages. Another is the Bona Vacantia Division, which sounds like a Newfoundland baseball league but actually deals with 10,000 cases every year of people who die without leaving wills and obvious heirs, as well as handling a number of businesses that fold. Overall, there are 722 staff in TSol.

Northern Ireland Office (NIO)

Factoids

- In 2006, the NIO bought an unusual asset – the SS Nomadic, a White Star paddle steamer.

- The auditors estimate that £151 million of Social Security benefits are lost to fraud and error every year in Northern Ireland alone. These are assessed to be "unacceptably high" and "can be reduced".

- Among the most valuable assets owned by the Department are; Hillsborough Castle (classed, unsurprisingly, as an "immovable"); an air conditioning unit that presumably recreates the Antarctic; a pathology machine; and a tractor.

- The NIO's Compensation Agency received 98,800 letters in 2005.

- One fifth of the 1100 page National Asset Register is taken up by this department.

- The NIO has spent £44,000 on its "Are you a victim of the Troubles?" Campaign. Well, are you?

The TaxPayers' Alliance has a particular regard for those who keep an eye on our tax money in Northern Ireland, where historically some very bad men have displayed a talent for siphoning off your dosh. Even today, rough types continue the tradition of "tiger kidnapping". This is nothing to do with Johnny Morris, but everything to do with taking hostages to carry out a criminal act.

Fuel smuggling has been a criminal tradition for some time locally, because of the differential tax rates north and south of the border. This provides us with another clear-cut example, to add to Prohibition and the Cornish smugglers of old, of the truism that crime flourishes where taxes bite. It is in any event a source of some pride that policing activity led to an increase of "legitimate fuel deliveries" by 6% over 2004-05, which obviously means more revenue. This was partly achieved by the discovery of an illegal fuel laundering plant in Armagh. For a mainlander reading all this, Camlough sounds more like the home of the fuel siphoning gangs of Basrah.

But this organised criminality and loss to the public purse is not symptomatic of all the waste that hits our pockets as taxpayers.

The auditors expressed concern at the increase in estimated fraud in the Province at a time when the Department had pledged to specifically target it. The following table shows the auditor's estimates. Remember as you review these figures that even though Ulster is, *per capita*, a high recipient of state welfare money, its population forms a fortieth of the UK as a whole. That gives you some inkling of the problems nationwide.

Estimated levels of fraud and error 2005-06		
Benefit	% Defrauded	Cost (£m)
Income Support	5.4	25.6
Jobseeker's Allowance	4.4	4.1
Disability Living Allowance	9.5	54.7
Attendance Allowance*	2.2	4.2
Carer's Allowance	9.0	7.5
Pension Credit	5.7	16.3
Housing Benefit	3.7	14.0
Pension and Bereavement Benefits*	0.8	9.2
Incapacity Benefit*	4.3	13.8
Social Fund payments and loans*	2.3	1.6

* Indicates error only

These levels are obviously a concern for the taxpayer. But so too is the way in which large amounts of money have been ploughed into the Peace Process.

The Patten Reforms, which covered policing in Northern Ireland, continue to have money pumped into them. The total estimate from 2000-01 to 2007-08, covering 'severance costs' or early retirement, runs to £233,640,000. 'Non-severance costs' are £146,949,000.

The merits and demerits of these changes and redundancies are debatable. Of far clearer concern for fiscal probity is the infamous Bloody Sunday Inquiry. At its height in 2003-04 it was costing over £30 million a year, with one estimate of the total bill running to £174.36 million – and rising with every new report. It will still cost £10 million in the two years after it has been wound up. That is a heck of a lot of legal fees. To put it into context, every witness who appeared before it could instead have been given £160,000 in compensation. We calculate the whole sum is twice what it would cost, at high street prices, to buy up every single copy of *War* on the planet, the multi platinum-selling U2 album that contained the eponymous song.

The Robert Hamill Inquiry so far has cost £7.475 million; the Billy Wright Inquiry has cost £3.922 million; and the Rosemary Nelson Inquiry has cost £8.134 million.

That makes a total to date of nearly £194 million. Of this, £99.483 million has gone to lawyers.

Indeed, the Bloody Sunday legal bill was so outrageous that the government has since changed the rules. There are now maximum hourly fee levels for publicly funded legal people; a 40 hour week cap; legal representation has been limited to those 'interested parties' or key witnesses whose evidence is in dispute; expense claims are checked every month; and bills of over £100 now have to be authorised.

It reminds one of the cartoon lawyer Lionel Schultz, whose courtroom tactic is "to introduce surprise witnesses, each one more surprising than the last". This might make for good drama. It may make for a better pension plan for the lawyers involved. But it is a serious waste of public money.

Frankly, there are plenty of atrocities that took place during the Troubles. A political decision was made to make examples of a handful of incidents, but to exclude others such as the bombings at Claudy. This sadly puts the value of all inquiries, legal aid and all, at a low base.

Department for Work and Pensions (DWP)

Factoids

- The size of the Department's estate is 2.447 million square metres – or ten times the public space on the ocean super-liner Queen Mary 2.

- The DWP has a communications manager on a £50,000 salary, with a £50,000 budget, to help the Health and Safety Executive "to position the HSE as a firm but fair regulator".

- In 2004, the DWP forked out £60,000 for a case of unfair dismissal, £59,000 for two cases of constructive dismissal, and £9,000 over a Public Interest Disclosure.

- Over 2005-06, the Department spent £31 million on part-time temps.

- In November 2005, a number of the Department's staff had their personal computer files raided by criminals through an e-portal supplied by Revenue and Customs. These were used to carry out Tax Credit fraud.

- The Department last year employed 130,000 staff, but owned 156,000 computers.

- There were 170 investigations over 2005-06, which revealed £193,000 worth of internal fraud.

- The Department's auditors have qualified (that is, made reservations about) its accounts for the past seventeen years because of the endemic scale of fraud and error.

- The DWP is entitled to take back overpaid benefits from your state pension when you retire.

- The cost-delivery ratio for major benefits has reportedly dropped over the last decade, so that the Department is now officially providing an eighth less value for money.

This year, the Department is "investing" nearly £1.3 billion in, er, things. Its annual report, unhelpfully, doesn't say how much is for long-term capital projects, and how much is just short-term fire-fighting. We understand, however, that "an extensive department-wide learning and development programme to increase resource awareness and resource management skill and capability within the department is rolling out," and that:

> *"This includes new learning and development products to ensure that the Department can fully exploit the capabilities afforded through the Resource Management System."*

So now you know.

A question mark hovers over the methods the Department is using to boost its quota of disabled workforce. Its policy suggests that it is spending money on getting existing staff simply to change their declarations, in other words, cook the books. A minister describes it thus:

> *"The Department is in the process of rolling out a new resource management system that will allow it to capture such information more effectively. To coincide with the rollout, a targeted programme of communications will encourage further staff to disclose their disability status."*

This sounds suspiciously like a PR campaign designed to encourage staff to register if they have a slight twinge when it gets cold, or wear glasses.

The Department has spent an inordinate amount of energy over 2005-06 on publicity campaigns:

- £1.4 million raising new legal obligations on small business concerning the Disability Discrimination Act.

- £900,000 on the effects of anti-age discrimination legislation.

- £7.6 million targeting benefit fraud ("no ifs, no buts"), seemingly – to judge from the TV ad – by warning people not to stutter if they get caught committing fraud, and that they might be interviewed under caution, which is hardly likely to deter.

- £1.4 million "maintaining the high level awareness levels of Winter Fuel Payments", in which case why is it needed (except to highlight a political policy)?

- £3 million encouraging "customers" to apply for money that they are due under the Pension Credit scheme.

- £700,000 encouraging people to claim Council Tax Benefit.

- £1 million advertising for a Pensioners Guide which lists government services.

- Another £1 million encouraging people to take out pensions.

- £800,000 informing carers to apply for extra pension credit.

- £900,000 to highlight State Pension Deferral.

The total figure runs to £18,859,000 worth of campaigning material, newspaper adverts, and radio and TV slots that may well be forms of public information, but which also serves indirectly to remind people of the hard work being done by ministers on your behalf. In other words, it also carries a net party political advantage. To put it in perspective, this sum is almost twice the amount that all the oil giants together spend on advertising in the UK every year, including addressing the concerns of the Green lobby.

A little known aspect of the DWP is the fact that it runs its own business empire of sorts. Remploy Ltd receives £115 million of public money. It is a worthy cause, a business founded in 1945 specifically to employ disabled war veterans. Now, most of its work consists of helping people move into private sector employment, but it continues to have its own holdings. It has opened a new household and toiletries factory in St Helens, which apparently has its own microbiology unit. Sounds like an ideal cover for SMERSH, in fact. Each year it mixes enough foam bath for 400 Olympic size swimming pools, and produces more than two million tonnes of shampoo and conditioner.

We note, however, that of the fourteen business sectors in

which Remploy operated over 2005-06, not one of its enterprises made a profit. The public money which went into Remploy simply goes in to support the losses (indeed, seem to fall short of covering them, since they were £136 million in 2005-06). This makes it a significant state-subsidised industry. It's reasonable to ask if these losses can be reduced without laying-off the workforce, which would of course completely defeat the purpose of the company.

We applaud the work being done to include people who have much to contribute to society. We note a further word of caution within the government's language, however. The NHS forecasts that one in three people between the ages of 45 and 61 will become disabled. This is a staggering assessment, not least in terms of its impact upon the economy at a time when the average age of the workforce is getting older.

The same report states that currently one in six people in the UK are disabled. This raises serious questions as to where the benefits line is going to be drawn in the future, because with that number of people qualifying for disabled benefit the impact on taxes will be massive.

And then there was...

- ☹ In 2004-05, like the Department for Education and Skills, the DWP binned 165,771 of its own publications after printing more than were needed. It also pulped 82,619 publications because they were out of date.

- ☹ The DWP over a two year period spent £33.8 million advertising government benefits.

- ☹ The Department spent £645,000 on staff costs for impact assessments on its Gender, Race, and Disability Equality Schemes.

- ☹ The Department has an unerring tendency every year to mistakenly pay out around £170,000 in duplicate Christmas Bonus allowances.

Department for Culture, Media and Sport (DCMS)

Factoids

- Local authorities spend £3.2 billion a year on culture and leisure, which is more than central government and the lottery combined.

- 139 of its civil servants received 'Special Bonuses' last year. 0.4% of the Department's pay bill is set aside to cover this cost.

- The nation has bought a brass foundry in Woolwich, and a Japanese bullet train. We also own a rowing lake and three National Sports Centres.

- In 2005, the Department sold off part of the Royal Garden Hotel land, once part of Kensington Palace Gardens, to the Imperial Tobacco Pension Fund. It had been in state ownership since the time of William III. The Royal Household were apparently consulted.

- It also sold two residential properties in Windsor, and terminated a shared lease on accommodation in Woburn Place which was costing a quarter of a million pounds a year.

- This year, the Department is selling off car parking space to the north of the British Library, worth £26.6 million. It is the old Somers Town Goods Yard, which was never built on when the Library was redesigned.

- It also plans to sell another five residential properties that it for some reason holds in Windsor. The occupants have long term leases. A neighbouring one was sold for £44,000.

- It intends to sell off the Tote. The last attempt to do this was halted when the excellent Adam Smith Institute challenged the deal, saying it was short-changing the taxpayer by £400 million. The Department had shockingly spent over £100,000 on consultants to evaluate it.

- The Secretary of State is also bizarrely *ex officio* the Minister for Humanitarian Assistance, and runs the Humanitarian Assistance Unit for Brits who have been hit by a major crisis.

- The Department is potentially liable for a whopping £6,884,783,704, as compensation to lenders if all its museums go up in smoke overnight. Most of this liability is in the Tate (£3 billion) and the National Gallery (£2.5 billion).

- The South Bank Centre meanwhile is covered for nearly £124 million, should it be torched, though some critics would consider it an architectural gain for the capital. It costs taxpayers £18 million a year to run, excluding a £400,000 grant for buying new work.

This Department is one of the most obvious candidates for having a chariot ridden through its corridors, its rider calling upon the Gods of ancient Britain to visit brimstone and thunderous retribution upon its many idle spendings and worthless frittering of public millions. And perhaps they'd give you a performance grant if you did.

The tone is set the instant you open its annual report. Right at the front is a two-page spread: a photo which, when cited in a parliamentary question, adopted the official title of 'Naked Man on Breakwater Wrapped in Lightbulbs'. NMOBWIL, as we refer to him for convenience sake, is apparently a still taken from a film entitled 'Andout', and funded by Arts Council England to the tune of £7,000.

Youth Music meanwhile is described as a national charity that has handed over £53 million to date, to "facilitate high quality and diverse music making for young people up to the age of 18". It claims to have created employment for over 8,000 music leaders and trainees, though it remains unclear as to how many of these are permanent jobs in the private sector. It receives Lottery funding.

£27 million is being spent on the Bookstart programme, which provides young children and their families with free packs of books, "advice and tips on how to enjoy sharing them together", and a "personal invitation" to join their local library. Yes, because when you are aged 8 months, 18 months and 3 years, which is when you receive your packs, you are really such a social wallflower that an invitation is just what it takes to encourage you to pooter off down to bookland.

In the period 2005-06, over 450,000 Bookstart baby packs were delivered, and the Bookstart+ and My Bookstart Treasure Chest mailings soon followed. An announcement has also been made that a free book will be sent to children before they start primary school, and again when they start secondary school. Presumably, these further three million books will be automated and chase truants down the street.

Some of the latest titles include *Peebo Baby, Go Wild With Colours, Wobble Bear Says Yellow, Little Kipper Splosh, Halibut Jackson,* and for the Welsh speakers among us, *Un Ted Mas o'r Gwely* (One Fell Out of Bed). Plenty of inspiration there for rock musicians in desperate need of a name for their band.

The Department is also responsible for keeping tabs on subsidies to the British film industry. Historically some outstanding films have been made with government help and the public interest has been well served by them. Think of Laurence Olivier breaking several bones in order to achieve glory in Henry V, and the stiff upper lip of Noel Coward's destroyer captain, both of which invigorated the public spirit in a time of national crisis.

We are not sure the same justifications can be made today for the £25 million distributed each year through the UK Film Council or the £19 million lavished on the British Film Institute.

According to the DCMS, the UK film industry in 2005 received £124 million through tax incentives, lottery and grant-in-aid funding. In return, tax receipts on "film-related activity" amounted to £850 million, while UK film added £3.1 billion to the country's GDP. So the film industry creates a lot of wealth and employs a lot of people. We like that. Our questions relate to some of the more specialist film support. We'll look at some examples later.

A new £12 million Cultural Leadership Fund has also been set up by Gordon Brown, "to benefit leadership in the wider cultural sector". We're not sure how. It reeks of statist intervention to groom a future artistic elite and make politicians look dandy (but watch out, Gordon: we all know what happened to Tony after he schmoozed with the Gallagher brothers). What does the Fund do with this money?

Well, firstly, there is the Clore Leadership Programme's short courses, costing £1,375,500 over two years. These deliver a series of 13 two-week intensive residential courses in selected universities and business schools "designed to cultivate the skills of emerging cultural leaders".

Then there is 'Catalyst ... Unleashed ...' in partnership with Unilever, costing £45,000, which are two pilot projects for a "commercial business and cultural sector collaboration in learning". £2.5 million is being spent on a two year scheme to establish a 'Creative Knowledge Lab'. This is to provide a "unique and comprehensive web based resource for cultural leaders at all stages of their careers to develop and manage their leadership progression and potential". A smaller sum is being spent on 14 test Leadership Development Networks, designed to "pilot leadership development through network activity and identifying shared ambitions".

The Fund spent £83,000 last year on central administration alone, a figure that will rise to £150,000 this year. Never let it be said that the Department is dictating to those it seeks to empower. This figure includes its 'Call for Ideas' programme, which ran for four months in 2005 and received a mighty 170 written responses.

The only true mark of the cost-effectiveness of these leadership training programmes will be the day when Parliament is stormed by mime artists, a revolutionary junta of empowered Dadaists takes over running the country, and the hallways of the Treasury echo to the sound of Folk.

It is also of some interest to note where VisitBritain has been spending money. The smooth-talkers of tourism have an annual budget of £33 million. In order to entice foreign visitors to these shores, £5.5 million has been spent advertising in the United States, £1.2 million in Japan, £1.5 million attracting the Aussies and Kiwis, £2.3 million in France, £2.7 million in Germany, £2 million on the Scandinavians ... and ... £6.9 million on ourselves. VisitBritain has spent £6,870,000 on domestic marketing, to an audience that is visiting Britain if it gets up and puts the kettle on.

Some of this went on targeting gay visitors in some rather brash official publications that actually offended gay tourists. They, like everyone else, wanted to visit the UK to go fell walking in Yorkshire or see the Tower of London, rather than visit nightlife that they can get in their home city.

The Department has also spent, to date, £3.2 million on an intrusive survey. 'Taking Part' is a questionnaire designed "to find out how people choose to spend their own time and their views on the leisure activities and facilities open to them", and to help with the Department's "understanding of people's lifestyle choices and the reasons behind their participation or non-participation in our sectors." This is done by sending someone round to doorstep you for 45 minutes. A market research agency has been hired to collate stats from 47,000 randomly selected people; some are blessed with a follow-up call to check that the interviewer was polite.

But hearts and minds are important. That's why the Department has its own crisis centre in case of a national incident. While the Home Office is dispatching dog teams and the MoD is prepping the SAS, the Secretary of State for Culture pushes a button. Out of hidden caverns below Whitehall storm the Tourism Industry Emergency Response Group. Established in 2001, "the group has an excellent record in planning for and responding to emergencies affecting the tourism industry", apparently. We are delighted to learn from a responsible minister that "it enjoys the full confidence of government and the industry" and that it won the *PR Week* award for 'Best Crisis Communication following the July 2005 terrorist attacks in London'. So we can all sleep soundly in our beds.

We do know who's to blame for all this. The Department has its own designated internal think tank within its Strategy Division, costing between £60,000 and £85,000 a year, and staffed by civil servants. It pulls in a variety of academics and members of private think tanks to suggest policy. Also invited are "external experts from the Third Sector", which we think is just left of the Orion Nebula.

But the real scandal involving the Department is how it has handled the switchover to digital telly. Consider for a moment: every household over the next few years will find that the box sets, before which they have happily vegetated for years gone by, will overnight become obsolete. They will need a magic box to upgrade it, or a brand new telly.

Never mind that when the British weather goes all electrical the reception of digital televisions will go down the pan. Or that 1.5% of households simply won't get full reception, whatever the weather. Consider for a moment what the government so far hasn't: the waste.

According to the government's own figures, three in ten households still haven't made any change. Heaven knows how many households have got one digitally-capable set, but also have old analogue sets knocking around various bedrooms, a portable in the caravan, a black and white set in the attic, a spare in the back room for when the mother-in-law wants to watch The Two Ronnies while the footy is on...

But there is no escape from the government's policy. Ministers have calculated that not much more than the present 70% of households will take up digital telly willingly. To quote the government:

"Until we turn off the analogue signals, we will not be able to increase the coverage of digital terrestrial much beyond 73%. Only full switchover will allow everyone who currently receives analogue TV to enjoy digital television."

So if you're one of the 27% of licence fee payers who is perfectly happy with your old set, tough biscuit.

There is some relief being offered. If you are an OAP or disabled (and haven't already been scared into the change by the BBC's pressureverts), you may be eligible to receive one of the 5.8 million free switchovers available to qualifying households in England alone. The downside is that the government has been given the legal right to trawl through all your benefits to find out whether you qualify.

Helpfully, under the legislation, if you are blind you get an upgrade free.

The switchover doesn't come cheap. The end cost to the BBC is estimated (currently) at £216 million. And the Corporation, by which we mean, of course, the TV licence taxpayer, will have to fork out an additional £600 million to support those millions of boxes going out.

But this massive sum, which doesn't include the costs of research, communications and programme support, takes no account of the hidden environmental cost either. As DEFRA acknowledges, disposal of the waste sets can't be done by standard landfill. The EU Landfill Directive entered UK law with a helping hand from The Landfill (England and Wales) Regulations 2002. Items such as cathode ray tubes are classified as hazardous waste, which requires pre-treatment. From October 2007, non-hazardous waste (i.e. the remainder of the telly) has to be pre-treated. Any set that is sent for landfill will have to be pre-treated accordingly.

From 1 July 2007, waste TV sets also became subject to the waste electrical and electronic equipment directive (WEEE). Local Authorities and retailers (and hence, ultimately, you) will pay for electrical goods to be stripped and bits recycled. Some official estimates have total WEEE costs rising to a third of a billion pounds a year.

What we are looking at here is potentially another fridge mountain fiasco. No one disputes the need for environmentally friendly waste disposal. But a changeover on this scale, done on a hope-for-the-best basis, risks ending up with sets being dumped all over the countryside in makeshift tips.

Keep your eyes open for the next fiasco. The European Commission is looking at harmonising the radio spectrum for short range devices. Heaven knows how this will whack your front door audio-visual kit or emergency service radios.

And then there was ...

☹ The Department spent £11 million over the last two years on its website, 'Culture Online'. This included support for 'Playground Fun', teaching things like clapping and skipping games, and 'Plant Cultures', which invites people to share what South Asian shrubbery means to them.

☹ To counter prejudice, the government spent £220,000 on an exhibition in Manchester looking at 1,001 Muslim inventions. A high point commemorated Abul Qasim Ibn Firnas, iconically if simplistically portrayed as a man on a turban on a hang glider.

☹ It also backed The Dark, an installation of total darkness with sounds in it. Insanely, it got turned into a website by the DCMS, 'The Dark Online'. You need headphones. And presumably a blanket over your desk.

☹ The Department has also splurged £4.1 million refurbishing its Cockspur Street offices, £3.96 million for a five year contract to manage its offices, and £1.5 million administering the Listed Places of Worship scheme.

☹ £25 million of lottery money went to refurbishing the Royal Festival Hall, excluding £5 million to cover closure and "change management costs".

☹ Last year, the Department spent £140,000 on adverts on BBC licences, and before that, £21,000 on adverts about the BBC Charter.

Foreign and Commonwealth Office (FCO)

Factoids

- In 2004-05, the FCO spent 3%, or £6.9 million, of its Estate Running Costs budget on consultants.

- In a three year stretch, it spent £22,000 advertising for an Assistant Librarian, £81,000 on general diversity advertising, £71,000 in one year advertising for accountants, £224,000 for four campaigns officers, £25,000 for a Head of the Polar Regions Unit, and £23,000 advertising for an ambassador to the Papacy (which was then awarded to a policy wonk).

- Only after a National Audit Office suggestion did the Department start to include medical staff with its rapid deployment teams.

- It has £20 million of antiques and works of art on its books, and over a third of a billion pounds of residential land and buildings.

- The UK is one of the five major financial contributors towards the Universal Postal Union, paying £960,000 in 2005.

- The FCO pays out around £3 million a year for VIP suites at Gatwick and Heathrow.

- The FCO and Home Office sponsored the Radical Middle Way roadshow for Islamic moderates to the tune of £250,400. These activists now claim they are being ignored.

- Last year, the FCO handed out £235,427.51 in compensation. £84,000 went to victims of the Istanbul bombing; the remainder was in small claims.

- The FCO wrote off £901,000 for a stockpile of out-of-date visa vignettes that were useless.

- Of the 20 biggest procurement contracts since 1997, one is the FCO's Berlin embassy, one is for refurbishing the Old

Admiralty building, one is its 'Knowledge Management Programme', and five are contracts in Iraq.

- Over 2005-06, the FCO hired 241 people on fee-paid contracts worth £7.5 million, working for an unspecified number of hours. This was up a fifth on the previous year.

- The Al-Qaeda and Taliban (United Nations Measures) Order 2006 freezes the assets of Al-Qaeda and Taliban terrorists. But the government can't spend them as they unhelpfully remain the property of the terrorist.

Britain is still a force to be reckoned with in the world. It is a position that confers status and privilege on its diplomatic staff.

This probably explains why the British Community in Rwanda was given the honour of naming a gorilla. The Embassy launched an official competition to choose the name at the Queen's Birthday Celebrations. Unfortunately, the only names that were suggested were Jack Daniels, Gin and Tonic, and Champagne. Thinking this wouldn't reflect too well on our nationals, the ambassador's daughter ended up naming it. Consequently, roaming somewhere around the Great Lakes region is a gorilla called Big Ben.

Names are a very important consideration in international politics. The FCO consults the Permanent Committee on Geographical Names, which tells government whether the correct name for Burma is Myanmar or not, and what other foreign places outside of Antarctica should be called. The lead section on geographical names in the FCO then makes the final decision. The Minster explains the mechanism thus:

> *"The policy for the application of geographical names is to follow the practice of the supreme administering authority of the country concerned. It is the FCO's policy to recognise changes of geographical name where these fall within the sovereign competence of a particular foreign*

government. For example, in India the name change from Madras to Chennai has been made according to due processes within the government of India and requires appropriate acknowledgement within the FCO. The name Madras would therefore now be considered a former name for this city, in the same way that Salisbury is a former name for Harare.

However, there will be a number of occasions where a geographical name within the sovereign competence of a particular foreign government is already known in a traditional form in the English language and it would not be unusual for this form to be used within the FCO for ease of recognition. For example, the Burmese geographical name Yangon has long been known in the English language as Rangoon, and that form continues to be acceptable today. However, the use of English-language terms can also alter over time. This could be considered to have occurred in the case of Beijing, where the name Peking is today rarely encountered as the English-language name."

In the period 2005-06, the FCO paid £59,826.83 to run this committee – a staggering sum, until you discover that the MoD paid out twice that as its share. Perhaps this makes sense on one level. If you are going to invade a country, best to make sure that you pick the right one on the maps.

Time was that an explorer like, say, George Vancouver would discover a place and name it after an admiral mate of his, which is how the volcano Mount Rainier got its name. Vancouver's lieutenant, Broughton, named a shoreline after his commander, later to become a City. Other places would be named after monarchs or after defining local features. A classic case is the capital of Saskatchewan, Regina – named in honour of Queen Victoria by her daughter, who was married to the Governor General. Before then it had gone by the name of Pile of Bones, after the remains of bison in otherwise empty grassland. But those were happier days when you didn't need to fork out large sums on an expensive committee.

It is an intriguing detail and an insight into how Whitehall functions. It's also a rather French way of doing things, expecting the public to follow the trend and appreciate that the proper spelling for Kiev is now Kyiv and Calcutta is Kolkata, just because some grandee expects it of them. We assume the BBC is brought to heel along the way.

The FCO is also our face in Europe, advancing our interests in the European Union. Or more frequently, according to cynics, the EU's interests in Britain.

Occasionally, however, the wheels come off the Rolls Royce. It recently fell to Britain to assume the six month long EU Presidency. One might have hoped that the FCO would avoid repeating its mistake of 1998, when it allowed schoolchildren to design logos for each of the member states, and upset the Italians by representing them as a pizza. Sadly not.

The logo its image consultants chose this time, at a cost of £30,000, was a flight of swans. According to the designers, the logo was a sign of leadership, teamwork and efficiency. Unfortunately for the Europe Minister, it was also the sign of the Bruges Group, a long-established British Eurosceptic campaign organisation. Doubly unfortunate, it was also redolent of the bird flu which hit a few weeks later.

It was not as if the symbol was barely used. The FCO spent a colossal £539,000 on special stationary for use at presidency meetings and events. It also forked out £251,000 on small gifts, such as mugs, umbrellas, bags, key rings, pocket-sized clocks and radios, watches, logoed desk items and the like, to hand out to diplomats and the press corps. Another £243,000 went on items of clothing, such as the deeply unpopular ties, plus scarves and lapel pins and such. A further £32,000 was spent on materials for dressing up venues, such as logo stands.

The logo thus turned out to be as helpful as another slogan the Department uses on freebie bags in some of its embassies:

"There is no such thing as 'abroad' any more." We assume this novel concept has something to do with lax Home Office attitudes towards asylum seeker applications.

It's not as if this mis-spending can be explained by a shortage of gatekeepers, either. There's a designated Europe Minister with his own civil service patch. Unfortunately, when the post was redefined it kicked off a turf war with the Foreign Secretary, ultimately leading to a public barney over who could answer which questions in the Commons. It didn't help his office's image that stories were circulating that the minister was preoccupied with buying a shiny new sign for his door simply to indicate he had the right to attend Cabinet meetings. On top of that, there is the potential for a policy clash with the European Secretariat, 28 people based in the Cabinet Office whose designated task is to coordinate European policy across government. Things could be better organised.

Tragically, our man in the Panama hat has been suckered more than once of late. In 2006, seven cases of fraud were reported to the Department's Financial Compliance Unit. £6,500 went for a wander in Albania, £17,000 in Outer Mongolia, £1,200 in Ekaterinburg, £25,000 in Japan, petty cash in Brazil and St Petersburg, but the real shocker was £186,000 swizzled out of staff in the Dominican Republic.

We have also found out a bit more about the case of the stolen paintings we mentioned in the last *Bumper Book*. You may recall we discovered that our man in Buenos Aires got burgled while in temporary residence elsewhere, and the thief wandered off with some of the decor. We now know that the lost works were:

- a painting by Michael Rocca called 'Offering to Jupiter', valued at £80,000;

- a £35,000 lake landscape by George Arnauld;

- a £60,000 painting by Anthony Higmore called 'St James's Park and Banqueting Rooms';

- a £60,000 landscape by Edward Charles Williams;

❦ and a £5,000 painting of the splendidly-named Sir Woodbine Parish by Edmund Dyer (after Thomas Phillips RA).

Those dark patches on the walls will be noticed.

The FCO has a generous allowance so that it can host parties and functions. We approve. There's nothing like stuffing the Austrian chargé d'affaires with a plate full of Lincolnshire pork pies to help export outboard motors to the Danubian riverines, nor anything so delicious as inflicting Yorkshire wine on the French cultural attaché. We note with approval that there has been a transfer of vol-au-vent funds from Old Europe to the New. But we still think you have a right as a taxpayer to know which of our embassies host the most swinging parties. The table opposite reveals all.

Expenditure on parties thrown by FCO

NATO only	05/06	Conversation over Ferrero Rochers
Ankara	£31,738	When are you letting us into the EU?
Bucharest	£13,290	Count Dracula
Oslo	£39,350	Skiing, fjords, tall blondes
Ottawa	£44,944	Maple syrup, secession, moose
Reykjavik	£18,514	Bjork
Sofia	£21,101	The Wombles
Washington	£121,729	Is Bin Laden in your basement?

EU only	05/06	Conversation over Ferrero Rochers
Dublin	£39,100	An introduction to black velvet
Helsinki	£37,211	Saunas and Santa
Nicosia	£33,726	Dissing the Turks
Stockholm	£46,233	Furniture
Valletta	£21,945	Humphrey Bogart movies
Vienna	£32,470	Harry Lime's whereabouts

EU and NATO	05/06	Conversation over Ferrero Rochers
Athens	£39,879	More dissing the Turks
Bonn/Berlin	£55,567	Not mentioning the War
Bratislava	£8,878	Where did the O go in Czechoslovakia?
Brussels	£40,526	Legumes, including ever-closer onions
Budapest	£34,648	Fiddling
Copenhagen	£28,093	Herringing
The Hague	£39,668	Who's next before the Tribunal?
Lisbon	£23,481	Fados and other words ending in -sh
Ljubljana	£19,100	Life in the Duchy of Carantania
Luxembourg	£20,326	Banking, radio stations
Madrid	£50,649	If Ceuta is Spanish, Gibraltar is British
Paris	£167,591	The charm of St Helena
Prague	£35,791	Bohemian living
Riga	£15,933	The art of amber
Rome	£41,673	Is the Pope a Catholic?
Tallin	£9,207	The Livonian crusades
Vilnius	£15,035	Teutons and swamps
Warsaw	£47,881	How to eat wonderful stodge

The FCO of course has a variety of affiliated bodies. The British Association for Central and Eastern Europe is one such (budget: £167,000). Then there's the Great Britain-China Centre (budget: £300,000), part of whose role has been to provide the fig leaf of an "honorary Chairmanship" to poor old John Prescott.

Within the service itself, Human Resources run the Disability Action Group, the Ethnic Diversity Advisory Group, and the Gender Advisory Group. These are distinct from two staff-run organisations.

The Gender Group published a booklet, *Inclusive Government: Mainstreaming gender into Foreign Policy.* No doubt this is a well-intentioned initiative by caring and sensitive people. However, they do not always seem plugged into the real world. Is the best use of resources going to be supplying water and a safe environment to the people of Southern Helmand, or alternatively is it following the booklet's guidelines and encouraging Afghan men to express their emotions? Good luck explaining that one to the patriarchs.

The most popular FCO quango has to be the 'Government Hospitality Advisory Committee for the Purchase of Wine'. It was established in 1922 to advise the Minister-in-Charge of the then Government Hospitality Fund on the maintenance of an appropriate standard of wine for use at government functions. This entails giving advice, after tasting, on the purchase of wine, the exchange of wines if necessary, the management and stocking of the GH cellar at Lancaster House, and advice on suppliers.

Members – who have to be Masters of Wine – attend business meetings, usually four times a year, to consider the state of the cellar, consumption trends and the current situation of the wine market. Their minutes are a delight. Apparently they are partial to Red Burgundy, and are quite prepared in blind tastings to give English grapes a run for their money. Running costs last year ran to just under £9,600 (excluding the staff time of the bigwig who runs the committee). This included the costs of samples, and the cost of four meetings and lunch for the committee and its guests.

"Hello Hello 0898 Lovechat? Is Foreign Office here."

Readers of last year's *Bumper Book* will recall the saga of the FCO's satellite phone. This rather key asset went missing, and several months later was found to have rung up a whopping £594,370 phone bill. Understandably, the auditors got a little concerned at how this could happen and looked into it. They managed to piece together a sad episode of departmental waste and confusion. This is the fuller story.

September 2003 . . . . . .
Ten satellite phones are sent to Iraq. No bills are received until the following June. They are signed off centrally in London.

Summer 2004 . . . . . .
An inventory in Iraq reveals that one of the phones used the previous September and October is missing.

August 2004 . . . . . .
All ten phones are barred.

September 2004 . . . . . .
A junior FCO desk pilot in the Telephony Section spots the high cost and useage. Nobody acts on the information and the bills still get paid.

March 2005 . . . . . .
One of the remaining phones packs up entirely.

29th June 2005 . . . . . .
The service provider expresses concern to the FCO about the high level of activity on one of the phones, particularly since the user had tried to activate a conference call feature instead of the normal satellite feed. They put a temporary bar on the feed while the FCO checks to see if it has been stolen.

15th July 2005 . . . . . .
The FCO decides to switch off all the phones and end the contract. An audit finds five of the phones, and staff work out that three others are in FCO hands. Two bought phones plus a rented one (which had already been barred) remain missing.

The investigators worked out that the satellite phones and their chargers were stolen at the same time, before they had been issued. It also seems, judging from the call pattern, that several people benefited. The plum choice for calls had been to the Wallis and Futuna Islands (a French dependency in the South Pacific), which cost £5.94 a minute.

We in the TaxPayers Alliance would like to helpfully point out that the islands have a total population of only around 15,000 people, in part it is said because the islanders of Alofi got eaten by their neighbours. This is a relatively low number of potential suspects. Columbo would start with the 1,900 people listed in the telephone directory.

And then there was…

- ☹ Despite the cloud hanging over Lord Levy when he left his position as the PM's personal envoy in the Middle East, a £6,000 farewell party was thrown at Lancaster House in London.

- ☹ More than £16 million of taxpayers' money has been spent on the creation and upkeep of VIP lounges in Heathrow and Gatwick. They are owned and operated by BAA but the FCO contributes to the cost of facilities, which are used by ministers, high-ranking civil servants and foreign dignitaries among others. They also charge a rather overpriced £230 per visit which, when compare to the £18 VIP lounge already present at Heathrow and Gatwick, seems rather steep.

- ☹ Ministers at the Foreign Office are receiving 'life coaching' at the taxpayers' expense, at an estimated cost of £250 per hour. The coaches are expected to act as 'critical friends', and help ministers 'download' their problems and stresses.

Department for Environment, Food and Rural Affairs (DEFRA)

Factoids

- The Department intends to improve safety with pesticides by "improving clarity and reducing jargon in public communicating and by engaging with stakeholders".

- In 2005, DEFRA staff had 3 major injuries, 70 minor injuries, and 20 that came under the bracket of 'Near Misses (Including Verbal Abuse)'.

- Its employees also had to avoid 13 attempted lynchings by angry farmers.

- Over a twelve month period, 18 laptops worth nearly £15,000 were stolen from DEFRA premises. A Victorian writing desk also went walkies.

- The government has put 182 solar panels and 75 wind turbines on its public buildings. The Leader of the Opposition is following suit.

- The Department spent £50 million last year on 'Envirowise', an in-house consultancy and marketing programme, encouraging people to send in amusing pictures of their bins, and businesses to run media stunts on waste.

- It also spent £16 million on 'travel' last year, which made it into the top twenty spends list of the decade. £9 million went on compensation for a stretch of mud flats at Fagbury, which was abandoned to the sea.

- The British Potato Council has assets of half a million pounds.

- The British Cattle Movement Service uses 4,000 square meters of office space to trace mobile cows.

- The pension plan of the former Director General of the Office of Water Services was topped up by an extra

£40,000 "in recognition of tax benefits lost" because of delays in approving his "by-analogy pension scheme". The analogy presumably being a mountain of cash. Unfortunately, the Office has no idea how much its pension pot contains for everyone else.

- The Department owns 1716 hectares of experimental farm land, Sea Fish House in Edinburgh, and a £1.6 million computer system on fly tipping.

- Other agencies own £8 million worth of Nine Elms Flower Market, and £735 million of woodland. They've just bought a Loch.

- Government departments across the board are wasting £120 million on expensive food, with milk, for instance, being bought at rates varying from 17p to 44p a pint, and wholemeal loaves from 32p and £1.10.

- The Department has an ongoing commitment to look after something built in the 1970s – an experimental "offshore reservoir". But happily, it probably won't have to pay up £100 million for seed potatoes that the Argentinians destroyed, alleging they were diseased.

There are signs of hope from this department. But it is not universal. When John Prescott surrendered his environmental briefs (steady!), his successor decided to prune one expensive element of them. It transpires that the former Deputy PM's environmental awards were rather more expensive than they were worth. The events were costing £300,000 to stage, three fifths of which were blown on consultants. Cancelling them cost another £55,000. At least, however, the new minister appreciated that the awards were just an ego trip for the department and cut her losses before yet more was wasted on a glitzy bash (even if most of the preparations had already, by then, been made).

One ongoing piece of research has long baffled MPs with farming constituencies. It relates to bovine TB, a serious issue. For many years now, DEFRA has been conducting research into the chances of cattle catching it from badgers. But the research project just seems to have gone on and on and on. . .

Over the last year, the Department has spent:

- ↻ £38.8 million on testing cattle for TB.

- ↻ £31.1 million on compensating farmers for experimenting on their cattle and then sending them for compulsory slaughter.

- ↻ £5.5 million on continuing administration for the Randomised Badger Culling Trial (RBCT) even though it has been wound up.

- ↻ £7.6 million on Veterinary Laboratories Agency work.

- ↻ £12.3 million on "other research" dealing with the issue.

- ↻ £1.7 million on admin overheads for coordinating all this.

This makes a grand total in just one year of £97 million. Yet MPs first started questioning the value of the research ten years back. That was 10,957 dead badgers ago.

DEFRA helpfully spent £1.15 million on a project working out badger density in the UK. This involved counting a lot of badger droppings near setts and keeping SAS-style surveillance on their neighbourhoods. Thanks to this essential research, and bearing in mind the model: group size = $\exp(0.99 + 0.71 \times [\log(FAR+1)])$ – we understand there to be around 300,000 of the monochrome chaps wandering around our country lanes. This means the government effectively has been spending £330 on each of them every year.

The problem is not one of spending money to protect cattle from the risk of TB. It's that the research seems to develop a life of its own. Exactly the same thing happened with research on rabbits. In the wild, rabbits can become a plague-infested livestock killer, so DEFRA needed to do some research to minimise the threat. Unfortunately, civil servants realised that the only real option was to conduct a mass cull, and that the sight of the cuddly denizens of Watership Down dangling from wires would not go down well with wishy-washy urbanites. The solution, one former minister tells us in frustration, was for the civil servants to ignore the problem by just reopening the research.

In fact, DEFRA is a department that seems to be built upon research. A staggering number of projects are run each year. Some of the hundreds that were run in 2006 included:

- ℉ Stickleback test method validation.

- ℉ Genetic structure of cod population in the English Channel and southern North Sea.

- ℉ Development of alternatives to methyl bromide fumigation for intransit treatments for alien invertebrate pests.

- ℉ Biorational alternatives to conventional pesticides based on insect hormones.

- ℉ DEFRA biosecurity chip.

- ℉ Designing an abattoir survey to determine the PrP genotype profile of the slaughter lamb population in Great Britain.

- ℉ Factors affecting transmission and protective immunity of European Bat Lyssaviruses.

- ℉ Colour and translucency of food liquids.

- ℉ Indo-UK collaborative research programme on climate change impacts and adaptation in India.

- ℉ Sludge – depthwise sampling and lit review.

- ℉ Illegal motor vehicle use of rights of way.

- ℉ Maintaining cracking-clay experimental platforms at Faringdon, Boxworth and Rowden.

- ℉ Evaluating the potential of carnivore and scavenger species as sentinels of new and emerging diseases in the UK.

- ℉ [Our favourite] Do bats avoid radar?

Let's not be too hasty in our condemnation. The £200,000 spent on sticklebacks will determine whether looking at these little fishes can prove if water is polluted. £380,000 will hopefully help resolve if your cat or nearby shrew will catch something contagious from whatever it brings in. And the £4,000 going on batty radar will help find a way of stopping the poor blighters getting sucked into wind generators.

The benefits of other projects are less clear – such as the £118,000 on how conflicts are resolved if cars drive all over the public footpath at the edge of your field, and the £280,000 spent trying to work out a definition of how see-through your apple juice is without just looking at it.

We shouldn't be surprised that officials get badger-vision and lose track of their senses. This is, after all, the agency that brought you the cattle hecatomb. It also signed up to European regulation EC 1774/2002 on fallen stock. In the past, animals which died in the field could be buried where they fell. But of course, to the tidy minds of the bureaucrat, this equates to pollution. So an additional administrative burden was created for farmers and for government.

Taxpayers' money is still today providing a temporary subsidy to support an industry of carcass removal men. Of course, if you live in the Styx (which means you are likely to be a subsistence farmer) you will be paying more for the call-out. Half a million cases have to be dealt with every year, covering everything farmed from sheep, pigs and goats, to alpaca llamas and apparently, now even fish. Picture it as a cross between Dr Doolittle and a piano removal man. Each cow costs on average somewhere between £50 and £100 to remove, depending on the region; a sheep between £12 and £40. Most of this direct cost falls on the farmer, but of course someone has to check that the rules are being followed. The government estimates that the cost of compliance is £20 million a year on top of the existing £30 million BSE arrangements.

DEFRA is also the department that botched the Single Farm Payments aid to farmers. The poorest farmers suffered most, but the effect was felt across the range of farmland holdings. By the end of 2006, 809 claims valued at under €100 still hadn't been paid – about 7% of the total. £15 million of owed money was still in DEFRA's hands five months after the close of the deadline. Ten people were still owed part of a payment of €300,000 or more. The Agency has been obliged to pay out £596,000 in compensation to cover the interest on the money not handed over. Note, however, that this 'compensation' is merely interest added to cover inflation and the like from the late payment. It doesn't take into account cases where a farmer has gone bankrupt or had a family split up due to the crisis this mismanagement has caused.

That's why we have particular sympathy for the cases that have been put into the 'difficult to resolve' category. This is where the Department is having problems deciding whom to pay because there is a partnership dispute, the farmer has gone bankrupt, or there is a divorce ongoing. Even though in some of the cases the Department may well be liable for the very difficulties that are delaying payment, it still refuses to consider paying proper compensation for the consequences of its incompetence.

There is a strong whiff of double standards in this. As a minister incautiously admitted, DEFRA has a robust policy of pursuing money that *it* is owed.

We do not as a rule of thumb support state aid, in farming or in other industries. Countries like New Zealand have weened themselves off it, to the benefit of ordinary families across the land. But it is no good either if a government department is so incompetent it can't pay what it has promised, and fails to deliver what a farmer has been told to expect as part of his business and bank plan for the year.

It says something about the level of incompetence that the British government has actually been fined by Brussels for its (mis)management of Single Farm Payments. At the time of writing, it looks like taxpayers are going to be surcharged a staggering third of a billion pounds for DEFRA's uselessness and the ineffectiveness of its Secretary of State (who was, Heaven help us, subsequently promoted to Foreign Secretary). The fine will not go to the farmers: it will go to the EU.

However, what really shocks us has been the Department's complacency on an international issue. The European Commission grants import licenses for stocks of foreign beef from southern Africa. Regulation 1380/2006, for example, allowed into the EU over 14,000 tonnes from Botswana, 7,500 tonnes from Madagascar, and 3,000 tonnes from Swaziland.

But it also includes beef exported from two of the region's nastiest governments, Namibia and Zimbabwe. Both, and in particular the latter under Robert Mugabe, are embroiled in land grab schemes. There have been many reports of farms being handed, not to poor but dedicated workers, but to cronies of the regime. The Namibians at least seem to offer some level of compensation.

Zimbabwe is allowed to export 9,100 tonnes of beef to the EU. We know £32,000 of meat and offal came in direct to Britain in 2005, and a similarly small amount via South Africa, but there is no government data on how much has been processed in other EU countries and imported to this country in pizzas and bratwursts from the continent.

Certainly, no one in DEFRA, or elsewhere in government, can say where the original beef came from. The British government profess total ignorance of what proportion is coming from farms seized by the ruthless Zimbabwean regime, and from stocks of cattle that, thanks to authorised EU exports, are paying for Mugabe to stay in power.

And then there was …

- ⊗ The Forestry Commission advertised for a £30,000 diversity chief to tackle the shortage of homosexual lumberjacks.

- ⊗ Environment minister Barry Gardiner put in claims last year for driving his car 10,852 miles around his constituency and to his home 12 miles away. The mileage allowance came to £4,213.

☹ Despite Gordon Brown's entreaties that we all fly less, the tax inspectors over at HM Revenue and Customs racked up a £3 million bill for flights in the last year, including £2.1 million spent on flights to Scotland, where the Prime Minister lives.

Department for International Development (DFID)

Factoids

- In its annual report, the Department claims:

  "DFID was ranked at the top end of Whitehall practice in a Treasury survey covering financial management and delivery planning."

  Curiously, Ed Balls denies the existence of such a report:

  "The Treasury commends DFID for the progress it has made in improving financial management and delivery planning. However the Treasury has not drawn up any rankings for Departments in these areas."

- Last year, DFID paid out £3,756 to a landlord in Nepal after the house it had rented was destroyed by terrorists.

- DFID also paid out £1,000 to a member of staff for "loss of personal effects", and £16,000 to "eight colonial pensioners" whose pension had been miscalculated over a number of years.

- DFID spent £12,934 advertising its free magazine, £3,642 on adverts in *Black History Month* magazine, and £26,000 on adverts promoting the role of trade in fighting world poverty (some of which oddly were carried in *Big Issue North*).

- DFID provides £59.4 million of aid to China, which itself supplies billions of its own aid to Africa to further its own international, and at times anti-Western, interests. China also supplies the loans that are indebting many of these countries again.

One item of major concern over the priorities of this department concerns its use of PR agencies. We have some data from the last two years.

The Department spent £16,890.13 commissioning an agency to come up with a corporate communications strategy and a three year plan. It also spent £2,700 on a video to record the April 2006 'DFID Public Information and Consultation Week' on St Helena, which ran to two hours of presumably top shelf horror. Staggeringly, it blew £203,918.56 paying an agency to provide media support for a conference in Asia.

The Department is notionally responsible for what happens with British money spent by the EU as part of its international aid programme. Remember, we contribute 17.5% of the overall Brussels budget. In 2004, the EC gave over £130 in aid per poor person in Europe and Central Asia; almost £90 per poor person in the Middle East and North Africa and less than £1 per poor person in South Asia. But then, of course, South Asia is less likely to join the EU one day. This explains why so much aid has been channelled into states that have applied to join the club (particularly the old Warsaw Pact states); countries which will no doubt do so once memories of the Yugoslav Civil War have receded; and countries which export boat people across the Mediterranean. Hence, according to the DFID books, 31% of EC aid goes to lower middle-income countries, 3% goes to upper middle-income countries, and 22% is unallocated by country and so may be directed away from the least developed states.

It's time then for some figures to put this into context. Approximately one fifth of the Department's budget – around £1 billion – also goes into the EC pot. In 2004, the EC spent £7.1 billion on aid. The five largest recipients were: Serbia and Montenegro, Turkey, the Democratic Republic of the Congo, Morocco, and Afghanistan.

Now you can begin to see our point about the politics of aid. In Brussels, aid is a means of building fishing ports, market places and motorways, and with it popular support, for countries to join the club.

Of far greater benefit would be to let developing countries sell us their goods. The EEC was set up as a trading bloc that encouraged internal trade and supported key sectors (like farming) with subsidies, while protecting them from outside competition. Of course, those walls are as much of a barrier to small farmers in developing countries as they are to subsidised South Korean shipping firms or dumpers of Russian steel.

Fifty years ago, when much of Africa's commerce was closely tied to France and the remainder was part of the Commonwealth system, the economic boundaries were less marked. There have been great bounds over the last few years as part of the WTO's millennium push, but third world importers to EU countries still remain constrained by protectionism in textiles, clothing and farming. These are precisely the industries that as taxpayers we are subsidising on our own continent, propping up uncompetitive European industries that one day will have to adapt or fail.

And then there was ...

- ☹ The former General Director of DFID, Masmood Ahmed, was paid £220,000 per annum until his departure in May 2006, and the Permanent Secretary, Suma Chakrabarti, was paid £170,000 in 2006.

- ☹ The Department greatly overspent on several of their capital projects including the Quest Electronic Document and Record Management system, which was supposed to cost £9m, but ended up costing £11.7 million – over 30% over budget. They also overspent on the Aries Finance, Procurement and Reporting System, which was supposed to cost £11 million, but ended up costing £13.5 million – an excess of £2.5 million or over 22%.

- ☹ Taxpayers pay £4.7 billion each year to the government's international aid programme but, according to Action Aid one third of this is given as 'phantom aid' which does not yield any benefits for the world's poor.

- ☹ DFID spends 12% of its annual budget (£0.5bn) on consultants.

Privy Council Office (PCO)

Factoids

- The Privy Council used to advise the king on how to run mediaeval England.

- It is historically made up of people who have the words 'Right Honourable' in front of their name, or alternatively 'PC' after it, who met in days of yore before democracy became the vogue. It still has a formal role in the royal succession.

- It is the smallest government department, with 70 members of staff.

- These days it deals with royal prerogatives, chartered bodies, and the older universities.

- The office of the Leader of the Commons, which draws its budget from the PCO, spent over £4,000 on taxis over a 12 month period. That's between twelve members of staff.

The Privy Council barely features on the TaxPayers' Alliance radar. It is a low key department. It is not, however, immune to the virus of public sector extravagance.

In the last few years it has spent:

- £82,424 refurbishing a ministerial suite.

- £44,828 on start-up costs for the Leader of the House of Commons website.

- £35,485 on start-up costs for the Privy Council Office website.

- £31,042 for a staff survey, conference and workshops (remember it's the smallest department…)

- £19,574 on departmental diversity awareness training and workshops.

- £18,844 for a correspondence database for the Leader of the Commons.

- £18,212 for a video conference facility for the Lords Chief Whip.

- £17,170 for a bathroom for Lady Judges at Judicial Committee.

- £15,267 for furniture for the Judges Retiring Room.

- £8,078 on a carpet for the Judicial Committee, and a similar amount for cupboards and cabinets (each would buy you 750 square yards of carpet at Carpet World).

- £7,451 for TV screens and video equipment for the Leader of the Commons.

- £7,401 on bathroom refurbishment at 2 Carlton Gardens, and a similar amount for third floor carpeting. We trust they are in keeping with the décor.

Ministry of Defence (MoD)

Factoids

- In 2005-06, around £5.9 billion was spent on equipment procurement. Until recently, only the big projects tended to be properly audited.

- The MoD made £486,000 by letting mobile phone companies place 77 masts in 57 Territorial Army establishments last year. Some are known to have been placed worryingly close to living quarters.

- Pity the poor staff, because under PFI, repairs on the army's 'white fleet' i.e. cars and minibuses, are governed under the equation $V<A+[H/5]+9$, which translates as "don't bother us until it's been bust for a few days".

- MoD Police and the Serious Fraud Office are investigating the sale of HMS Coventry and HMS London as scrap to the private sector for £100,000 each. The Romanian government then bought them for £116 million.

- The MoD is the department with the biggest assessed value of assets, running at £93 billion of the government's total of £337 billion.

- In 2005-06, the MoD wrote off £463,583 in pensions it had overpaid – eight times as many cases as the previous year.

- Ministers bought 14 specially armoured vehicles for £4.5 million, then sold them for £44,000, including to a private security firm working in Baghdad, at a time when the MoD was short of them. One, sold to Estonia, was reportedly used to rescue British soldiers in Afghanistan, wounded in a gunfight in an unarmoured Land Rover.

- The department does *not* own a Uranium PU-36 Explosive Space Modulator.

Not all of the MoD's problems relate to how it spends money on things. Some relate to the strange impact of laws from other departments.

These are often unquantifiable. For instance, one can only guess how much it will cost if every Land Rover in the army has to have seatbelts fitted in the back for health and safety reasons, or how much it will cost to have to use other vehicles in the meantime.

Another example is the legislation on driving licences. Thanks to a wonderful piece of EU legislation and the ineptness of the civil servants who are supposed to stymie these things, modern driving licences do not include the right to drive much more than a bog standard car. Time was that your average youngster could leap into the driving seat of the students' union minibus and pooter over with the lads to play rugby against the neighbouring college.

These days, however, safety is paramount. What the bureaucrats failed to factor in, however, was the impact upon the armed forces, and especially upon the Reserves. Most young soldiers have driving licences that don't allow them to drive a minibus, and it is only the older fogies who have 'grandfather rights' because they retain the type of driving categories from before the changeover.

In practical terms, this means that it's the senior officers and sergeant majors who have to drive the soldiers around when they go on training exercises. These busy people have better things to do with their time than chauffeur junior ranks around. On top of everything else, if they have a prang at that rank, the paperwork gets horribly official.

It's not a problem that's easy to resolve either, because the conversion course takes a week. This, obviously, has a cost in time and money, and there are a limited number of courses available, even if TA soldiers can take the given week off from their day job. Ask the army management and they recognise there's a problem. Ask the MoD ministers and they say they are "not aware" of it. This is before even taking into consideration another problem for people behind the wheel – the paperwork and regulations governing the number of hours driven in a week. The armed forces are not exempt from the regulations, and for the TA it is a particular problem. Professional drivers, like truckers or posties, will simply not be able to drive over the weekend. Some businessmen in the transport sector have said they will not allow employees to join the Reserves as a result. So one problem snowballs into another.

There are many other problems. The Astute Class is the Navy's new type of Attack Submarine. It has been one of the worst offenders for budget creep. Despite measures to keep costs under control, last year the forecast costs actually increased by £164 million – which now means a final bill of £3.6 billion rather than the £1 billion forecast. It gets worse. The House of Commons Defence Committee was shocked to find that the prices for boats 2 and 3 hadn't even been agreed, so the end liability was completely unknown, and the future of boat 4 was in question.

Then there is the helicopter botch. Eight Chinook Mark 3s were procured. But at a time when the armed forces are desperately in need of heavy lift aviation in Iraq and especially in Afghanistan, these airframes are sitting unoperational in hangars in the UK. It seems that legally the terms of the £259 million contract have been met, but they don't actually meet the operational requirements with their flight software.

Some of the smaller procurement deals have also run into problems which some lateral thinking could and should have addressed. The armed forces are shortly to get the new General Service Respirator (GSR) to replace what people tend to call the gas mask. Obviously, it is a key piece of equipment if you hunt down Weapons of Mass Destruction, appear in SAS drama documentaries, or attend raves. Unfortunately, tests in Australia on the experimental batch of 500 revealed a problem that seems to have been overlooked. Retrial, and a ten month delay ensued. At least we can thank the Aussies for our respirators when they eventually turn up.

One of the other small projects currently being researched is a thermal sighting system for an air defence missile. Apparently, £72 million is being spent to modify the missiles in a way which will allow troops to fire them when it is cloudy or dark. This is helpful, because the enemy doesn't always bomb you after elevenses. The wonderfully named 'Operations Director for Information Superiority' told MPs that the reason why this technology gap had existed was because they hadn't been sure that they could technically do it and the risk of failure was too great to spend the money: even now there was a five month slippage. This just goes to show that not all waste at the MoD consists of rooms wallpapered with money.

Though, judging by the reports of the palatial new MoD offices, a lot is. At a cost of £2.3 billion over 30 years, in a new PFI outrage, the civil servants' building contrasts obscenely with the shoddy accommodation servicemen often find themselves in.

We referred to the case of the Nimrod MRA4 in our last book; the way in which it was still being delayed – it is currently seven and a half years late – and how the government was cutting costs by cutting the number of aircraft on order. This surveillance plane is an excellent tool (one of the authors has been up in one in theatre), and it is currently doing sterling work in overseas deployments and protecting our maritime zones. But the version in service has been flying for decades, a fact tragically brought home recently when one crashed in Afghanistan killing all on board. It is a salutary reminder that slippage in delivering the kit can have an impact not only on the public purse, but also on people's lives.

That same admission of policy failure has been repeated elsewhere. £114 million in 'savings' have been made simply by cutting back on the number of rockets the army will buy as part of its Guided Multiple Launch Rocket System project. In other words, the threat assessment hasn't changed, but the army will have fewer reserves of ammunition to face it.

It gets worse. The number of rockets was cut from 6,204 to 4,780, but as this didn't match the cost overrun for the project, the Defence Management Board cut the number even further to 4,080. Even the Board itself considered it a "shortfall in capability", albeit in its view an "acceptable" one.

A word of context, then. The army today has 63 multiple launch rocket systems (MRLS) in service, each delivering 12 rockets. Allowing for each vehicle to reposition itself after firing in order to avoid counter-battery fire, and the time it takes for each to reload, we estimate that the British Army could fire off this entire stock in five and a half hours.

We hope the next war is a short one.

Fortunately, the army is so short of manpower these days that artillerymen are having to do regular tours in place of the infantry. So our bombardiers will by then be well practised in throwing rocks at the enemy once they run out of missiles.

The same approach, cutting back on the asset rather than getting to grips with the overspend, has been used on the Brimstone anti-armour weapon. And on the Trojan and Titan vehicles, where the prototypes were supposed to get turned into Driver Training Vehicles, but £1 million was scrimped by scrapping this modification. Then there is the reduction in numbers for the new Support Vehicle. This is particularly controversial given media coverage of the effect of mines and other forms of attack on the army's Land Rover fleet. £5 million was also saved by cutting back on the ability of the new Airbus A400M to be loaded with civilian as well as military pallets, a shortcoming which will no doubt exercise some poor logistician come the next humanitarian disaster.

Another fiasco has been the handling of the Joint Strike Fighter (JSF) programme. Our boffins have been part of a massive programme with the Americans to build a plane to fly off our aircraft carriers. It is a capability gap right now, because the government scrapped the Navy's Harrier fighters (as seen in the Falklands War) before having a replacement ready. This is a concern, as it leaves the Fleet reliant on other countries to defend it from air attack.

However, because of the UK government's recent tendency to get involved with EU defence projects, many in Washington DC fear that any technology they share with the British will be passed on to the French, who will then, based on past form, sell it to the Chinese, Iranians, and other sundry types who are less than enamoured of apple pie and episodes of *The A Team*. So Capitol Hill put a bar on key microchips being implanted into the fighters that we would buy. This is equivalent to selling us X Boxes that can only play a cruddy 1980s version of Asteroids.

What's even more ridiculous is that British Ministers allowed key UK technology to go into the plane, including wizardry for take off and landing, flight control, the engine and lift fan, the ejection seat, flight simulators, and parts of the weapons systems. The Commons Defence Committee had some trenchant words to say on the subject:

> *"We have no doubt that the Minister for Defence Procurement, the Chief of Defence Procurement and MoD officials have made considerable efforts to ensure that the United States are fully aware of the information required by the UK on the Joint Strike Fighter to allow the aircraft to be operated independently. However, it is still uncertain whether the United States is prepared to provide the required information.*
>
> *If the UK does not obtain the assurances it needs from the United States, then it should not sign the Memorandum of Understanding covering production, sustainment and follow-on development. Such an impasse on a procurement programme of such strategic importance to the UK would be a serious blow to UK-US defence equipment cooperation, which has hitherto been of such positive benefit to both our nations. If the required assurances are not obtained by the end of the year, we recommend that the MoD switch the majority of its effort and funding on the programme into developing a fallback 'Plan B', so that an alternative aircraft is available in case the UK has to*

*withdraw from the Joint Strike Fighter programme.
We must not get into a situation where there are no
aircraft to operate from the two new aircraft carriers
when they enter service."*

Even if we buy a version of the fighter, it seems that the US
Congress might now cut its own order, which means an
increase in costs by up to a third.

The risk is that the government has engineered its own crisis.
The price of its decision to support European Defence
integration with technology partners who are less capable is
that the US may well not sell us kit which we helped develop,
because we might indirectly pass it on to somebody who our
forces might one day be fighting. As a result we could be forced
to buy an alternative off-the-shelf product to cover for a
capability gap from which our forces already suffer.

The big picture procurement planning policy clearly hasn't been
thought through.

Would that wage money was being spent more carefully. Take
the Oil and Pipeline Agency, which deals with storing and
transporting the government's petrol. Our sources tell us that
the post of Chief Executive, lately advertised as vacant, has
been up for grabs. Back in 1986, the General Manager got
£34,430 plus £1,320 lunch allowance. In 1997, he was on
£73,700 plus £1,070 lunch allowance. Now, the post of Chief
Executive that has replaced that role is being advertised at up
to £120,000, plus £1,320 allowance, plus a further unknown
performance bonus to boot. If this job has seen its salary leap
so massively, what has been the total cost to the taxpayer of
similar rises across the board?

Scandal comes in many scales. It costs £38 to buy an Iraq medal
in a shop. The MoD press department, or more likely Number
10's, knows value for money when it sees it. The qualifying
criteria for the award of the Iraq medal are set out in a small
document called Cm6135, and amended in Cm6936. This said
that MoD accredited war correspondents, photographers,

cameramen and sound recordists were eligible for a gong. But in the original context, this could well have been an error – a poorly worded reference to the Department's own broadcasters who are brought in on government contract to put together products for the MoD's website, newsletters and such like. In any event, even if it was a botch up, the Defence Council (five ministers, five khaki, three civil servants) subsequently decided categorically to award the medal to any and all war correspondents who were accredited to the MoD. Any journalist embedded with British troops for a week would be getting a medal, and indeed would get the campaign clasp as well for participating in the invasion.

There are several things that are simply not right about this. Alright, it isn't an issue of waste. But it is an issue of fraud – defrauding the honour of soldiers who put their lives on the line for their country. Firstly, these reporters received their gongs faster than a number of servicemen (some of whom are still waiting three or four years on to be awarded their own). Secondly, the journalist is not serving his country in the same way as a soldier, who is receiving recognition for putting his life on the line: the journalist's reward comes in job variety, global travel, nice hotels most of the time, and a fat pay cheque denied your average trooper. Thirdly, the journalist (by definition, unarmed) is not putting himself into the same type of danger as the soldier, and can claim a degree of immunity from the horrors of war. On top of that, there is the question of the service to the nation. Some journalist reporting has been looked on less than favourably by squaddies as increasing the risk to their own lives.

There have been 35 MoD policemen seconded to the Iraqi police force. None of them has been awarded the medal. There's even a Ministry of Defence Iraq medal specially designed for the contractors who cook the food and fix the electrics. But, no, journalists got the frontline one.

And what of the journalist's integrity? A journalist who receives a campaign reward is by definition being rewarded for being part of the victor's side in the campaign, even if in the case of some broadcasters and journalists that clearly wasn't true. Look up the BBC lexicon defining terrorist and insurgent to see the point. To accept the medal is to take an undeserved award that belongs to the fighting man, and to the person who strives to support his campaign. The government has debased the award. It knows its cost, it even knows its value on eBay, but it does not know its worth.

Now, if only we knew if any were awarded to journalists from al-Jazeera.

We do know that some journalists refused to accept the gong. Seventy four people accepted the offer, though a dozen have taken some time to provide their forwarding address. But five more notified the MoD that they did not wish to be considered for the award.

If we knew who they were, we'd buy them a drink. But the government refuses this request, because it says when journalists were contacted they weren't told their names would be put in the public domain, and so to do so would breach data protection rules. Never mind that this interpretation of the regulations has been ignored by the government when it suited them in other instances, such as over paternity rights from sperm donations. Or more obviously, the minor detail that half of the journos appeared on world TV saying where they were reporting from.

On a lighter note, let's turn back to the troops. Perhaps it is just as well that so much attention is placed by the armed forces on training people in first aid. Even in peacetime, the vigorous outdoorsy fighting machine occasionally trips over a tree root. The MoD puts together a weekly list of dozens of accidents and incidents, probably just like BP or a big trucker firm. In any given week, you might see: someone being blown off the top of a vehicle by a gust of wind; a twisted ankle from situation awareness training; people in a rush jumping out of accommodation; bad rugby tackles; someone falling out of their bus; a mock rioter who gets a hernia or is trampled on; a dog handler who gets bitten by his dog; someone falling off a bridge; serial plummeting on assault courses; falling off a bicycle to avoid a rabbit; an unexpected attack dog waiting in your office; falling off the back of a lorry and so on.

Many aren't at all funny, and relate serious injury and deaths by people doing their daily bit to make this country secure. But still, a rabbit...

And then there was ...

☹ The order for the new stealth Nimrod plane has not only been cut nearly in half, from 21 to 12, but the cost of the project has also risen from £2.8 billion to £3.5 billion, with the project now 7 years behind schedule.

☹ The new computer payroll system for the armed forces has caused errors in almost one in three wage packets, despite being part of a £2.3 billion revamp of the way the MoD operates.

☹ Defence chiefs spent £18,000 on a mystic powers experiment to find Bin Laden's lair. This included conducting experiments to see if volunteers could 'see' objects hidden inside an envelope.

☹ Compensation claims arising from low flying aircraft topped £4.1m last year.

☹ The MoD paid £30,000 for the sex change operation of Sergeant David (Deborah) Penny.

HM Treasury

Factoids

- Last year, the Treasury taxed other government departments £4 million in Stamp Duty Land Tax, costing an estimated £8,000 to administer the receipts.

- Over 2005-06, the Treasury taxed other government departments £3,478 million – nearly £3.5 billion – in VAT. It is not known how much it cost the government, in wasted administration and inflation, to tax itself.

- The Treasury has issued £272 billion of gilts since May 1997 and redeemed £173 billion of this national debt.

- The Treasury spent £3.6 million advertising its tax credits scheme in 2006.

- Between 2002-05, 1.6 million fake sterling banknotes were removed from circulation globally, mostly twenties, with a total value of £28.7 million.

- Over 2002-06, 2.2 million fake Euro notes with a value of £117 million were removed, mostly fifties and hundreds.

- The Bank of England has its own sports ground, sports centre and pavilion at Roehampton, with buildings alone worth £16 million.

- The Treasury does in fact have its own tax cutters. But only in the old sense. They are HM Customs boats, called *Sentinel, Seeker, Searcher, Vigilant* and *Valiant*.

- The Paymaster General has a current account for day-to-day use, presumably for office tea bags and milk. At the year's end it contained £400.

- Council Tax inspectors from the Valuation Office Agency in 2006 attended conferences in Vancouver, Kuala Lumpur, and Disney World.

In December 2006, a number of MPs received emails purporting to come from HM Revenue and Customs. The emails claimed that recipients were entitled to a tax rebate and asked for credit card details to which the rebate could be refunded.

The Parliamentary computer people were quickly on the case, warning that the email was not genuine and should be deleted.

We suspect that anyone in the political arena who had received the message already knew it was fake, as a tax rebate these days is as likely as seeing Sting and Sir David Attenborough cropdusting the upper Amazon with Agent Orange.

It's much more likely you'll be contacted by the taxman with a demand to pay up more. Revenue and Customs conducted a sample of tax credit awards covering 2003-04, and came up with findings that indicated an overpayment rate of about 3.4%. In other words, they calculated the Treasury was overpaying credits by £460 million. It also assessed that these results were subject to a wide margin of error, and that in subsequent years there would be far more claimant error and fraud.

Customs were also found to have spent a lavish sum on rebranding themselves. £720,000 has been reportedly spent on giving themselves a new image, which in all likelihood means a slightly different logo.

The Treasury is less likely these days to be popular with your average public sector employee. Some have been cushioned to varying degrees. The Department for Constitutional Affairs alone has an additional bill of £9.6 million to cover the Treasury take on its judicial pensions scheme, after changes in the 2004 Finance Act.

Just in case you were wondering, the ten most valuable pieces of art at Treasury installations, and at 11 Downing Street, are:

- a George IV mahogany breakfront bookcase (worth £40,000);

- a demi-lune console George III carved giltwood table (circa 1780) (£25,000);

- a fine George III mahogany longcase clock (£25,000);

- a George I style carved giltwood table (£12,000);
- two similar side tables (£17,500);
- two Japanese lacquered 18th century cabinets (£17,500);
- a Victorian mahogany dining table (£7,000);
- and a carved giltwood George I period mirror (£4,000).

And then there was ...

- ☹ The Bank of England has revealed it had to hand over €56,187,041.67 to the European Central Bank as its share in the reserves of the Eurozone, a currency in which Britain is not even participating.

- ☹ The Treasury employs four staff on its websites; its agencies employ 34 more.

- ☹ Every year, thieves swipe an average of five computers from the Treasury, costing £1,675 each.

- ☹ It is phasing out its food subsidy for staff, which used to cost £130,000 a year.

- ☹ Nevertheless, last year's spend by the Treasury and its Agencies on accommodation and food allowance had leapt to a whopping £56 million. £5 million of this was overseas.

- ☹ £8.1 million was spent on advertising the Child Trust Fund – money which will be invested by the government anyway if the parents don't invest it themselves.

Department for Trade and Industry (DTI)

Now the Department for Business, Enterprise and Regulatory Affairs... the acronym won't catch on

Factoids

- The Department's various Research Councils have assets valued at £1.2 billion.

- The DTI has its own navy, the research vessels *RRS Shackleton, RRS James Clark Ross* and *RRS James Cook*. It also has telescopes in the Canaries and Hawaii.

- The government last year paid a subscription of £580,000 to belong to the International Bureau for Weights and Measures, as agreed in the Metre Convention of 1875.

- The National Weights and Measures Laboratory costs £3.9 million a year to run. Yes, carry on there, that's still a kilo. But best call the International Organisation for Legal Metrology (OIML) to check. After all, we pay for that too.

- The Department is spending £80 million over three years putting windmills and solar panels on its buildings.

- £2.7 million was budgeted for external legal fees last year.

- Over the decades, the Department has sold 309 ships that were sunk during World Wars One and Two. This raised £53,000. It allows salvage rights from the superstructure, courtesy of Admiral Doenitz. If you want to buy a gun emplacement from *HMS Compass Rose*, don't call Jack Hawkins, call the DTI.

- Regional development agencies now handle combined budgets of over £350 million a year – a doubling in half a decade.

- The department runs SPIRE, a £2.2 million package to automate export licensing. Hopefully the computer will be clever enough to spot superguns. Its predecessor was the Export Licensing via Internet Service Project, or ELVIS.

- The National Physical Laboratory has an apple tree planted in 1953 by the Director of Kew, and descended from a graft of an old tree at Woolsthorpe Manor, where Sir Isaac Newton saw the tumbling fruit.

- The International Lead and Zinc Study Group costs around £10,000 in membership fees a year. The DTI is, excuse the pun, the lead department. So too for the International Nickel Study Group, which sounds like a no-holds-barred riot, well worth the £25,000 sub.

The DTI is the department that is lumbered with the government's liabilities in Outer Space. Under UN Treaties, if a crazed Brit ever decides to take out France with a giant orbital device, it is our responsibility to sort him out and send in Austin Powers. But if his mojo isn't up for it, our government has certain liabilities.

This is why under the Outer Space Act 1986 our orbital scientists (mad and otherwise) have to be licensed, which means the government can pass on the damage bills to them. The space company has to provide £100 million insurance cover in case a bit of space debris demolishes the Taj Mahal. If the claim is a whopper and the licensee can't pay the excess, the taxpayer then becomes liable. So if you bump into a bald guy with a white cat at an electrical store, don't sell him anything, otherwise you'll be getting a big tax bill next year.

Overall, we question whether the DTI needs to exist at all. Even the department has its doubts, as it confirms when it declares in its annual report:

> *"Generally, businesses succeed through their own efforts. Businesses not governments exploit market opportunities."*

So why spend £267 million on staff costs alone in defiance of this evident truth?

The Department and its agencies spent £381 million on Business Support over 2005-06. This ranged from funding research and development (which is what businesses should be doing) to providing in-house consultancy (which is what banks do) and grants on renewable energy (which is what the market should be capable of doing).

The DTI is another offender in the jargon sin bin. Take this example from its annual report:

> *"2.124 The 2005 Gender Equality Steering Group Event focused on improving the domestic violence indicator through raising awareness of the need for robust reporting systems for individual police forces, as scope exists for real improvements in this area. It also highlighted the requirements of the forthcoming gender duty, which strengthen the case for high quality data provision across the public sector. Although legislative changes have since affected the proxy measure for this target, the need for consistent good quality data remains."*

Last year the DTI spent £3.2 million, excluding VAT, advertising its activities. This included £329,000 selling the minimum wage. The previous year it spent £2 million, including £706,000 plugging Consumer Direct. You would think that the money it spends on advertising campaigns would infuse some plain English into the departmental lexicon.

The Department funds the National Consumer Council, plus its Welsh and Scottish counterparts, to the tune of around £6 million, a sum which is rapidly increasing year on year. This is a group that campaigns on behalf of the perceived needs of consumers. The London office alone employs a policy team of 15, five in the National Social Marketing Strategy for Health, two in human resources, and six in the media office. This seems rather excessive when other solutions have been to establish an ombudsman and not a state-funded lobby group that establishes its own agenda. It also replicates the Which? campaigners, who don't take public funds.

The number of research papers that these councils have come up with over the past ten years runs to fourteen pages of titles alone. These include:

- *Consumer's Knowledge of Their Health Rights*
- *Preparing for the Euro in Scotland*
- *A Consumer Agenda for the Scottish Parliament*
- *Gender and Bus Travel in Wales*
- *People Without Cars*
- *The Good, the Bad and the Healthy*
- *Learning Lessons from Disasters*
- *The Stupid Company*
- *I Will if You Will*
- *Companies Branded 'Out of Touch' by Consumers* (and which probably didn't read the report)
- *Food Access Radar Toolkit*
- *Survey of 10-19 Year Olds Timed to Coincide with the Buy Nothing Day*

The DTI is responsible for the UK Research Councils. These august but slightly nerdy bodies might be worthy, but they soak up a fair amount of public money. Opposite is a list of the twenty biggest budgets.

Research Councils Budgets	£ (m)
European Space Agency	£101.9
CERN	£79.1
Diamond Light Source	£74.0
British Antarctic Survey	£44.9
ISIS Target Station 2	£42.4
ISIS Operations	£35.6
MRC National Institute for Medical Research	£33.6
Subscription for European Southern Observatory	£32.9
MRC National Institute for Medical Research: Purchase of Land	£28.0
Synchrotron Radiation Source Main Facility	£27.7
British Geological Survey	£27.5
Centre for Ecology and Hydrology	£22.6
MRC Laboratory of Molecular Biology	£20.9
Fusion	£20.6
James Cook Research Vessel	£15.9
International Subscriptions, Institut Laue Langevin, Grenoble	£15.2
MRC Clinical Science Centre	£14.7
MRC Laboratorie, The Gambia	£9.6
MRC Human Genetics Unit	£8.7
High Performance Computing	£8.2

That's over £660 million on space age level research, or as it is known in episodes of Quatermass, *Meddling In Things That Man Should Leave Well Alone*. This might explain why there is something called the Dunn Human Nutrition Unit in Cambridge. But if you want to uncover the secrets of the universe or stop some dreadful pandemic that gets Dustin Hoffman in a sweat, then this is where your tax money goes. The African research units are conducting research into the mass killers like malaria, TB and AIDS: all worthy stuff. Meanwhile, we think that the poor science chaps stuck up on the Svalbard islands, or building a new station at Halley in Antarctica, deserve a warm round of applause. Google Earth them on Bird Island, South Georgia, and give them a wave.

We also think it's quite cool that the DTI has its own airforce. It owns a Dornier aircraft for "earth observation work". Yes, it's still down there, so we can still land.

We are more circumspect, however, on the merits of other budget lines. There is EHLASS, which sounds like a northern greeting, but in fact is the European Home Leisure Accident Surveillance Survey. There is the £300,000 of EU taxpayers' money (i.e. our own) for a conference on Corporate Social Responsibility and for the Gender Equality Programme of the UK Presidency. £3.3 million was spent ensuring that employers and employees were made aware of their rights and responsibilities under legislation about the National Minimum Wage and various EC directives, and boosting the monitoring of these laws.

A recent discovery has been the US/Canada Marketing Scholarships Programmes, part funded by the department's UK Trade & Investment unit. This pays for some small businessmen to be awarded scholarships to attend an intensive marketing course at the Kellogg School of Management in Illinois, and three more at the Richard Ivey School in Ontario. The individual then gets one week at a prominent North American business. Each sponsorship is valued at £7,500 (excluding expenses), so that the Department's 28% share of the overall cost comes out at £53,000. Is it value for money for the Department? Possibly. But only because of the unusual level of sponsorship. And it rather depends on the frat parties.

Then there was ...

☹ £33,500 paid to three staff members whose employment was "terminated on efficiency grounds" and another £18,000 for a senior official who was allowed to take compulsory early retirement after the Department had first tried to sack him.

⊗ Departmental compensation claims last year of £614 for lost property, £71 for damage to clothing, £249.23 for robbery, £886 for damage to property, £132 for stolen property or clothing, and £803.94 of stolen money. Plus the £290.50 paid out for damage to suitcases.

⊗ The Department's science bodies this year are spending a total of £46.2 million on 'Policy Advisors'.

⊗ It subsidises the excellent Citizens Advice Bureaus, or bureaux, or bureauses, to the tune of £24 million a year.

⊗ The DTI spent £126.5 million on MG Rover after the company failed in the middle of a General Election, most of this on redundancy and supplier bills. £5.2 million of a £6.5 million loan to administrators to seek a going concern sale has effectively been written off.

⊗ This year begins a massive funding splurge on the National Consumer Council – £15 million this year, £30 million next. Hence government is paying a lobby group to lobby government.

⊗ The Department also spends around £1 million a year supporting SITPRO, which lobbies against red tape, and in favour of free trade.

⊗ In 2005, the Department and its agencies spent £12,895 on Christmas cards.

⊗ £300,000 is spent annually supporting the Women's National Commission.

⊗ Over four years, the Department spent £37 million advertising policy initiatives.

⊗ The Equality and Gender annual budget will quintuple from last year to reach over £20 million by 2007-08.

⊗ £1,776 paid out for cars the Department pranged.

Cabinet Office

Factoids

- The Cabinet Office also covers the admin for Number 10. The ministerial residences in Downing Street are valued at £7.1 million, but then they are within walking distance of London's top nightspots.

- Number 10's staff budget last year came to £11.8 million.

- Chequers cost the Department £900,000 to maintain, plus another £150,000 for military personnel stationed there.

- Number 10's Press Office employs 18 civil servants, and costs £1.6 million.

- Number 10 also now has a £50,000 House Manager. We think this is a posh butler.

- The Department's watchword is "Making government work better". Yes, you can blame them.

- Children who write to the Prime Minister get sent the 10 Downing Street children's pack, containing "a wealth of information, games and activities".

- The Department proudly boasts that 2.8% of people at Senior Civil Service level are disabled, up from 2.1% on two years previous. This appears to be because the stat compilers have encouraged more disabilities to be declared, though whether they are all genuine remains a moot point.

- Departmental pensions cost £3.2 million in 2000-01. They now run at £6 million.

- PA Consulting, PricewaterhouseCoopers, Accenture, CAP Gemini, Boston Consultancy Group, Frontier Economics, Demos, Timebank, and KPMG all seconded personnel to the Cabinet Office last year.

- The Cabinet Office paid out £27,000 in compensation for payroll errors, a fall in the office, the use of some land, and two cases where staff generously cancelled their private lives to work late.

The amount of money the Cabinet Office spends has increased significantly over the last few years.

- In 2000-01, it was spending £19 million on "supporting the Prime Minister". This year it's spending £46 million.

- In 2000-01, it was spending £62 million "supporting the Cabinet". This year it's spending £95 million.

- In 2000-01, it was spending £12 million "strengthening the Civil Service". This year it's spending £19 million.

Two other budget lines intrigue us. £2 million goes to what are called 'Independent Offices'. On top of that, another £1 million or so is going, each year, into a new budget line called the ERM Project, which while it sounds suspiciously as if it is something to do with joining the Single Currency, is actually a new electronic filing system.

Some other expenses stand out. In 2002-03, the Cabinet Office spent just over £2,000 maintaining Admiralty House, including a flat where the Deputy Prime Minister lived. But the following year it went up to £30,000, then £158,000, and then £225,000. It seems a large chunk of this has been spent on fitting disabled toilets in this Grade I Listed Building (to comply with an Act dating back to 1995) and redecorating the basement. Presumably that gives the Prince of Darkness somewhere to stay over when visiting from Brussels.

A showcase budget line run by the Cabinet Office covers spending of £100 million over the next three years. Most of this is being channelled to V, which is Gordon Brown's toy, and has nothing to do with alien lizards. It is an institutional amalgam of charity funding directed through the sinister sounding Office of the Third Sector, and intended to match charity money raised privately pound for pound.

However, of the £13 million on record as having been given by the state, £2,285,000 has gone to websites, £1,770,000 for marketing and communications, and another £2 million on strategic funding. Is this value for money and is it reaching frontline projects, or is it simply a gimmick that is diverting money through new admin costs that was already going to charities with established and successful projects? The jury is still out.

This department spends a further £716,000 a year "advising government centrally on spending matters and associated non cash items." £2 million now goes to the Office of Public Sector Information. If you want to know where the money that pays the spin doctors comes from, it's the Central Office of Information. Here's what they say about themselves:

> "The Central Office of Information (COI) is the government's centre of excellence for marketing and communications. COI works with Whitehall departments and public bodies to produce information campaigns on issues that affect the lives of every citizen – from health and education to benefits, rights and welfare."

It has nine Specialist Groups and six Client Account Teams, plus the Informability Team who focus on the disabled and those with reading problems. The groups and teams hire in expertise from one of 31 private PR agencies as required.

The COI advises government departments and their associated agencies on their PR work, and is expressly authorised to give advice which "may be against the COI Trading Fund's own commercial interests" – in other words, it would be cheaper to get someone else in.

The COI does not work all the time, however. The gap between when an election is announced until after the election is held is colloquially known as 'purdah'. During these weeks, as throughout Whitehall, "any activity which could call into question the office's political impartiality or could give rise to the criticism that public resources are being used for Party political purposes is suspended for this time". It is a rare acknowledgement of an inherent flaw in government communications.

The COI also conducts research into the sort of people it

intends to speak to. In official speak, this is known as "common good research conducted into the hard-to-reach target audiences to whom government needs to communicate its policies and to inform about rights and benefits". These can be less than inspiring. Take this example covering youth culture:

> *"Common interests for young men included playing and watching sport, going to the gym and cars. They liked surfing the Internet, online gaming and Playstation. Increasingly, they 'talked' to their friends in chat rooms, by email, by MSN Messenger or via text messaging.*
>
> *Young women also liked music and were interested in fashion, cosmetics, hairstyles, celebrity gossip and soaps. They talked animatedly about which male stars they 'fancied' on TV and in the movies. Young women were also keen on using the Internet for communicating with friends."*

We consider this research to be money less than well spent.

And then there was …

☹ The Number 10 website has a new section encouraging people to submit petitions. This has been a daft PR move, as witnessed by the roads pricing backlash. But a great way of getting a voter's email address to send them propaganda.

☹ The Department also spent £1 million on the two month 'Get Started' campaign, introducing OAPs to the internet.

☹ It spent a further £2 million telling people how to prepare for emergencies (buy tins and bottled water now), £250,000 trying to recruit staff, and £21,000 encouraging more women to apply for an MBE.

☹ The Cabinet Office spent £649,000 on hospitality and entertainment last year.

☹ Over 2005-06, it spent £73,000 advertising in the *Guardian* newspaper.

☹ Over the course of an eighteen month period, the Blairs hosted 56 receptions at Number 10, including ones for Allied Health Workers, women's magazines, children's authors and illustrators, the World Cup football team and officials, and the World Cup rugby team.

☹ In June 2006, civil servants spent a reported £280,000 on a conference addressed by Messrs Blair and Brown on value for money in the public services.

What's in a name?

🖉 Renaming the Department of the Environment as the Department for the Environment, Transport and the Regions cost £176,690.

🖉 Renaming the Department of the Environment, Transport and the Regions as the Department for Transport, Local Government and the Regions cost £25,250.

🖉 Renaming the Department for Transport, Local Government and the Regions as the Office of the Deputy Prime Minister cost £52,117.

🖉 Renaming the Office of the Deputy Prime Minister as the Department for Communities and Local Government cost £12,000.

🖉 John Prescott then spent £645 on a new sign and £726 on new business cards, renaming his department from 'the Office of the Deputy Prime Minister' to 'the Deputy Prime Minister's Office.'

The Gershon Savings

Not all the savings made by departments under Gershon are meaningful. Take the Office of the Deputy Prime Minister's Efficiency Programme. It reported £244 million of savings to date, but only £53.7 million were what they call "cash-releasing" – i.e. money released back into the Treasury coffers. Against a target of removing 240 posts out of London and the South East by 2010, 93 posts had been moved by the last count, but the process actually led to the establishment of new "local service facing" posts in London, Guildford and Cambridge.

The reasoning is expressed by a Northern Ireland minister thus:

> *"Sir Peter Gershon's independent report into public sector efficiency did not require that efficiencies be recorded net of upfront investment costs."*

In other words, if you spend money in order to save money, you count the money saved but not the money you have spent in the process. By this logic, scrapping posts and hiring in consultants counts as a total saving.

In fact, the Treasury itself estimates that only 60% of the supposed savings will be cashable – which means that over £8 billion of supposed savings will just be shuffling money from one account to another.

This comes at a time when the Exchequer is encouraging local government to take on debt. It has established what it styles the Prudential Borrowing Scheme, allowing more space for local authorities to borrow for 'capital investment'.

Furthermore, the government has still to reveal if there are any major liabilities that have been added to departments as a result of FRS17. This is not a 1950s rocket, but it is just as complicated. It is not altogether clear to what extent these changes in pension accounting have led to extra costs lying off the balance sheet, how much departments are having to pay for it, and what new departmental liabilities exist. We leave that analysis to the arch-wizards of accounting.

We are intrigued by the books of the Treasury itself. The **Treasury Group** is cutting 150 staff over the four years to 2008, and yet we still find in 2005 that in addition to its internal promotions it recruited 27 Grade D policy analysts and economists, 6 Range B business support staff, and ran 36 other individual recruitment campaigns. In fact, it recruited 265 new staff. While accepting that many or indeed most of these would be replacements, you do wonder whether some prime opportunities to allow natural wastage through retirement are being missed.

If so, a large part of the blame would fall to the **Office of Government Commerce** (OGC), whose mission is to work with the private sector to create value for money. It is the key institution when it comes to finding the £21.5 billion in economies the Chancellor wants from government.

But is it delivering? Are its designated 'Change Agents', for instance, achieving an impact in procurement and productivity? Are changes delivering money back, or simply swapping one set of bills for another? For instance, how much does it cost the OGC to pay for what it itself acknowledges is a "large team of independent consultants", and is there no one already within the public sector with the mindset required to effect this change? Ironically, the Office of Government Commerce has identified one of its own failings as "use of consultants".

Meanwhile, it has been announced that the Treasury's UK **Debt Management Office** is not subject to the Department's drive to reduce headcount, so it intends to recruit another 47 people by 2007-08. On the plus side, it has decided to save £100,000 by not paying an outsider to do transactional processing which, it has realised, can be done more cheaply by one of its own staff.

Meanwhile, the **Government Actuary Department** has identified a saving of £117,000, achieved through moving a fifth of its staff within the building and renting out a floor to the Human Tissue Authority. Hence one government department is paying another, and this counts as an efficiency saving. It also counts as a profit because the new sub-tenant is buying the Department's services. Indeed, one of the department's very benchmarks of success is to increase the number of other departments spending more than £10,000 on them. It is hardly surprising then that their pay bill has gone up by a third since 2000-01.

It is quite difficult to ascertain how many head count savings have been made at the **Department of Health**. Leaving to one side the whole business about ward closures, what the statistics reveal is that of the 1,240 'gross reduction' in head count in core departments, only half were actual job cuts. 680 staff are being shunted sideways into other department agencies.

Also unusual was the caveat attached to plans by the **Office of National Statistics** to relocate posts to Newport. Someone was tasked to carry out a Race Equality Impact Assessment "to minimise the impact of relocation for our staff from minority ethnic communities".

Planned savings have also failed to materialise in the **Northern Ireland department**. Ministers there had targeted a reduction of 1,318 'public servants'. A rather disingenuous target, because the people they had in mind were not civil servants in the normal sense, but low-hanging fruit. The ministers were relying on all members of the police force's Full-Time Reserve (FTR) leaving by March 2008. Unfortunately, these 'peace dividend' cuts failed to materialise when the Chief Constable said he needed to keep 680 officers on the books.

In **Communities and Local Government,** there is a surreal attempt to identify £8 million pounds as savings on Firelink – which procures a fire and rescue radio system – by "replacing high risk items through an initial risk assessment process". We read this as cutting items or capabilities from a £350 million procurement budget. These were spent as part of the Firelink programme, replacing nearly a thousand old fire and rescue radio systems with new ones. It seems this qualifies as Gershon Savings because the old equipment might break down and need money spent on it to be replaced, which, of course, is precisely what is happening to it. But £8 million is a step closer to the required savings so, outrageously, onto the blackboard it goes.

The **Department of Culture**, meanwhile, has fulfilled its savings targets by focusing on the British Museum where it saved £6.8 million by getting rid of 127 members of staff. The only problem is that, as with other museums after cutbacks, rooms have had to be closed to the public because there are not enough people keeping an eye of them. Management figured this detail out when it noted an increase in items being stolen or broken by latter-day vandals. A further net loss, our BM insiders tell us, is that a jobsworthy management culture has taken the place of one of a learning and academic establishment, to the detriment of an internationally renowned institution.

The **MoD's** method of making savings by cutting equipment purchases is something we have already referred to as a dangerous luxury. But we are also shocked to discover that £448 million, or 57% of its latest designated procurement savings, was achieved by either re-classifying expenditure from procurement to support or by transferring expenditure to other sub budgets. As the National Audit Office revealed:

> *"These re-allocations do not represent a saving to the Department as a whole. By transferring the costs elsewhere the Department potentially will have to forego other activities, which previously could have been provided, or make corresponding efficiency gains to accommodate the expenditure."*

One example, for instance, is with the Trojan and Titan projects, where spares were just reclassified as consumables to save £4 million on the books.

On one level, this is not a new practice. The FCO was "sponsored" by Wales Trade and the BBC in cash and equivalent services worth £23,000 when it hosted an event in Tokyo. In the civil service mentality, this counted as outside sponsorship; in reality, it was just shuffling of taxpayers' money from one part of the public sector to another.

The Government has certainly accelerated its sale of assets. New Labour has come a long way from its root hostility to privatisation. In 2004-05, central government sold off £1.138 billion worth of fixed assets. Last year the figure was £1.673 billion. This is the reverse of the trend for local authorities, where asset disposal is down from £5.169 billion to £4.207 billion. Nevertheless, the Chancellor made a commitment to sell off £30 billion of public sector assets over five years.

At the end of the day, the whole Gershon project is founded on a Brobdingnagian nonsense. The Chancellor expended cost and effort trying to find ways of cutting 84,150 public sector jobs. If he had maintained a staff freeze for five of the years he had been in office, he could have reached that objective without having to pay out for any redundancies in the first place.

An example of
POINTLESS
GOVERNMENT
STATISTICS

Lord Oakeshott of Seagrove Bay asked Her Majesty's Government:

"What evidence they have to support the statement by the Lord Drayson on 1 November that morale among British forces in Iraq has improved by 14 per cent since March; and, if the statement was based on a survey or opinion poll, whether they will place the full questionnaire, sample selection, data and results in the Library of the House."

The Parliamentary Under-Secretary of State, Ministry of Defence (Lord Drayson) replied:

"I welcome this opportunity to correct a data point in my answer to Lord Craig of Radley in the Question on Iraq on 1 November. The percentage increase of 14 per cent in soldiers' morale that I quoted from information briefed to me by the department was not correct. The correct figure is 16.7 per cent."

SECTION 3

Other Areas of Waste

We've looked at government from an elevated, top-tier vantage point. Now it's time to scoop into the blancmange and dig down to the yummy tasty bits of excess that you know are bad for you but you just can't help yourself.

Before we do, we'd like to doff our hats to two other books that have highlighted waste in their own way. The first, by Ross Clark is called *How to Label a Goat* and provids a lurid exposé of the rules and regulations that government is churning out every year. The hoops that roof thatchers have to go through these days to get the 'right type of grass'. The precise legal definition of what makes an island an island, which can be changed if one more person emigrates to it. The way paper warriors went about building an international airport so planes fly right over a crowded city. The crime of selling lobsters 1mm too long.

We challenge anybody to read a chapter of the book while holding a paper cup without scrunching it through outright frustration at the lunacy of government.

We also pay tribute to PC 'David Copperfield'. Several policemen over the past couple of years have been running successful blogs detailing the conspiracy of idiocy that operates within the police system, showing how mad rules are getting in the way of attempts by the Fuzz to simply get on with their job. Mr 'Copperfield' (whose identity, quite understandably, has remained a secret) made the leap into publishing. *Wasting Police Time* is crucial for any outsider who is looking for an insight into why morale in the Force has plummeted; it gets you pondering on how it is that coppers can never seem to be able do anything even when they are able to escape from the mountain of paperwork at their desk; and makes you think about the serious rebooting of the system that is required. Rather, that is, than leaving them acting as "the administrative service for the insurance industry".

One of the most comprehensive chronicles of government waste is the *Burning our Money* blog written by Mike Denham. Denham is a retired Treasury Civil Servant so has an in-depth knowledge of government finance issues. He puts that experience to use helping his readers understand just how government burns their money. He has also made a series of "It's That Bloke Again..." videos to explain particularly dismal examples which are available on his blog.

Top notch, chaps. But that still leaves absolutely miles upon miles of examples for us to share with you now. Which, let us never forget, is not a good thing.

Auntie Beeb

The BBC is an institution. Some think it should be institutionalised.

All members of the public who don't spend their lives reading books beside a toasty fireplace have a telly. They are therefore obliged to pay a cathode ray tax to maintain the privilege of tuning in without facing all those irksome adverts. Except, of course, for the gratuitous product placements that directors occasionally slip in. And the adverts saying how wonderful the BBC is. And the adverts telling you how you have to go digital. Not to mention some dancers shot in primary colours on a far flung beach performing a politically correct dance (costing over a million quid).

The Corporation is understandably unsure of itself. Its angst is evident in the sums it spends gazing at its own navel. One consultation exercise alone cost £1.1 million, and the only obvious outcome was that the TV division got renamed BBC Vision, and the radio renamed Audio and Music. £76,000 was spent on six consultants (one of whom was the former BBC Controller of Strategy), £17,000 on stationery, and £140,000 on hotels, hospitality and travel. Not forgetting, of course, £11,000 in expenses.

It's quite likely that this expenditure falls into a different wasted budget line from the £20 million the BBC spent on taxis and car hire, and the £24 million on expenses claims, and the £17 million reportedly given out in staff bonuses, and the £232,000 *The Sun* newspaper reported was handed over as a bonus to its top ten salary people.

We quite understand that a journalist in the field may need to take someone out to lunch to get the background to a story. We complement on an individual basis the renowned drinking skills of certain journos. We recognise that laying on a courtesy car is money well spent if it entices a reluctant interviewee into the studio. But £20 million! It seems like an awful lot of travel expenses, and it's strange that the spending on taxis is going up when the number of staff is going down. Can't more people follow our example after last year's *Bumper Book*? The BBC offered to send a car to each author's home to collect us for an interview at White City, which we felt more than a bit guilty about, so we arranged to travel in the same car to save money. It's not rocket science.

Perhaps an iconic symptom lies in the story of the neon sign. The BBC Television Centre found one of its 'i's on the blink. Instead of getting someone to fix it, the management brought in two outside contractors to consult with its own facilities people – one to set up a hydraulic platform, another to write an assessment of the damage – and awaited the regular personnel to mend it in due course. Nothing got fixed for weeks. Insiders meanwhile moaned that a couple of workmen could have been sent up in a cradle and just sorted it.

Then there was the report of the emergency studio audience. The story goes that the organisers behind the *Paul O'Grady Show* didn't fill out the forms properly, so they had to spend £16,000 on in-house unionised staff just to fill out the audience because members of the public weren't written into the licence. Even shows like *Top of the Pops* had to bring in the hired help.

With stories like this breaking, morale amongst the lesser paid obviously needs to be maintained. One option, of course, is to blow £125,000 on an office party for your staff, with free champagne, dodgems, and waltzers. Lovely. Pity licence fee payers weren't invited, though.

One of our moles in the Beeb also tipped us off about a story to do with the late Pope which has been doing the rounds. Apparently, the BBC was one of a number of news agencies that had long planned ahead for the ultimate demise of John-Paul II. Realising that a turf war would erupt between the global news agencies the minute the news was out, BBC managers decided to hire roof space in Rome for a prime camera shot of the Vatican. They also reportedly started to rent accommodation for the reporters who would be required to turn up for the event.

The problem was, the Pope keeps a different diary from the BBC. He didn't die for several more years. This meant wasted rent. Or perhaps not entirely. The White City rumour mill has it that middle ranking managers would occasionally disappear off to Rome and use the accommodation themselves, to help justify its continuing cost.

But the problem is much broader. Robert Aitken was a reporter for 25 years at the Corporation. He has written about some serious failings that beset our public broadcaster. In his book, *Can We Trust the BBC?*, he points to institutional bias towards the left; a predilection to argue in favour of increased public spending; the recruitment of journalists with 'progressive' agendas; a failure to address 'old consensus' issues such as multiculturalism unless politicians from the left attack it first; the small numbers of staff from opposing views in key positions and programmes; in-built bias towards Sinn Fein and against US Republicans and Israel; a refusal to accept criticism; blindness to Islamic fascism; and selective use of facts in support of the political agenda.

Obviously there are noble exceptions to the rule. We make the ovious point, however, that any agency which recruits only in certain newspapers will recruit more often than not the type of person who reads those newspapers. The BBC uses the *Guardian*.

We don't object to left wingers presenting programmes. We don't object to right wingers presenting programmes. We don't object to political atheists presenting either. But there should be fair representation for all views, and a variety of presenters who are open about where they are coming from. If, for example, Peter Snow holds strident views that may colour his presentation, we shouldn't have to check out the colour of his socks for biased swing-o-meter analysis. And if there isn't variety in the world views of presenters, the public shouldn't have to pay a licence fee and be taxed for the privilege of listening to the political agenda of a metropolitan elite.

Superstar Wallets

Two thousand years ago, vast wealth could be made in the arena or in the circus. Some Roman nobles even sank to the depths of playing the role themselves in order to win acclaim and gold from the benevolent mad Emperor of the day.

These days, the big money lies in football. Staggering, indeed ridiculous, sums are handed over to people who are able to kick a ball around.

At the end of the day, however, you have a choice whether to contribute to footballers' wages or not. You can choose not to buy the season ticket, not to buy the football shirt, and not to subscribe to Sky Sports. You can, if you prefer, go and watch pétanque instead, for free. But you have no choice over how much you are forking out for the public servants who get superstar wages.

The TaxPayers' Alliance published the *Public Sector Rich List* in November 2006. It presented a list of the 171 most highly paid people in the public sector – people earning above £150,000 a year in government departments, quangos, other public bodies and public corporations.

The key findings of the report were:

⅄ There are 3 people in the public sector who earn more than £1 million a year.

⅄ There are 14 people in the public sector earning above £500,000 a year.

⅄ There are 46 people earning above £250,000 a year.

⅄ On average, the 171 people on the list had a pay rise of 8.4% between 2005 and 2006. This is double average earnings growth (including bonuses) across the country, which is 4.2%.

⅄ The average total pay of the 171 people on the list is £259,701 per annum. This works out at just under £5,000 a week. Although many people on the list are likely to work longer, based on a 35-hour week, this is equal to over £140 an hour.

⅄ The 10 most highly paid people in the public sector earn on average around 40 times the amount earned by someone starting out as a police officer, nurse or soldier.

⅄ The 12 highest paid NHS people earn an average of £183,000. (Starting salary for a nurse: around £19,000.)

⅄ The Chief Executives of 9 Regional Development Agencies earn an average of £178,000 each. None of these Regional Development Agencies is based in London.

⅄ Gordon Brown is only the 88th highest paid person in the public sector.

Top 10 public sector salaries

	Organisation	Person, Poistion	Pay (2006 or 2005-06)
1.	Transport for London	Bob Kiley, Commissioner	£1,146,425
2.	Royal Mail	Adam Crozier Group Chief Executive	£1,038,000
3.	Network Rail	John Armitt Chief Executive	£1,027,000
4.	Network Rail	Iain Coucher Deputy Chief Executive	£924,000
5.	Royal Mail	David Mills Chief Exec. Post Office Ltd	£816,000
6.	Network Rail	Ron Henderson Group Finance Director	£683,000
7.	Network Rail	Peter Henderson Projects & Engineering Dir.	£678,000
8.	Royal Mail	Maria Cassoni Group Finance Director	£656,000
9.	British Nuclear Fuels	Michael Parker Chief Executive	£635,751*
10.	BBC	Mark Thompson Director General	£619,000
		Average	**£843,047**

* 2005 or 2004-05 figure

The Town Hall Rich List was published in March 2007, just after inflation-busting council tax rises had been announced. It revealed details of 578 of the most highly paid people in local government – people earning above £100,000 a year in 230 councils right across the country.

Local authorities refuse to state in their annual accounts which of their senior staff are earning these high salaries, so the TaxPayers' Alliance was forced to use the Freedom of Information Act to obtain details. In so doing, we came up against a co-ordinated cover-up attempt from a number of councils that didn't want local taxpayers to know how their council tax was being spent. Despite these attempts, we succeeded in obtaining responses from the majority of councils.

The key findings of the report were:

- 5 people in local councils earn more than £200,000 a year.

- 64 people in town halls earn more than £150,000 a year.

- The number of people earning above £100,000 in local authorities is increasing at an alarming rate. There are now 578 people on these 'fat cat' salaries, compared with 429 people the year before, an increase of 35%.

- Consequently, the total pay bill for these senior staff stands at £72 million, compared with £53 million the year before, an increase of 36%.

- Senior staff turnover in local authorities is rapid, but there are 350 people who feature on the *Rich List* in both 2004-05 and 2005-06. Their average pay rise was 6.09%, three times the official rate of inflation and far higher than the 1.9% pay award granted to nurses earlier this year.

- The average remuneration is almost £125,000 per annum – almost £2,500 a week. Although many on the list are likely to work longer than the standard public sector 35-hour week, this equates to almost £70 an hour.

Top 10 Town Hall Salaries

Council Position	Person and notes	Total Remuneration (05-06)
1. Renfrewshire	Tom Scholes Chief Executive	£233,029 Included redundancy of £113,015 and £161 travel expenses
2. Kent	Peter Gilroy Chief Executive	£229,999
3. Wandsworth	Gerald Jones Chief Exec. & Director of Administration	£227,424 Included health insurance and health check - £1,156 on average; performance bonus of £18,033 (avg. 8.66% salary)
4. Surrey	Dr Richard Shaw Chief Executive	£207,843
5. Norfolk	Tim Byles Chief Executive	£204,165 Included performance-related payment of £16,813; mileage & sundries: £2,991
6. Cambs.	Ian Stewart Chief Executive	£199,999
7. City of London	Chris Duffield Town Clerk	£190,270 Salary bands incl. London weighting: £4,370 for 05-06
8. Kensington & Chelsea	Derek Myers Town Clerk & Chief Executive	£190,000 Includes undisclosed annual performance-related bonus
9. Kent	Graham Badman Strategic Director Educ. & Libraries	£189,999
10. Herts.	Caroline Tapster Chief Executive	£188,500 Included £3,500 alternative to a lease car

London 2012

There is a celebrated science fiction movie called *28 Days Later* in which a comatose man awakes in a deserted London, whose streets have been trashed, public services have vanished, and transport is non-existent.

There is a near parallel: the Olympics. But they are only going to last nineteen days and there are no planned killer zombies. What kind of deal is that?

Assuming London 2012 follows Athens 2004 and that the Games cost £3.5 billion – which we don't believe for a moment – that would mean each day of the Games costing around £185 million. That's quite a lot.

Assuming that there are 10,500 athletes, that would mean a third of a million pounds per competitor, including the hopeless ones. The final bill will, of course, be vastly higher. In fact, we are now looking at sums approaching £9-10 billion. Think about it for a moment. Nine billion pounds. That is enough to pay for the entire schooling of four million Third World children.

Time was that spectators would get to see events with real broken bones and fatalities, charioteering Ben Hur style, and even people pounding around the track in full armour and carrying a shield. These days you get synchronised swimming, and women prancing around a sports hall waving a loo roll on a stick. So much for progress.

At least someone has found a decent use for the Millennium Dome in all this. It transpires that the white elephant will host the basketball finals, artistic gymnastics, and trampolining events. Thank goodness for that £1 billion roof space.

Let's turn to some of the hidden costs, as government looks at spending money outside of the events themselves. One example is the extra tax money being spent on winning medals for the Olympics in the Talented Young Athlete Scheme.

Talented Young Athlete Scheme (TASS)

£1 million has been allocated to a new fund called the TASS 2012 Scholarships, supplying one hundred 12-18 year olds with £10,000 of support each, specifically with the aim of increasing medal chances in coming Olympics and Paralympics. £17 million has been earmarked to TASS over four years, in addition to other athletics funding, to support about 3,000 youngsters.

There have been successes for TASS athletes – one silver medal at the Turin 2006 Winter Olympics; three medals at Gothenburg 2006, and 21 at the 2006 Melbourne Commonwealth Games. But there is no clear evidence that state money made the difference to the athletes' performance. Arguably, the money just kept a few people fit at public expense. Is our national sporting prestige worth the money, or is it not better to push for the targeted £100 million sponsorship fund to come entirely from the private sector?

Payroll

We can also look at the cost of London 2012 from a payroll perspective. If you are a seasoned veteran of organising ticker tape parades, you are going to make a mint. The 2012 Head of Culture, for example, got a "six figure package" on joining the team. It is a four year appointment. We expect the lucky incumbent will get a gong too (providing we don't see a repeat of the Seoul Olympics, when the doves of peace got barbecued as the beacon was lit).

The DCMS itself has advertised for a Director General to manage the department's own staff, with a salary package "designed to attract world-class candidates". We expect other interested parties will throw large amounts of salary money around to correspond with their own bid for a bigger share in how the Games budget gets spent.

Nearer the time, LOCOG (the Games organising committee) will be appointing a veritable host of salaried staff. Consider one small element alone. A Chief Medical Officer will be appointed to put in place dope testing procedures to test an estimated 5,000 Olympians during the course of the proceedings.

Questions to the London Mayor

Damian Hockney: *"Will the Mayor consider erecting on top of City Hall a solar-powered illuminated sign to keep Londoners informed of the ever-rising budget estimates of the 2012 Olympics?"*

Ken Livingstone: *"No."*

LOCOG, as of early February 2007, had 114 employees, eight seconded employees, and retained 13 consultants, on top of five temps. The Olympic Delivery Authority (ODA) employed 90 people, had another 24 secondees, and 77 temps. It has 21 Board and Committee members, presumably the ones on the top pay grades.

As a guide to how much this whole fandango is going to cost, by the end of January the ODA had spent over three quarters of a million pounds on recruitment, and it's barely got going on its target of recruiting 2,500 staff.

It is not clear how much it has even spent to get this far. Pay costs for the Olympic Games Unit up to the award of the games ran to three quarters of a million pounds, but that only counts the unit's 13 staff and not those from other departments which were providing support. Right now, the DCMS has 37 full-time civil service staff working on the games.

In Summer 2006, the Department for Culture ran a 2012 Roadshow. This ra-ra event was designed to "ensure that as many people as possible were made aware of and able to take part in the unique opportunities that the 2012 Olympic Games and Paralympic Games can bring", though it is hard to find any real benefit from this operation. In addition to unknown costs borne by regional government, the Department spent

£22,600, Transport for London £9,000 and Sport England £5,000 on this three week jolly, excluding staff, travel and accommodation costs.

On top of that there are the generous consultancy costs.

Consultancy costs

In 2002, Arup was paid £81,131 for a report called *London Olympics 2012, Costs and Benefits*. In 2003, PricewaterhouseCoopers also wrote a report on *London 2012 Costs and Benefits*, costing £38,000, and then a report in 2004 as an *Olympic Cost Review*. In addition to these projects, KPMG were also commissioned in October 2005 to provide advice on the cost of the Olympic Games, for which it billed an exorbitant £1,017,593.

Yet the government's own figures are inconsistent in that another set of figures, released the same day, said that the Arup report actually cost £190,830. It also transpires astonishingly that the KPMG advice is part of an ongoing set of advice that has not actually been written up as a report, which sounds remarkably odd. Whatever the reality, it has been revealed to us that when new management took over in 2006, one of its first acts was to terminate the practice of repeatedly employing expensive consultants to rework the same figures.

Problem areas – identified in 2003

We have in front of us one of these reports, dating from 2003. This places it in the period when the London bid was very much ongoing. What is particularly interesting is that at this relatively early stage, even the people coming up with the figures for the pro-bid government were pointing out some areas of concern.

One lay in a possible surge in building costs due to "scope creep", as builders modify planned structures in order to make them more permanent investments, and to avoid a 'Dome legacy syndrome'.

Another was the unknown costs of the mooted 'Elite Sports

Programme', where money would be spent on "initiating and maintaining an elite sports programme to boost performance at the Games"; in other words, up to a quarter of a billion pounds spent on making the UK win a few more golds. This is rather more than the figures the government like to cite.

In fact, we have since learned that the Elite Sports Programme is bigger still. For the games in China we are looking at £215 million going to support athletes in its World Class Performance Pathway (WCPP). For London, it will be £400 million. Amateurism, it seems, is very expensive.

Then there was the estimate on security costs, which said that the Operational Command Unit might require funding of up to £280 million (this was before the Underground bombing atrocities). Next, up to £60 million spent on beautifying London under the 'Look of London' scheme.

Again, there is the roughly half a billion pounds identified in administration costs, which states that there is a "high level of uncertainty in this area, especially salary/resources", and indicates that it may have missed hidden costs such as those of salaries for local government officials involved. (They might also have usefully mentioned how much it costs to hire temps and consultants during a vacancy glut.)

Massive uncertainty surrounds the costs of upgrading infrastructure to cope with the number of people getting to the venue. Intriguingly, the Government Office for London seems to have identified through its own consultations at this stage that there would be an extra direct £13 million in costs for main road route management, £2 million extra costs for City Airport, and a shocking £20 million for "publicity planning" – which presumably refers to the report's subsequent comment that "background demand must be suppressed". We assume this means spending taxpayers' money telling people not to travel at peak time, involving what is styled "possible displacement of alternative transport schemes".

So far it does not bode well. Add to this the assumption that revenue is achieved through every seat being successfully sold "through price adjustment if necessary" – i.e. slashing prices and therefore expected revenue – and an acknowledgement that "public willingness-to-pay has not been market tested", so nobody had an idea how much money might be raised through ticket sales. Up to a third of money raised from local sponsors, meanwhile, would be lost by having to be ploughed back into the deficit side of the balance sheet as the cost of looking after them.

So what we have is an early acknowledgement that all might not be so rosy when the hidden costs and negatives of staging an Olympics are felt. It is further stated that extra issues might also surface, such as the risk of building work "being held to ransom"; there might with the administration side of things be a "lack of control in salary of experts and committee members"; public expectations in 'Elite Sports Funding' (i.e. the prospect of winning golds) would by inference require managing; and there were questions over "seat kills" – a curious term redolent of a Frederick Forsyth novel, which just means sales of tickets.

This is not even going into the section dealing with "congestion costs measured by loss of productivity", which are guesstimated at an astounding £100 million. And on top of all this, we need to factor in inflation.

House of Commons worries

A House of Commons committee looked into costs much more recently. One of its first observations was to note how, 18 months after winning the bid, many of the cost figures it contained were already seriously outdated. The programme contingency as set by the Treasury "could amount to an almost open cheque". Of £900 million new costs, amazingly £400 million was being spent on 'cost control'!

Major uncertainties remained. One was over costs to decontaminate the land, which planners today seem in danger of becoming fixated by. Another was on how exactly £1 billion was going to be spent on linking the Olympic Park to local infrastructure.

Legacy issues

Nor are we any clearer on what is going to happen after the Games to some of the assets, what with reports of athlete accommodation being kept extremely low-rise so competitors don't have to wait too long for lifts, and a £134 million press centre left over after the event. Even the main sports venue will have most of its seats ripped out. This is patently absurd. The venue only needs maximum capacity on two days – for the Opening Ceremony, and when the Games close. The rest of the time the stadium will be half empty. Far better to host it on those days at the showpiece Wembley Arena, rather than build a useless venue that more money has to be spent on to remove afterwards.

We are doubly incensed to learn of the Olympic impact locally. Manor Garden Allotments are going to be concreted over in order to allow extra pedestrian access at the Lea Valley site for these two days. So much for the Games leaving a legacy for the local community. Shame on the planners.

Optimism bias

The big fiascos to date have been laid at the door of the Treasury. One detail which we uncovered was that the Chancellor deliberately failed to fully factor in its standard 'optimism bias', which is a formula to help cover overspend in massive government projects. There's nothing new there. The same 'oversight' added £140 million to the wonky maths for how much benefit the government thought ID cards might bring.

VAT

Another charge has been that the consultants completely failed to factor in VAT. It's unclear whether this was because they assumed the Treasury would let them off the hook, or just slipshod accountancy. In either case, it caught the Culture Secretary by surprise. Even more embarrassing, when challenged she didn't even twig that even if the government wanted to, there was an issue as to whether ministers could now ignore VAT rules under established EU law.

Police costs

Police costs are reported to have soared. Obviously there is the security threat during the Games itself, with memories of what happened in Munich to add to concerns. One ballpark figure pushed the bill up from £190 million to £1.5 billion. Even the initial back-of-a-fag-packet security report will cost the Met £4.6 million to produce. But what has also had to be factored in is security during the building work. It seems that the prospect of large amounts of building material and equipment lying around the East End proved tempting to locals, and so extra security and police officers have had to be taken on to guard the gaff. Only time will tell, of course, if all the contract money itself is being put to properly audited use. We hope skeletons don't turn up in the concrete when buildings are demolished in the future.

We suspect prices will soar as the project goes on. It is not particularly reassuring to learn that the government is looking into PPPs and PFIs (more later) to help finance building work.

We can't say we haven't been warned. The chairman of the Olympic Delivery Committee resigned spectacularly after claiming that the cost of the Games would rise exponentially. Curiously, he was given a £150,000 pay off to keep his mouth shut, which of course made his point eloquently.

If only . . .

Back in 1948, London hosted its last games. The nation was still recovering from war. Flour rationing actually ended as the Games began, but you still had your coupons for tea, clothes, soap, sugar, and food. This made the games a pretty straightforward kind of affair.

We have an opportunity to get back the spirit of the old Olympics, to drop glitz and focus on the pursuit of excellence. Rather than throw money at glamour, why not cut the razzmatazz and just recall the soul of those athletes throughout the last century who have excelled despite the lack of decent facilities, from the Ethiopian runners to the Eddie the Eagles of this world? Why not dwell on some of the sportsmen of the past, such as the extraordinary stories of German Lutz Long's sporting advice to Jesse Owens during the Berlin Games; Eugenio Monti, who gave a crucial spare bolt from his bobsleigh to his British competitors in the 1964 Winter Olympics; or Karoly Takacs, who lost his shooting hand in the war and learnt to win gold with his left.

The London Planning Committee at least has an eye on something approaching this internationalism. LOCOG is providing £26,000 to every national team to allow them to use facilities from an approved register. Obviously this will be of greatest help to the athletes from the smallest and poorest nations. Go Liberia's weightlifters!

But they are still set to blow £10 billion of tax money in a shameful extravaganza, a corruption of the spirit of amateur athletics.

On the 27th of July, with five years to go until the start of the 2012 Olympic Games, the TaxPayers' Alliance launched its *Olympics Watchdog*. The cost of the games has already spiralled from £2.4 to £9.35 billion. The Olympics Watchdog will alert taxpayers to any further rises. It will also investigate the hidden costs of the Olympics. In the Athens Olympics, for instance, most British taxpayers were probably unaware that they wound up paying a subsidy for the games by proxy – through the European Union.

Public Art Grants

We first thought we ought to include a few words on public support of the arts when we came across something supported by South East Dance.

SED is a regular recipient of Arts Council Funding. Last year, it commissioned a new dance film by Jane Mason called *Hard Told*. In the SED's words:

> *"Hard Told is a journey of suffocating intimacy and isolation. Through the eyes of an elderly deaf man, a dance emerges. Bare feet ... a muddy field*

> *... a distant tree ...*
>
> *... A woman.*
>
> *Taking pedestrian movement through barren landscape, Jane Mason's film searches for boundaries of time and space, guided by her protagonist's deviating narrative."*

It sounds gripping. But is it something you wanted your tax money spent on? And what other similar projects are being supported on your behalf which you might not want to see at the box office? Even at gun point?

Let's start with the UK Film Council. The government likes to fly the flag. Since 2000, the UK Film Council has distributed grants to the film industry, both for production and distribution. 108 films in all have been subsidised.

The first thing we note is the definition of British. Many of the films, particularly the ones supported on artistic merit alone, aren't really British. They are sometimes not even in English. So why are we funding them, if most taxpayers won't even be able to understand them?

Some have been bigger hits than others. The UK Film Council, for instance, has supported *Gosford Park* (worldwide box office takings: £112 million), *The Constant Gardener* (£84 million), and *Bend it like Beckham* (£94 million). There was also *The 51st State* (£21 million) and *28 Days Later* (£86 million) amongst others. Good on them.

However, for many of the subsidised films, the notion of profits is a pipedream. Among recent flops are *Miranda* (worldwide takings: £107,000), *Sex Lives of Potato Men* (£1.6 million), *Diameter of the Bomb* (£3,000), and *Emotional Backgammon* (£4,000).

We don't deny the powerful drama of such outstanding films as *Sophie Scholl, Shooting Dogs* or *Pierrepoint*, or even the brazen anarchy of *Churchill – the Hollywood Years*. They have artistic merit even if the box office has disappointed. We'll even forgive

C.R.A.Z.Y. for being a Canadian film, in French, because it's quite thought-provoking. Let's focus, however, on money spent backing films that simply never drew the crowds.

Films that flopped at your expense

- *Aaltra* – Belgian film apparently about annoying farmers who are mostly silent (investment £17,000, box office £18,000).

- *Awesome; I F#ckin' Shot That* – US home movie shot by the audience at a Beastie Boys concert (investment £40,000, box office £12,000).

- *Cockles and Muscles* – French seaside coming-of-age film (investment £22,000, box office £31,000).

- *Dear Frankie* – mum hires stranger to pretend to be a deaf boy's father (investment £100,000, box office £133,000).

- *Emotional Backgammon* – tortured relationships (investment £60,000, box office £2,000).

- *Frozen* – unresolved and ghostly grief in Morecambe (investment £21,000, box office £23,000).

- *Iqbal* – Indian film about cricket (investment £50,000, box office £13,000).

- *King's Game/Kongekabale* – Danish film about spin doctors (investment £47,000, box office £32,000).

- *Lobo* – Spanish film about ETA (investment £39,000, box office £20,000).

- *Murderball* – US film on quadraplegic rugby (investment £45,000, box office £36,000).

- *Princesa* – Brazilian transvestite in Milan becomes prostitute to finance sex-change operation (investment £10,000, box office £3,000).

- *Rock School* – About the Philadelphia School of Rock (investment £39,000, box office £10,000).

- *The Magician* – Australian film about a hit man (investment £43,000, box office £23,000).

- *Unknown White Male* – an amnesiac on Coney Island (investment £15,000, box office £12,000).

Some of the films in the table opposite may be classics, and not just in their own lunchtime. Unfortunately, the paying public didn't think so as individuals, even if collectively their representatives holding the public purse strings thought they should.

Who are these connoisseurs? The UK Film Council has 90 people on its payroll. Unfortunately, Jonathan Ross isn't one of them (despite being paid £18 million by the BBC). This might explain the above choices.

On top of these finances, of course, there's the support to the film industry offered by the state-funded BBC and Channel 4.

We said that the government likes to fly the flag. This obviously does not mean, in its eyes, that it should refrain from subsidising films that attack our country. *Bloody Sunday, The Wind That Shakes the Barley,* and *The Road to Guantanamo* are three films that almost certainly did not help the cause of the United Kingdom government overseas. Should they have been made? That's entirely an issue for the artists. Should we as taxpayers have subsidised them? That is a different matter altogether.

What if state support for UK films is made on one of two conditions; firstly, the government, as a business partner, gets a full share in profits based upon investment, and secondly, no public money gets handed over for politically-motivated films that damage Britain's reputation? By all means make the movie – and good luck to you – but don't expect the British taxpayer to act as your backer.

Let's turn to the non-cinematographic. You would not believe how many arts projects are funded from public money. We have a list that just covers just one year of grantees. Page after page after page of scores of names. Overleaf are some examples, chosen pretty well at random. We swear we haven't made any of them up. Scout's honour.

Programmes

- £644,000 on *Own Art*, interest-free loans for people to buy artwork.
- £665,000 on *Take It Away*, interest-free loans for people to buy musical instruments.
- £490,000 for *Joined Up Music for People in Somerset*.
- £1 million on *Artsmad*, introducing art to a rough housing estate.
- £2.9 million on reducing carbon emissions from South Kensington museums and colleges.
- £875,000 on using art to introduce new health opportunities for overweight primary school children.
- £250,000 for *Mission, Models, Money*, "to address the challenges faced by individual arts and cultural organisations and their funders in developing mission-led financially sustainable businesses."

Lottery Grant Awards

- £4,950 for Fluid Groove
- £170,000 for Hoipolloi
- £13,230 for Inky Fish
- £4,335 for the Rufford Wood Firing Society (presumably pottery rather than arboreal kalashnikovs)
- £9,351 for the Unique Coffee Bar
- £33,662 for Gob Squad
- £5,000 for Dante or Die
- £75,000 for Greenpeace (sounds politically controversial)
- £4,874 for Network of Stuff Theatre
- £36,711 for Queer Writers and Poets
- £21,800 for Stacked Wonky
- £35,636 for Stan Won't Dance
- £96,720 for Emergency Exit Arts
- £43,000 for Flying Gorillas
- £60,850 for the Poetry Translation Centre
- £344,000 for the Belgrade Theatre Trust (Coventry)

- £3,500 for Bloodaxe Books
- £26,000 for Chaplaincy to the Arts
- £124,820 for Dodgy Clutch
- £10,000 for Falling Cat
- £4,871 for Kipper Tie
- £32,485 for the Mad Alice Theatre Company
- £2,420 for Neighbourhood Watch Stilts International
- £4,935 for the Dying Frog Arts Network
- £4,471 for Electricwig
- £69,500 for Excellence in Crewe
- £75,000 for Fat Northerner Records
- £15,817 for Pickleherring
- £34,980 for Queer Up North
- £6,435 for HM Prison Albany
- £4,525 for I am the Mighty Jungulator
- £4,950 for the European Union Chamber Orchestra
- £64,205 for Gonzo Moose
- £193,940 for Moby Duck
- £59,472 for Rhubarb, Rhubarb
- £3,760 for Swamp Circus

The list above is your fault for buying a Lottery ticket. But overleaf is a random picking from the list receiving direct state aid.

Recipients of direct state aid

- £4,500 for the Department of Health
- £2,000 for Smart Team – Arrest Referral Unit
- £139,000 for Viva: the Orchestra of the East Midlands
- £55,000 for assorted BBC projects
- £199,000 for BBC Pebblemill
- £45,000 for Lincolnshire Dance
- £95,000 for Artichoke Trust
- £69,000 for Told by an Idiot
- £63,037 for Bigga Fish
- £220,632 for Oily Cart (sic)
- £1,770 for Creeping Toad
- £9,800 for Don't Feed the Poets Productions
- £8,000 for English Martyrs
- £12,500 for the Shysters Theatre Company
- £10,000 for the British Antarctic Survey
- £31,519 for Lawnmowers
- £800,000 for MAO (Museum of Modern Art Limited)
- £11,347 for Open Hand Open Space
- £34,925 for the Ann Peaker Centre for Arts and Criminal Justice
- £75,000 for Barfly
- £7,550 for Create – Scarborough
- £2,500 for the Institute of Crazy Dancing
- £42,200 for Yorkshire Women Theatre
- £930,000 for the Yorkshire Sculpture Park

We wanted to find out a bit more about these grants, especially those to the BBC. Why, we wondered, was the BBC even applying for Lottery money? If successful, wouldn't that just be a case of a state-funded organisation taking money away from good causes, when it already has its own tax money to rely on? It transpires that those projects are as follows:

BBC client	Title	Amount
BBC Pebblemill	*Roots*	£199,000

Eleven cultural workers based in BBC local radio stations in England. Developing Black and Minority Ethnic talent producing and researching pieces for BBC programmes and supporting diverse arts events within communities.

BBC	*Open Tales*	£25,000

Researching and creating digital storytelling pieces with several Creative Partnerships Coventry schools.

BBC Radio Kent	*Arts Audiences Coordinator*	£15,000

Developing audiences for contemporary arts and culture within the BBC Radio Kent broadcast area.

BBC Sheffield	*Trimedia Test Station*	£13,500

A pilot partnership project to produce radio, video and web content with young reporters aged 14-17.

BBC Hull	*Exploring Multi-Media Rich English*	£11,000

Investigating views of young people, teachers and creative practitioners as they participate in creative learning through the added value of an intense multi media rich English curriculum. To build capacity of schools and teachers to work effectively and creatively.

BBC East	*Every Picture Tells a Story*	£3,540

A collaboration exploring questions about children's understanding of the media and what children learn from visual representation of themselves and their world.

BBC Home Service	*Roots Leicestershire*	£2,000

The continuation of Roots work in Leicestershire until March 2006.

This is all dandy, but how frankly does it differ from what the publicity or careers people in the BBC are doing anyway? Or is it a case of funds being applied for because the projects cannot be funded under licence fee regulations for some reason, in which case why is the BBC doing them this way?

We were also intrigued to find out more about the money that goes towards arts in the British Antarctic Survey. After all, the canvases would surely lean rather heavily on blacks, blues and whites when you get your palette out. In fact, it transpires that Arts Council England provided a grant of £10,000 (now £12,000) annually to the British Antarctic Survey to cover a stipend award to the artists participating in the Artists and Writers in Antarctica Programme. The aim of this BAS programme is to raise awareness and understanding of the extensive scientific research it undertakes in Antarctica. This award covers the costs of travel to and from the Falklands, accommodation, medical examinations and support for the artists towards exhibitions and outreach work. I hope you like pictures of penguins.

Are any of these projects any good? Who knows. We doubt the civil service came round and evaluated whether the money had been spent to any qualifiable benefit. The lists alone cover £350 million of grants, not counting another quarter of a billion provided by local authorities. Perhaps some wonderful pieces of art were generated. But perhaps, too, some of it was wasted on being pretentious in a small room with a limited audience.

There is nothing wrong with public art, including performance art, unless your money is paying for it involuntarily. We are quite happy to attend events like these, and are always delighted to observe artists at work and judge them on their merits. But why are these shows and performers selected and not others? Why, for instance, is stand-up comedy not subsidised in quite the same way? Is it because it is profitable, because it is actually popular? The problem simply is this: no one seems to be accountable for millions of pounds of our money.

One final word on the subject. We reserve special praise for greengrocer Michael McElderry, who hit the national news for striking back. His local council in Wansbeck spent £1,600 for a week hiring a performance artist to dress as a commuter and stand still in the street. Mr McElderry decided to stage his own event, a sprout on a saucer next to the artiste. It apparently demonstrated "a symbolic expression of resistance to the totalitarian state which is now Wansbeck District Council". But locals got that display for free.

The Government Art Collection

Of course, ministers are not to be deprived of art either. That's why the state has a government art collection (GAC).

Last year we told you about some of the wonders that are being held in Whitehall in your name, their purpose being to impress visiting dignitaries in ante-chambers while they waited to deliver declarations of war. We have since learned more about the GAC:

Did you know, for instance, that the GAC spends approximately £130,000 from its annual budget on transporting and installing some of its collection in government buildings in the UK and around the world?

A lot of it is spent moving works to and from the offices of ministers. On taking up a new post, a minister gets to select the paintings and such like that decorate his surroundings.

In Tony Blair's various cabinets, sixty-seven ministers had such public works in their offices. Some, like Margaret Beckett and Alistair Darling, had a penchant for taking their artwork with them when they changed jobs. Others, like Charles Clarke, filled in the paperwork to change their artwork but had resigned before it got to them. Some, like Jack Straw, decided to remove items that they were unhappy with. But many others liked variety, and at public expense requested a new selection of art now and again. One of the worst offenders was Tessa Jowell over at Culture, who made changes in September 2001, January and October 2003, January, March, October and November 2005 and February 2006.

We know fashion changes in the creative arts, but be a trend-setter please and not a slave to the moment. Those specialist removal vans cost money.

Devolved Government

Devolution costs. It costs the taxpayers locally and nationally, to support an extra tier of government with all the buildings, civil servants, and politicians. It costs to supply all the extra budgets that these politicians insist on spending in order to justify their jobs.

This probably helps to explain why the number of people working for the Welsh Assembly has grown by 20% in four years.

It's bad enough even without the bureaucracy. Scotland gets subsidised by the English taxpayer to the tune of £11 billion these days. This means several things. Firstly, that Scots get around £2,000 more spent on them per person than the English for tax take. Secondly, that this irritates the English and does no good for national harmony. Thirdly, that it discourages the people who spend the money in Scotland from having 'ownership' of the tax money, and if you want to know what we mean by that, look at some of the great financial scandals that have taken place in Scottish politics over the years. Finally, the state spending means dependency, with people who have been bought by the state through bread and games, with no incentive to participate in the kind of business-supporting and job-creating society that is really needed in order to make the country thrive. It's a little bit like the pet owner who kills the poor wee timorous beastie through endlessly feeding the thing jam doughnuts.

We would wager a bet, however, that if Scottish taxpayers felt that the expense and waste was coming from their own pay packets, the mood in Edinburgh and Glasgow would change quite dramatically.

Meanwhile, the Westminster side of Scottish politics continues to be busy in its own right. The Scotland Office funded a number of events at Dover House over 2005, including the Advocate-General's summer reception, and the Secretary of State's lunch held in honour of the Moderator of the Church of Scotland.

We suppose these events have to be held to give the Secretary of State something to do. His empire has been devolved from him, and quite an empire it is once you examine it. Why the Scottish Executive owns two arable stud farms comprising 12 properties and 366 hectares, or 14 farms for agricultural research when London government has its own, is not altogether clear. There is nearly £2 billion held in business loans and shares, covering island ferries and crofter industry but especially for water. There's also a £2 million oceanographic research vessel, the *Sir John Murray*.

Meanwhile, the Welsh Department, you will be delighted to learn, has a £3 million National Wool Museum in Carmarthenshire. And devolution has its toys: the Welsh Assembly government sanctioned spending taxpayers' money to buy 32 acres of rain forest in Ecuador. Apparently, it's a gift to the "young people of Europe". If you're a "young person of Europe", we hope you wrote to the Welsh Assembly (on recycled paper) and thanked them.

The Assembly government has also started its programme to create mini embassies in some of the world's most expensive cities. The first opened on March 1st, 2004, in the Chrysler Building, New York, at an initial cost to the Welsh taxpayer of £252,000 (including a refundable rent deposit of £93,000) and an annual running cost of £262,000.

Wales International Centres have also been established in San Francisco and Tokyo in co-location with Wales Trade International, the Assembly government's overseas business arm. The annual running costs for these are £95,500 in San Francisco and £110,000 in Tokyo.

Welsh Assembly Culture Minister Alun Pugh also spent £3,000 on legal advice to find out whether his scrabble Christmas cards would infringe Mattel's copyright – even though Mattel had already offered to waive their licence fee. Here are some tiles we found: M_3 U_1 P_3 P_3 E_1 T_1.

It seems to have become the accepted wisdom in politics now to accept such waste. We disagree. That's why we support people like Newport Councillor Peter Davies, who have quite shamefully been criticised by their own party for pointing out some basic home truths, namely that these assemblies are bad value for money and, certainly in the case of Wales, should be scrapped entirely.

Regionalism

Regionalism is a growing trend.

These days, everybody is into the regions. You have Regional Assemblies (also known as 'Regional Chambers'). You have Regional Arts Boards and Regional Biodiversity Partnerships. You have Regional Centres of Excellence (procurement bodies) and Regional Climate Change Partnerships, Regional Cultural Consortiums and Regional Development Agencies. Regional Fire Management Boards and Regional Fire Control Rooms do their work alongside Regional Housing Boards and Regional Industrial Development Boards. Regional Museums, Libraries and Archives Councils, Regional Observatories and Regional Public Heath Observatories ply their trade, while Regional Resilience Teams and Regional Resilience Forums work with Regional Rural Affairs Forums to assist Regional Social Inclusion Partnerships, who might ring up Regional Sports Boards to complement the effects of Regional Tobacco Control Managers, while members of Regional Transport Boards and Regional Waste Technical Advisory Boards confer in the corner.

And of course they send their united delegations to Europe and the Committee of the Regions. When, that is, they are not attending meetings of the new super regions – the Arc Manche Regional Assembly unites delegates from Southern England, Northern France, and Western Belgium. The North Sea Regions, Atlantic Region, Ireland-Wales Region and North Periphery Regions with associated quangos and hangers-on will soon follow.

It's just a shame that we don't have any real regions to go with them. We invite our critics to wear a black and white strip in Sunderland to see what we mean.

Some government departments play up their regional groups. Take the DCMS, which has regional boards. The Culture West Midlands team spent £5,600 on a jolly, in which 26 people with interests ranging from Stoke-on-Trent Council through to the Birmingham Opera Company went to Brussels to learn more about waffles. The team also spent £2,500 rebranding itself when it became a company limited by guarantee.

In England, such constructs are a peculiar development whose only real meaning comes tenuously from a review of Dark Age maps. Counties with no affiliation are banded together for the sake of adding an extra tier of devolved government. A good example of this is if you go to the Four Shire Stone in the Cotswolds. If you stand to the south, looking over to Four Shire Stone Farm, you are in the South West Region that stretches down in single governance to the Scillies. A step to the East and you look down on Heath Farm and South East Region, at one in governance with Dover. Pace around the stone to the North and you are in the same territory as the West Marches. But if you were to ask the local farm residents whether they feel any special affinity with the people of either Bristol, Guildford or Birmingham, you would get short shrift. Regional government is a fake construct, and has been since the suppression of the marcher lords centuries ago. More to the point, it is expensive.

As much as anything else, when people talk about regional spending, they are referring to the work of the Regional Development Agencies, or RDAs. These are recent constructs, set up a decade ago. Spending on them over that time has gone up massively. Each now employs around 300 to 350 staff. Even so, there are increasing reports of a reliance on consultants, particularly former employees.

The whole thing is just gravy. As *Yorkshire Post* journalist Simon McGee, who has witnessed regionalism in his patch, tells us, "Small level government doesn't mean cheap government."

Not surprisingly, over the last five years, the average cost of running RDA offices has gone up from £95 million to £132 million, and the accompanying and useless talking shop of the regional assemblies (which do exist, regardless of the failed referendum in the North East a few years back) now costs us £18 million, up from £5 million. That's just the money that comes from central government, though – it excludes local levies.

A large chunk of regional money dealt with by RDAs is EU funding, meaning UK taxpayers' money recycled via Brussels. This amounted to £278 million in 2004-05. On top of that there are individual snippets, like the £100,000 each region received to come up with some strategic policy on energy locally. Add up the rest and an agency can be dealing with sums of up to half a billion pounds. But is this money being well spent? Given that a tenth of the budget gets eaten up by administration before it's even dealt, it seems unlikely. And we hear instances of the RDAs using old-style practices of trying to pick winners, setting up business parks and then vetting who can and can't put their businesses there. Far better, as one MP has observed, to shut down these agencies and use the money saved to cut corporation tax and the burden of business rates on small businesses.

Look at another case – a revealing snapshot of the North West's priorities. The North West Development Agency spent £488,000 on encouraging the BBC to move to Manchester and Salford. In other words, it spent nearly half a million pounds on projects designed to move jobs around rather than create them.

How much then is this whole project wasting? More than you can shake a stick at. For starters, there is the £4.4 million that the RDAs spend on their quasi-embassies around the world, in places like Australia, Belgium, China, France, Germany, India, Japan, Korea, Norway, Sweden and the United States – where, of course, each office is competing against those from other regions. The South East Regional Development Agency (SEEDA) was even reported to have spent £10,000 hiring a yacht to launch its development strategy.

It's not even as if this is obviously doing much good. A

Yorkshire MP said laconically of his own regional office in Brussels that it was a useful place to drop off his suitcase before he went into the European Parliament. As store lockers go, it is quite expensive. But then, with this regional RDA office in Brussels accompanying the region's Assembly Office, adding to the UK's Embassy, and the assembly of civil servants from sundry departments that make up our national delegation to the EU (UKREP) also based in Brussels, that means Yorkshire – like other English regions – is represented by four separate delegations in one city, not counting all the professional organisations and quangos too.

This absurdity is only surpassed by Scotland's utter cacophony of representation, with Scotland Europa, the Scottish Executive EU Office, West of Scotland, the East of Scotland European Consortium, the Convention of Scottish Local Authorities, and Highlands and Islands. In a perverse sort of way, London's representatives offer better value for money: at least Ken Livingstone's people, the London Councils, and the Foreign Office have three different policies on the go at any one time.

Back to Yorkshire for a moment: when the extent of the county's over-representation first became public in 2004, council leaders found out to their surprise how much they had been funding these burgeoning organisations. The £1.5 million a year subs have since dropped by six sevenths as outraged councillors have slashed their contributions. But the money from central government keeps flowing.

It might not last. One left wing think tank, the New Local Government Network, has challenged the trend, in a move at least partly (if warily) endorsed by two Treasury ministers.

Cynics say that the whole jamboree was a framework for the time when the government would (supposedly) win referenda on forming elected regional assemblies. Unfortunately, they then realised afterwards that regionalism in England was massively unpopular. The result is that we've been cursed with a temporary set of quangos that were supposed to be stopgaps for an extra tier of government, which at least would have had a democratic input, even if it would have been unpopular and expensive rubbish. We have been lumbered by government incompetence with the worst of both worlds.

A Local Case Study

Even if you doubt that you'll ever find yourself running a government department, you may well be in a position to make some difference to waste on a local level.

Many people are indifferent about local politics, but forget, or aren't aware, that their local council has a budget of millions of pounds. True, it might be boring to figure out how your bins get collected, but this sort of decision can have a real impact on how much money you fork out to pay for its staff and services every year.

Here's one example. Tim Pollard is a local councillor who has taken on Finance and Regeneration in his patch. His experience could be echoed and repeated in councils up and down the country, regardless in many cases of the party politics involved. Here's what he writes of his experiences.

The Croydon Council story

Croydon Council has only changed political allegiance twice: once in 1994 and then back again in 2006.

In 1994 it had reserves of around £24 million, low levels of borrowing and a culture of efficiency.

Twelve years later, when it changed hands for the second time, the picture was completely different. Reserves were almost non-existent, expenditure routinely exceeded income and the Council's 27% increase in Council Tax in 2003 had stimulated the reintroduction of a national capping regime from central government.

What had gone so catastrophically wrong? In the main, the problem was that the pre-2006 administration had forgotten the golden rule of local authority finance: if it is a recurring expenditure, it must be funded from recurring income. Income which is one-off or time limited must not be used to subsidise regular expenditure, for this simply exacerbates the problem when the funding stream dries up.

The pre-2006 administration had found itself running short of cash around the year 2000. Reserves were fast disappearing and expenditure each year was consistently greater than forecast and in excess of income. Faced with this problem they resorted first to widening the scope for capitalising revenue expenditure and then to living off the proceeds of asset sales. When this income, too, had dried up, wholesale cuts were the only option. This included the closure of residential care homes for the elderly and the axing of a sheltered workshop for workers with disabilities.

Under these circumstances it is perhaps unsurprising that the local election of 2006 saw a change of administration.

As an incoming administration in May 2006, there were clearly a number of key priorities, but top of the list was to restore financial stability. A programme to re-engineer service delivery so that quality standards could be maintained but the services delivered in a much more cost-effective way was launched. A wholesale review of budgets, including discarding the assumption that next year's budget for each department should be this year's plus inflation, saw costs driven down throughout the organisation.

We have also launched a campaign to challenge the government to review the financial model which allocates resource so unfairly across the country. Croydon does particularly badly under the current system and, by way of example, we receive £115 per head less than another London Borough which the Audit Commission says is 97% similar to us. That £115 per head equates to £40 million per year. This cannot be fair.

All this work is now beginning to pay off. Our Audit Commission 'Financial Standing' score, as measured five months after the change of administration, has risen to 'Good'. We have been able to set a balanced budget that protects key services and has even allowed the expansion of recycling and law enforcement. We have set a Council Tax rise of 3.99%, the lowest rise for many years. And most importantly, for the first time, we are working to a five year financial horizon rather than taking each year as it comes.

It is this longer term financial plan which will give us long term stability and the means to address the significant challenges that the current government funding system poses.

What's sauce for the goose is sauce for the gander. If you think that your local council is wasting money or blowing sums in ways that aren't sustainable, then you're not powerless. Set up a local campaign; stand for Council yourself; or join the local branch of the TaxPayers' Alliance. A note about our local activities appears at the end of the book.

The Kost of Ken

London has a regional government. It is not a local government, because that is your borough and your local councillor. It is not national, because that is a minister before Parliament. It is regional, because it covers a defined region of the UK – Greater London.

It is not a very good form of regional government though. Accountability is nominal. The incumbent can scoot off on field trips to distant countries and open mini-embassies in far flung corners of the globe without so much as a by-your-leave. The only time accountability comes into it is when some unelected quango takes issue with the mayor over comments that may or may not be of questionable moral worth.

Even the Assembly which is supposed to keep the Mayor accountable on a daily basis is a waste of good money. The Mayor can push through whopping council tax hikes, and the Assembly can vote against a billion pound budget by 16 votes to 9, yet still (because of a two thirds majority rule) nothing happens – so much for democracy and accountability.

At the TaxPayers' Alliance, we see the whole system as a waste of good money. We'd like to see the whole tier of government banned, and power handed over to the boroughs acting in concert. That's why one of the authors of this book, Lee Rotherham, put his money where his mouth is (campaign expenses at time of book's first draft: £10.89) and put his name forward for selection on an abolitionist ticket, to re-inject local democracy and slash waste in London's administration.

By looking at the cost of Mayor Livingstone, we are looking at the costs not simply created by the consequences of our individual choice of mayor, significant though those are. There was, for instance, the incident when Mr Livingstone was hauled before the Standards Board for accusing a Jewish journalist of acting like a concentration camp guard. That cost the Board £63,000, plus £14,000 at adjudication, plus the costs incurred by the Mayor himself – estimated by the BBC at £80,000. Quite a bill for one comment in poor taste.

There is a wealth of tittle tattle out there that raises all sorts of questions to which we would love to know the answer. Such as precisely how much the refreshment bill came to when Ken Livingstone and Transport supremo Bob Kiley met to thrash out strategy for the first time. No doubt it was money well spent. But we leave such vintage for others. No, we are looking rather at policy costs, and the price of administration.

Take the Congestion Charge. According to the National Audit Office, an average of 165,000 penalty notices are issued every month. Each one is billed to Transport for London at a cost of £4.90. It also costs the taxpayer £800,000 a year through the work the DVLA has to do (for free) to supply information from its databases.

In 2004-05 the scheme generated total revenues of £190 million, of which £72 million was enforcement income. Transport for London incurred annual costs of £92 million out of which the private sector contractor expected to earn a cumulative £230 million over the next five years. Nice to know someone's making money out of it.

London Underground Limited has been a major component of the Livingstone Empire since 2003. Aside from the controversy about what the Mayor could do with it, there's the question of the debt. Transport for London (TfL) is allowed to operate what is euphemistically called a Prudential Borrowing Scheme. This means it can borrow vast sums of money to buy new stock, put new rails in, increase staff wages, and so on, all on the never-never. Of course, in the long term the traveller and the taxpayer will have to pay for these loans.

The Underground is managed under a PPP agreement that even

the Labour Mayor seems to take regular issue with. Three companies run the infrastructure and rolling stock, which lease the assets and are supposed to return them in 30 years time in good nick. Notwithstanding this, the government is still pouring in an average of £1 billion a year up to 2010.

In 1992-93, 728 million journeys were made on the Tube. By 2004-05 this had gone up to a record 976 million. One would think that the increase in passengers and the increase in income would mean that the system could improve and make a profit at the same time. But fares have shot up. You wonder if it is no coincidence that in 2005-06 five million fewer journeys were made than in the previous year.

London Underground passenger journeys: 1986-87 to 2005-06

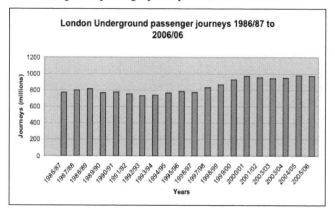

Source: Department for Transport - Annual Report 2005-06

Transport for London, by the way, are the same people who had the bright idea of conducting roadside interview surveys on the six major central London bridges. For thirteen hours on consecutive February days, travellers first on Lambeth, then Westminster, Waterloo, Blackfriars, London and finally Southwark Bridge, were subjected to a clipboard interrogation. While we pity the eleven interviewers and three policemen who at the close of play told us they were "feeling the cold now", we wonder at the final cost and the actual value of a project whose statistics would almost certainly have been politically interpreted to support a pre-decided policy. At least they had the common sense to only bother traffic heading into work, and not those racing home.

Perhaps the effort should have been spent sorting out the mess surrounding free bus passes for kids over 11. First off, we are not sure why the taxpayer should have to fork out for this. Even on public health grounds, the policy discourages children from exercising by walking or taking a bike for the equivalent of a couple of stops. Meanwhile, the habit now is for bus drivers to allow teenagers on without swiping their special Oyster cards, which means that even those who have been barred for aggressive behaviour are using public transport at public expense. Bus drivers who try to apply the rules don't get the support they deserve. When troublemakers do get apprehended for causing a public nuisance, they very rarely have their cards removed; and even if they do they still get to travel with a discount. A tool to encourage a small number of selfish people to behave responsibly is being wasted. This rubbishy system is reported to cost us £55 million a year. It is one giant freebie that Londoners pay for and which brings nothing but aggro in return.

Worryingly, the DfT is thinking of extending the Mayor of London's powers in relation to rail services outside the GLA boundary. Passports to Pimlico here we come.

Reading the various accounts and reports that come out of the London offices can be a delight though. Let's treasure together some of the ways the London Mayor has spent public money, as revealed in answers to questions from Assembly Members Damian Hockney and Roger Evans.

- The Mayor held a Peace Reception for CND and Stop the War, costing taxpayers £5,637.10.

- £215,000 has been spent over five years in bringing birds of prey into Trafalgar Square to deter pigeons. Two hawks are trucked in; they work in shifts. 121 pigeons have been killed in the process. Dastardly and Mutley have an alibi.

- The Mayor has also reportedly authorised a grant of £3,600 to campaigners who want to keep the pigeons fed. We assume none of his £110,000 a year advisers was behind this spectacular demonstration of joined-up government.

- Recycle for London spends £30,000 a year on promotional material. These are things like leaflets and stickers. The sort of things you put in the bin.

- Over a one month period, TfL detected a bus fare evasion rate of 1.06%. This translated as £2.3 million in lost revenue (more if you discount the Oyster card reduction). Thanks, Bendy Bus.

- Meanwhile, 2.63% of Tube travellers were dodging fares. You pseudo-Parisian shirkers cost honest people £1.86 million that month. A stupid ticket price is no excuse.

- In 2005-06, the number of TfL staff being paid more than £50,000 a year rose from 621 to 821.

- Over the same period, the number of people being paid over £50,000 in the London Development Agency rose from 46 to 66.

- Public funds contributed £215,000 to the Mayor's Caribbean Showcase, and £100,000 to Europride.

- In 2006, there were 1,363 reported accidents involving bendy buses. To put this in context, there are currently 337 bendies in the fleet.

- TfL is spending £450,000 in two boroughs offering free personalised travel advice, along the lines of 'take the bus' and 'walking is good for you'.

- TfL has a huge advertising budget. M&C Saatchi got £3 million per year including production. For media planning and buying, Mediaedge CIA received £11 million per annum. For "creative design for direct communications", Chemistry were given £2.2 million per annum including production. Printing of posters and leaflets saw another £6 million per year including production going to publicity firms. So now you know where the money is coming from to show you Bob Kiley standing in the Underground with a hard hat on telling you TfL is "investing" in the network and best check to see if your train is still running. (Next time you're on the Tube, count how many times you see the logos for TfL and the Mayor on adverts above your head. Our record is 12.)

❦ London also has its own Climate Change Agency, costing taxpayers £815,000 last year.

Even when our GLA representatives retire, we still pay for the privilege of having them. As we revealed to the *Evening Standard*, the Mayor is expected to be awarded a pay-off of up to £127,000 when he stands down or loses an election. All members of the London Assembly will also get severance pay under the new rules of between half and all of their £50,000 salaries.

So all told, London government is about tax. It's about whacking you with the Congestion Charge, which is really another vehicle tax, and which is now being targeted against a social class – people who drive 4x4s. Are you being anti-social driving a vehicle like that through town? Maybe. Is it a humvee? No. Is it a little tax jump? Definitely not. It's a hate tax directed against people who would never vote for the Mayor in the first place.

It's about tax, but it's also about waste.

We looked through the GLA's 2006 budget, and it raises all kind of questions. Here are some questions we would love to see answered:

?! Throughout the budget, we see repeated reference to fees. What is the sum of those fees; who is paid; and for what purpose? Is it more money for consultants?

?! Why is it costing £27 million pounds a year extra simply to re-role PC officers already on the beat?

?! How much is going to be spent on pushing for diversity within the fire service, and will diversity be the priority over individual capability for the job?

?! How much does it cost to actually run the various administrative authorities and agencies set up by Mayor Livingstone as part of his fiefdom?

?! Why is there a quarter reduction in budgeting for firefighter pensions? Is this just going to cost us more down the line?

?! Who is the London Fire and Emergency Planning Authority receiving interest from? It looks like they've issued loans.

?! How does the Fire Service intend to reduce hoax calls by a precise 5%? Stop making them themselves?

?! Will the extra six fire and rescue units to be set up for 'major catastrophic incidents' be dedicated solely to that task (i.e. mostly idle) or on general call (i.e. potentially unusable)?

?! How much is the new Fire Service headquarters costing in sum, is it needed, and is waste being avoided?

?! What proportion of the Mayor's own £11 million office allowance is spent on personnel, including advisors and consultants, and who are the top ten highest paid?

?! Why are we spending £300,000 a year on an 'elections' budget line when we are not having any elections?

?! Why does it cost £13 million to run an election in London when a whole general election for the entire nation costs only three times that much? Is any spent on advertising?

?! What are we spending over £40 million a year on below the line 'management and support services'? Are these consultancy fees?

?! Why is the GLA receiving £2 million in interest from other parties, and who are they? Why haven't they paid up yet? Are any of a political or campaigning nature? Who authorised it?

?! What exactly are we spending £57 million of Olympics money on next year?

?! Why do we need an extra £500,000 per year for advisors to Ken Livingstone on the Olympics?

?! What is the average daily pay of a quango member?

?! What exactly is costing £300,000 per year as a Health and Safety cost for the people in City Hall, or in terms of new contracts with the maintenance people? Is everyone in the building getting a personalised bungee cord in case they fall over?

?! As part of the efficiency review, what has been found to have been the average number of sick days taken per year, and how does that compare with the national average for both the public sector and indeed the private?

?! What proportion of the TfL budget goes on debt servicing, now and in the future? If the ludicrously-named 'Prudential Borrowing' rate will indeed be £3.3 billion by 2009-10, what is the liability for the average Londoner? How much will ratepayers be paying simply to service the debt? If it is indeed one quarter of a billion pounds, do we pay that from higher taxes or some form of cuts?

?! How much is spent by TfL on branding, including advertising and sponsorship?

?! Who has made the official assessment that the large underground price rises will have no impact on income from tickets? What assessment have they made about fare dodging, or ordinary people having no alternative but to suffer the price hikes?

?! How much money does TfL hold from Oyster card or similar card holders from the obligatory deposit? What interest did they make last year on the money that they hold, which is actually our money?

?! How much money has been spent on advertising health and safety in transport? What attributed reduction has followed in the number of fatalities? What is the expenditure per fatality averted?

?! How much has TfL spent on consulting the public in hearings, particularly those where it ignored its own findings?

?! What funds have supported social occasions, particularly those at management level? Did they enjoy themselves?

?! What costings have been made of the impact of the Olympics on London transport, including road usage, and consequently on business? Do they support the 2003 PricewaterhouseCoopers assessment that the cost could run to £100 million?

?! What happens if the inflation rate of 2.5% is not met?

?! What is the hidden off-balance sheet cost of the PPP and PFI sets referred to?

?! What is the total pension liability, and what is being budgeted in advance?

?! Have any of the London Development Agency's activities been cost-effective? Has anyone even looked at the cost value? Does anyone in the Agency care?

?! How many affordable housing units has the Places and Infrastructure scheme built on brownfield land? Was it real brownfield land, or was it residential?

?! How many enduring private sector jobs has London's People generated, at what unit cost, and how does it deconflict this role with other agencies?

?! What exactly is London's People doing "to create maximum benefit from the Games in terms of skills and local procurement and ensure that London makes best use of its talent pool by working towards reducing sexist, racist and other prejudices"?

?! How many private sector jobs has London's Enterprises generated, and at what unit cost?

?! How many businesses has London's Enterprises attracted to London, that were not going to be established elsewhere in the United Kingdom? Has anyone in the office received any phone calls from miffed people in other development agencies who wasted money locally trying to attract the same business?

?! What attributable and measurable benefits have London Marketing and Promotion provided to the London economy, and at what unit cost?

?! What is the legal basis, and value added, of the £1 million spent on 'Health and Sustainable City'?

?! Why is the Mayor running an office in China? Can he get duty free? Is it a freebie crash pad for staff during the Peking Olympics?

?! What exactly was bought during the £11 million refit of the HQ of London's Enterprises, and why? What proportion was it of that year's total office budget?

?! And finally, how much did it cost to translate the budget into the various different languages; what decided which languages would be selected; and who decided not to use, for instance, Portuguese, Italian, or Hebrew? Or for that matter, if there are 50,000 Welsh speakers in the Capital, why not print it in that language as well, since unlike the others it is an official national tongue?

We could be here all day if we started looking at the budget. So let's concentrate on one aspect – *the waste*.

And let's start with the Mayor's propaganda budget. Tens of millions of pounds are spent every year by the Mayor on little more than self-publicity. Step onto the Underground, pass a bus stop or walk beside a billboard and you see useless advertising all the time. Transport for London spent £2.6 million on one single pointless brand awareness exercise.

Not that it's without controversy for all kinds of reasons. One hoarding showed the London skyline with Orange and Green strips. In a different climate, that would have raised an outcry, given the Mayor's past controversial comments on Irish politics. Or from the subcontinent, because the London Eye placed centrally made the advert look from a distance like the Indian flag.

But let's focus in even tighter to make the point. Before the Christmas holidays, one of the authors was randomly handed a free copy of the *Londoner* newspaper in the street. We understand it costs around £2.8 million a year. You can assume the person who was handing it out was being paid, as it's not exactly volunteer work, so there we have the first hidden cost. But let's examine from an academic perspective the actual content, as if an outsider were reading it for the first time, and see what impression he would take away from it.

▥ Page 1 – lead article on a poll, commissioned by Mayor Livingstone, supporting the grant to him of more powers. Livingstone is quoted. (Secondary article is advertising a competition, designed to attract readers inside.)

▥ Page 2 – lead article on more polling data, supporting the grant of yet more powers to Mayor Livingstone. Secondary article sells Oyster card increases under the principle of 'investment'; another trumpets a purported Livingstone policy victory over London Councils, with a Livingstone quote.

▥ Page 3 – advance notification of New Year's Eve fireworks and travel options over the holidays (fair enough, though costs are not discussed, and the funding source of the fireworks display is plugged).

▥ Page 4 – full page advertisement, cost unknown, of special Oyster card deals for cheaper access to museum exhibitions, cost of implementation unknown. So Oyster cards are good; we must have one.

▥ Page 5 – Article on the *Tour de France*, with Mayor Livingstone quote; day conference advertised (cost unknown) in which Mayor Livingstone is a speaker; piece indicating Mayor's taskforce for 2012 will cut unemployment; op. ed. by Mayor Livingstone.

▥ Pages 6 and 7 – Article on TfL East London rail link

referring to how Mayor Livingstone had successfully argued for it, with an indirect quote on his policy position; a line map with artist rendition entitled 'the right track'; five views from members of the public which are all positive; an advert on recycling carrying the logo of the Mayor of London; and a piece on Hannukah in which Mayor Livingstone is quoted and identified as participating in person in an event. There also are two items which are politically neutral – an appeal to register to vote in borough elections and an invitation to carols in Trafalgar Square.

▦ Page 8 – On police advice to minicab users, and on a new leading figure in the Public Carriage Office. Politically neutral.

▦ Page 9 – Contributions from invited commentators; the choice of comments compliments the op. ed. of the Mayor earlier in the paper.

▦ Centre pages – At first sight, these look like simple adverts, but on closer examination we find a quote from Mayor Livingstone, and details on TfL benefits, including Oyster card advantages.

▦ Page 12 – Photo competition (justifiable indirect advertising for a sponsoring company); appeal for recycling by Recycle for London (unclear who runs this, so politically neutral).

▦ Page 13 – Major piece on ice skating rinks, but the page footer sells the London Development Agency.

▦ Page 14 – Letters to Ken (two are open questions, one is supportive of Oyster, one is questioning with a tinge of criticism: the latter gets the longest reply); box indicating that the Mayor is receptive to input.

▦ Pages 15 to 19 – Four of these pages are propaganda neutral. Page 16 carries a second full page advert for Oyster cards, masquerading as an instruction to pay the fare when you travel.

▦ Back page – Full page advertisement for the CabWise scheme, with prominent Mayor of London and TfL logos.

Overall, the reader is bombarded with name dropping and quotes dealing with Mayor Livingstone. But it's overwhelmingly one-sided. Most of the advertising comes from GLA bodies, and only the last few pages of the paper provide neutral and useful information for Londoners on events going on in the City, which *Time Out* covers much better anyhow.

Frankly it looks like a massive waste of public money used for political benefit. But we are nothing if not fair. We thought it might be a one-off. So we checked a subsequent edition and found it was even worse in terms of choice, of bias in language, selection of supportive material, name dropping of the Mayor, direct quotation, backing of declared policy, and absence of criticism. Just in case there was any doubt remaining as to the direction of the message, we spotted that 29 Across in the crossword read 'Fidel Castro's Island Republic'.

Around £3 million a year that costs you. *Gracias, y que le vaya bien.*

The Quangocrats

Earlier in this book we dipped into the dismal world of quangos – dismal, that is, for taxpayers, though not for their well-rewarded members. We covered them a lot in last year's book, so we won't go over old ground now.

Nevertheless, it is worth a moment's reflection to put these unelected bodies into a broad perspective.

The amount of money that flows through quangos is phenomenal – one study puts it at £124 billion. We object to them on several levels.

Firstly, on accountability. These bodies can get away with murder – figuratively, of course, we don't think there's a Public Council for State Assassination (yet) – but so few of them have anybody on them who is accountable to any elector if they botch things up. The tendency more often is to reward failure with a pay-off and give the culprit a new job somewhere else.

The Peter Principle says that people rise to one level of

promotion beyond their limit of competence. But in the public sector, that law is probably a rosy interpretation of events. More commonly, people are promoted several levels above their competence.

Our second issue concerns the way appointments to quangos are made. The evidence suggests that some of the best quangos are used to reward friends of the government. One MP is currently being criticised for the suspicion that he is going to accept a plum role in a new environmental superquango in order to be able to free up a seat in the Commons for a close colleague of Gordon Brown who is about to have his own seat merged. Others provide rich pickings for people with a track record of supporting the party in power, either as politicians, former in-house advisers, or in giving donations.

Our third gripe concerns the pay. These quangos are financially supported in a seemingly random way. Some are run by unpaid volunteers. Others are run by people on the public payroll. We disapprove of non-jobbers being paid masses of public money for doing nothing of added value to society or the economy.

This takes us onto our final point. Do we really need these quangos? If they had stayed firmly within the sponsoring department, we suggest that many of them would have been closed down and the civil servants transferred somewhere else. But what benefit accrues from the third of a million pounds spent on the Women's National Commission, whose mission is to ensure women's views are taken into account by government and heard in national debate? This is government lobbying itself.

What about £380,000 spent on the Home Grown Cereals Authority? Can't selling grain be left to the farmers?

What about the £44,000 spent on the Advisory Panel on Beacon Councils, which spots good councils and pats them on the back?

Or the £580,000 on the Advisory Panel on Clinical Excellence Awards?

We propose that a future government looks at each quango in turn, and considers whether scrapping it overnight would materially affect anyone other than the quangocrats employed on it. A mass cull would free up money that could make a real difference to people elsewhere. When he was Secretary of State for Health, John Reid suggested as much with the NHS.

A Culture of Consultancy

"Surveys of companies that have used consultants found that people at the top were close to 100% satisfied – hardly surprising, since they would be the ones who took the decision to call them in – but satisfaction rates at the bottom fell to 17%."

Bryan Appleyard, *Sunday Times*

Consultancy is not of itself pernicious. It can reinvigorate, it can share, and it can bolster. But it is not a permanent prop for management. This is where our public sector is going wrong.

The exact cost of consultants is a moot issue. Even the Postal Services Commission spends £3.5 million a year on them, so the total sum must be astronomical. One NAO report estimates that the annual bill has gone up from two to three billion, which would mean that you are personally handing over £50 to consultants this year. The National Audit Office observed that:

"Consultants, when used correctly and in the appropriate circumstances, can provide great benefit to clients – achieving things that clients do not have the capacity or capability to do themselves. On the other hand, when used incorrectly, consultants can drain budgets very quickly, with little or no productive results."

We concur. We also note the NAO's comment that it found it hard to qualify how successful these consultants have been, because the departments themselves tend not to assess performance.

This might explain why consultants are able to make twice as much profit out of a public sector deal as they do on a private sector contract. One story that reached us was of a consultant who was invited to tender for state work. The civil servant asked him how much it was going to cost over the phone; over a cupped telephone receiver, his business partner joked that he should ask for a sum four times above the going rate. To their shock they got it.

The biggest spending departments were:

- International Development (£255 million)
- Defence (£213 million)
- DEFRA (£160 million)
- Home Office (£129 million)
- Health (£126 million)
- Environment (£110 million)

A significant slice of these were for IT contractors, but there's also over £600 million for advice on various aspects of management and change, and £100 million for advice, ironically, on 'outsourcing'.

And who are the lucky recipients of this largesse? The big winners over the past three years were:

- IBM (£749 million)
- Logica (£431 million)
- Accenture (£350 million)

But even the National Audit Office's £3 billion assessment could be optimistic. The NHS was later discovered to have banked £172 million for consultants – a third more than the auditors had thought. If that is replicated across the board, the consultancy spend is even more staggering.

Education and Skills (DfES) is seen by the auditors as the worst offender. It was given a red traffic light for failing to grasp when to use internal staff rather than consultants, and for handing out contracts on the basis of a single tender. It was also, ironically, one of three departments red lighted for failing to transfer skills within the department. At least the Home Office directly employed asylum seekers.

We know from other sources that in March of 2006, the Lifelong Learning and Skills Directorate had six senior consultants attached on a part-time basis at an average daily rate of £1,129. There were another 25 people working full or part time on secondment from the private sector, on salaries ranging from £11,064 to £99,636 a year. Meanwhile, in the Higher Education Directorate there were five more consultants working part time on an average of £1,164 a day.

And yet, there are critics of the system who say that the NAO report was a whitewash. Neil Glass, aka David Craig, the author of the excellent book *Plundering the Public Sector*, estimates that over the past ten years we have forked out £70 billion for the state to hire consultants, including the IT wonks, with zero or negative benefit. As one former chairman of a consultants committee puts it:

> *"Men in smart suits turn up and tell doctors and managers what they know already and charge a fortune."*

Glass and like-minded whistleblowers provide several examples. Consultants who advised cutting the number of high street job centres, which turned the remaining ones into "war zones", so more consultants were brought in to suggest potted plants and sweets. Consultancy theories about stockholding in the MoD that led to soldiers not having enough body armour. Blair hiring the consultant Lord Birt to advise him on consultancies. HM Revenue saving £105 million of Gershon cuts by spending £106 million on consultants. IT consultants who get paid 80% of the contract regardless of whether or not the system works.

Let's delve deeper into this murky area. Put your galoshes on. You'll need a torch.

For a department based on international relations, the FCO hires a surprising number of consultants – over £24 million worth in 2004-05. Some expenditure items seem comparatively innocuous, such as bringing in outside specialists to help with IT. Others raise all sorts of questions. Here were the big five recipients:

✍	Fujitsu Consulting	£3.2 million
✍	ATOS/KPMG	£2.8 million
✍	Morson Human Resources	£2.1 million
✍	Parity Resources	£1.6 million
✍	Logica UK Ltd	£850,000

The Welsh Department has been more circumspect, in part because it doesn't do as much as it used to since devolution. But even it spent £13,566 on consultants for its website, £18,815 for a review of its staffing, and £37,699 to "help in drawing up and taking forward our change programme".

The **Department for Transport** hired consultants to deliver its employees equality programme. This cost an unknown share of a £95,000 budget. The Department also spends an average of £4 million a year on outside consultancy research on road safety issues.

We have also found out what **DEFRA's** ten biggest consultancy payments have been over the last few financial years. Rather than induce tedium, let's simply state that those ten alone cost us £13.8 million in 2002-03, £18.2 million in 2003-04, £19.2 million for 2004-05, £24.1 million the following year, and in the first six months of the last financial year £8.3 million. This is the department that burns cows for a living and botches farm payments. Perhaps it needs the outside help after all.

One example in the health sector relates to 'turnaround teams', or people brought in by **NHS Trusts** to work out what services should be cut when the hospitals overspend. We have long suspected that this is a milch cow, and it seems judging by the example of Surrey and Sussex Healthcare Trust that we're right. It is reported that they paid out £700,000 to consultants for three months' work, figuring out what needed to be cut.

A Yorkshire Trust was also reported to have spent a cool half million on a team of accountants, who advised them to ... cut spending. A word of advice – lose the consultants, and sack the people who hired them.

The **Department of Culture** has got the consultancy bug. Its top payments since 2000 are:

- £1.34 million on a feasibility study for Culture Online.
- £255,000 double checking the costs of the Olympic Games.
- £224,000 on a review of how its associated public bodies are managed.
- £240,000 on Project Management Training.
- £205,000 on a BBC Consultancy Requirement.
- £151,000 on a study to identify the priorities of local communities.
- £136,000 on the provision of a 'Skill Audit Solution'.
- £130,000 on the 'Management of a 360 Degree Feedback System'.
- £128,000 on an Olympic Games Impact Study.
- £126,000 on Ceremonial Requirements for the Department.
- £100,000 on the Promotion of International Arts in the UK.
- £100,000 on a public awareness campaign on digital switchover.
- £100,000 on a review of standards in public libraries.
- £96,000 on a review of BBC News digital services, which also analysed the BBC's license bid (and so in itself raises interesting questions).
- £89,000 on an evaluation of national regional museums.
- £87,000 on research on 'indicators of mental health and social inclusion outcomes'.
- £85,000 on the Touchstone Change Management project 'to develop and deliver a cultural change strategy for DCMS'.

Some of the studies done by academics in the last year alone are: Measuring Elasticity of Tourism Demand; Independent Technical Review on Sport and Leisure Facility Equity Indicators; Sport's Contribution To Achieving Wider Social Benefits.

And from consultants: Live Music Impact Study; Willingness To Pay For Work To Inform License Fee Setting; Exploring Creative Industry Spillovers; and Scoping Links Between the Creative Industry and the Rest Of The Economy.

We know from similar costings that these studies come in at an average of over £40,000 a time. With bedtime reading like this, Tracey Emin starts to make sense.

The Department for Culture has also commissioned a review of academic literature and best practice on how to meet peoples' needs in an emergency. And, of course, it spends a lot on internet projects. Take ICONS, which is a Culture Online project that cost £43,500 a month over two years to set up with Cognitive Applications. It is designed to act as "a creative collaboration between cultural institutions and individuals". In fact, it is just a glossy list of images that people identify with, from the bowler hat to the Routemaster bus. We put Churchill's two fingers up to it.

> *"We helped them out when they came in. We were naïve about all this. But then we got the report on our desk, and looked at it, and 90% of it was mine. Our research, our stats, everything. And they got a six figure sum for it."*

Some mystery surrounds how government brings in outside experts to support its work, as the case of immigration numbers illustrates. During the time of the accession of eastern European countries to the EU, government ministers claimed to have an authoritative figure for how many eastern European citizens would use their new right to come and work in the UK. They even claimed opponents were scaremongering in an irresponsible way. When it later emerged that the official figure was a wild underestimate, the embarrassed ministers distanced themselves from the study and said it had nothing to do with them. It later transpired that the Home Office had actually commissioned the study. It is not too surprising when you have government rubbishing the people who attack its own report, then refusing to even acknowledge it, that there is a lack of clarity on how government hires in academic advice.

> *"Without a proper justification for the use of consultants, there are risks that resources are not obtained in the most cost-effective way or that resources currently available are wasted."*
>
> DfES/NAO, Engagement and Use of Consultants
> Good Practice Guide

At least we know how the **Department of Constitutional Affairs** hires its consultants. A head of branch can approve a budget holder's request to spend up to £25,000 on an outside study; a head of group or division can sign off a request of up to £250,000; and a single tender of higher value or anything over a quarter of a million pounds has to be signed off by a departmental board member. This suggests that there is a lot of money available for a sexy piece of research and a glance at the DCA's top ten consultancy suppliers since 1999 confirms this:

- *PricewaterhouseCoopers*, £2,162,000 (2004-05) to provide support for the conclusion of phase 1 of the consumer strategy project part of the DCA five-year plan falling in 2004-05.

- *Deloitte MCS Ltd*, £1,603,700 (2004-05) for implementation of IT Shared Services including the creation of a new DCA IT delivery organisation.

- *PA Consulting*, £1,307,196 (2005-06) to develop the national implementation and roll-out of the Courts Act and improvements with regard to community penalties.

❧ *PA Consulting*, £1,304,050 (2004-05) for consultancy support in relation to Courts Act Pilots data/performance analysis and identification of best practice procedures.

❧ *Deloitte MCS Ltd*, £888,688 (2005-06) for development of a financial management function including payment mechanisms, review of payment and change management activities and creation of a new change management operational process.

❧ *KPMG*, £817,751 (2004-05) for consultancy support connected with the successful reorganisation of the DCA and subsequent transition planning.

❧ *Towers Perrin*, £627,893 (2005-06) for HR consultancy to investigate potential options to support the Transformation Programme – including Pay and Grading Project and Performance Management.

❧ *Barkers Advertising*, £561,458 (2005-06) in return for provision of a specialised suite of advertising material for use in future campaigns across the country by the magistrates' recruitment team and local advisory committees during recruitment periods.

❧ *C International*, £522,000 (2001-02) under Revenue Grant Allocation Project guidance on best practice implementation.

❧ *Arthur D. Little* £504,488 (2001-02) for development of a financial costing model.

With money like this, the TaxPayers' Alliance formally announces it will be putting in a cut-price bid come the next baksheesh bidding round. Ours will be better. We'll have a model made of toilet rolls to go with it.

These accounts compare with the stats available from the **Northern Ireland Office** for last year. The bills for the ten most expensive consultants ran to £1.6 million. Or to put it another way, over the last ten years the Department expended £4.6 million on consultancy fees for its ten biggest projects, and they're only a third of the way spent yet.

The **DTI** is also a major sinner. Since 2003, the top ten recipients of departmental moolah for consultancy fees have been Deloitte & Touche (total payments of £9.5 million), Serco (£8.4 million), PricewaterhouseCoopers (£4 million), Fujitsu Services (£3.7 million), Amey Business Services (£3.5 million), Hedra (£2 million), KPMG (£1.6 million), Herbert Smith (£1.5 million) and QinetiQ (£1.5 million) – a total of over £35 million in advice for the top ten alone.

Work and Pensions seems to prefer not to do the work but to pay for someone else's pension. From April 2004, we know that the top ten fees paid by this department to consultants added up to £233,697,452 – approaching a quarter of a billion pounds. But if you are a shareholder or a member of the consultancy team at Booz Allen Hamilton (£109 million), Capgemini UK (£42 million) or IBM UK (£49 million) in particular, go for it. All you need to do is understand the vocabulary of "strategic planning and business change", what is involved in a "change programme", "managed service provision of interim transformation managers", the "Operational Readiness Review Gate", and "processing, resource management, learning and reward management". A lexicon of these and other essential terms follows shortly.

We could boggle you with a mountain of similar stats to show how endemic the consultancy mindset is in government. But you deserve mercy, poor reader. Let us provide just a few more examples and then draw the line. Next up is the **Department for Communities and Local Government**, which has a top ten list of consultancy fees since 1997 that adds up to £50.8 million. The DTI has two research councils known to hire in consultants costing £1.2 million. It seems likely that the embarrassing discovery that £11.7 million has been spent on consultants on fire service reform will provoke some cutbacks in that budget at least.

It is a little harder to judge value for money with **DFID**. But we do have some information about its twenty biggest procurement projects since 1997. These cover such worthy campaigns as fighting AIDS in Nigeria, supporting the fight against the drugs trade in Afghanistan, research on crop protection, and developing schooling in South Africa. Between them, they had an original budget of £361.8 million.

So far, £195.8 million of that figure has been spent. Fees (including expenses) come to . . . hold on to your seat . . . £52.7 million! That's about a quarter of the budget that should be going to the poor. At this rate, £90 million will be lost on fees before it reaches the front line.

> "The use of consultants can be costly and therefore
> it is good practice to be highly selective in their use."
>
> DfES/NAO, Engagement and Use of Consultants
> Good Practice Guide

Perhaps the most damning indictment is the record of the Treasury, the supposed enemy of waste. Its position is as follows:

The Treasury does not have a fixed, recurrent, annual budget for consultants. Budgets for line items such as consultants are allocated internally on an annual basis, as part of the business planning process, and flexed in the year to accommodate changes to priorities and circumstances.

Last year, the Department per se spent £6.1 million on consultants. But that's only part of the picture.

The Treasury's **Office of Government Commerce's** mission is to get the best value for money from procurement. It has been tasked to identify over a third of Gordon Brown's Gershon savings. The OGC is supposedly at the forefront of the culture of change.

Guess what? Over 2005-06, the OGC entered into 190 consultancy contracts at a total cost of £11.1 million.

Which takes us back to the report by the auditors. It's clear from the above examples that the true scale of consultancy in government is extremely difficult to assess. If the Department of Health defends itself by saying the auditors' figures are "back of the envelope" estimates, it only has itself to blame. But if the auditors are right, then reformers could immediately start saving £270 million a year just by changing working practices, a figure that leaps to £540 million in three years time.

MPs have for some years been receiving plenty of anecdotal evidence about civil servants being laid off for cost efficiency purposes, and then rehired as contractors to do the same work at a vastly increased rate, but on a different budget. Then there was a phase which involved waves of staff voluntarily leaving to go private. It is not at all clear from government figures to what extent this is going on today, despite moves to block at least the senior civil servants walking straight into private sector jobs with civil service contracts and links. But then, the government itself doesn't seem to want to know.

Management Speak for Beginners

If you aspire to the lofty pay grades of the manager, or have put in for a hefty consultancy contract, you'll need to be able to obfuscate with the best of them. Here's a short lexicon to help you on your way.

Outsourcing – hiring in people at three times the price, who can slopey-shoulder the blame away from you.

Right-shoring – exporting your workforce to Delhi.

Downsizing – (i) sacking, or (ii) employing elves around Christmas time.

Slippage – outright failure to meet deadlines.

Workshop – a place of indoctrination.

Service provider – a company that you expect to deliver but instead you have to treat like the French.

Solutions – a word tagged on to make a transaction look like a Nobel Prize bid.

Dashboard reporting – regular updates; or the process when you keep looking at the fuel gauge after you realise you're dry.

Empowerment – subsidiarity in avoiding blame.

Value-added – an essential factor that was overlooked when running the initial assessment.

Framework – a plan that falls apart when leaned on.

Public stakeholder – the taxpayer, as represented by someone whose pay is provided through your taxes.

Benchmarking – a comparison chosen to make the end result look good, like when a jogger might time himself depending on reaching "In Memory of Maureen" when he should be aiming for the bench with a tramp sprawled across it.

Baselining – the actual point at which you realise things can only improve, so you set it as the comparison point.

Recalibration – moving your benchmarks just enough to look as if you are making an annual improvement.

Business as usual process – a modus operandi which allows failure to be blamed on an institution rather than yourself.

Human resources – people who deal with people, who appear at the alpha and the omega of your career.

Risk owners – the people who cop it when you make mistakes.

Stakeholders – the people who you will pass the blame onto when things don't happen, as intermediaries towards the Risk Owners.

Management of risk – as in Health and Safety, the paperwork required to imagine a world without the disaster which is pending.

Risk resolution – covering your posterior for when everything goes wrong.

Risk register – a list of future press releases.

Risk appetite – an analysis of whether the rug in the room is big enough to hide a crisis for your successor to have to handle.

Strategic risk – the threat to your knighthood on retirement.

Change facilitator – an outside consultant brought in to fire people.

Driver of value – the impulse to make big numbers seem small by dividing rather than subtracting.

Cash equivalent value – the attempt to buy off an employee who has just realised he would get a bonus in a private sector job.

Investment – spending taxpayers' money on something which has no quantifiable return, but expressed so as to make criticism seem mean-spirited.

Non-Jobs

The TaxPayers' Alliance's annual 'Non-Job Report', which examines the most pointless and wasteful public sector jobs advertised in *Guardian Society*, is always published over Christmas. This year it found:

The total salary bill for the jobs advertised in *Guardian Society* in 2006 was an incredible £767,343,282 (excluding pensions and perks). This is marginally less than the £787,319,556 total for 2005, but it shows that the government is still failing to tackle bureaucracy and waste.

The average starting salary for a full -time position advertised in *Guardian Society* is £11,405 more per annum than the mean private sector wage in 2006 (£36,894 and £25,489 respectively).

> *"We have a system that increasingly taxes work and subsidizes non-work."*
> **Milton Friedman**

Two of the most ridiculous jobs advertised in *Guardian Society* were a Diversity Programme Manager in Redbridge council on £39,126, and a Diversity and Inclusion Manager for the Qualifications and Curriculum Authority on £38,000.

Since the report was published, the TaxPayers' Alliance has been monitoring each weekly issue of *Guardian Society* to find further examples of pointless public sector jobs. Highlights in the last few months include a Carbon Reduction Officer on around £30,000 a year at Islington Council and a Welfare Rights Officer at Southwark Council, whose job is actually to encourage benefit take-up.

First we had the non-job, now we have the non-conference. The Public Sector Project Management people teamed up to put together a conference, paid for by taxpayers, which looked at how they run things. Or, in management speak:

> *"This is a networking event which is designed to bring together professionals from the public sector to discuss their projects and the ways they successfully undertake those projects, whether this is by using 'traditional' project management methods or tools or by using 'new' ideas or methods."*

We hope at least that the bar was good.

Flights of Fancy

There is a bit of a vogue these days to criticise key figures for flying places, as their jet fumes add to greenhouse gases. We've never seen a 747 in our Aunt Mavis's rotunda, but we'll take their word for it.

Every year, it costs around £6 million pounds to fly ministers and their entourages overseas. It's difficult to tell if that is a conservative estimate, and to know whether the figure includes only tickets bought from commercial airlines or also includes the full price of using RAF planes. But ministers do like to travel. Over the course of six months, even the junior ministers at the Department for Constitutional Affairs scooted off to Belgium, Bulgaria, Finland, France, Germany, Ghana, Ireland, Luxembourg, Poland, Romania, and South Africa.

It doesn't stop at central government. Welsh Assembly ministers in the past have: selflessly undertaken "trade missions" to Japan and Australia; attended a food fair in France; flown back to *Showcase Wales* in Australia (£13,885.50); attended the

125th anniversary of Rourke's Drift (cost: £9,288.90; number of Zulus: thousands of 'em); spent nearly £1,200 attending St David's Day celebrations in Paris; blown £1,300 on a trip to Sweden to study legislation for banning punishment of children; wasted £1,100 to study renewable energy in Navarra; spent £850 on a food fair at Barcelona. Oh, and £12,000 to launch the Wales International Centre in New York. Not a bad way to escape from the office if your department can afford it.

As for Whitehall, here are some of the more interesting trips from 2005-06.

★ The Secretary of State for Foreign and Commonwealth Affairs flew to Sarajevo to commemorate the 10th anniversary of Srebrenica. He was also flown back from a holiday in the States at taxpayers' expense to attend Robin Cook's funeral.

★ The Secretary of State for Work and Pensions did a little whirlwind visit of Washington, Chicago and Vancouver as part of a series of welfare reform fact finding visits.

★ The Home Secretary flew to Jordan, Egypt and Libya to discuss 'Home Office issues', which we take to mean the deporting of suspected terrorists. In July, he was flown at taxpayers' expense "to meet up with family" – apparently, he had missed his pre-booked family holiday flight "due to essential Home Office business". We would applaud it, had this one-way ticket not cost us £4,000.

★ The Secretary of State for Culture flew to a Zambian Conference on Sport and Social Development; went to Rome to further sport and cultural links with Italy; to Japan to do likewise there; furthered British film links in Dublin and Lisbon; spent 6 days in Singapore as part of the 2012 bid; spent a week in India, Sri Lanka and Thailand discussing a film treaty with India and visiting Tsunami areas; made a flying visit to the Winter Olympics in Turin; and spent ten days at the Commonwealth Games.

★ The Deputy PM went to Moscow for the VE Day anniversary (where, according to protocol, although the representative of a Big Four country he was so junior compared with the assembled presidents he was stuck at the back). He also went on a tour of Washington, Austin, Denver and Los Angeles to meet local bigwigs; went to Munich to speak to the Congress of European Urbanism (not: Urbaneism); attended six sessions of the European Parliament in Strasbourg (despite not having been an MEP for 25 years); and spent several days flying around China. We eagerly await news on what it cost the taxpayer to put him up at the Grand Garden suite at the five star China World Hotel, which has 24 hour butler service.

✈ The Leader of the Commons spent four days in Prague, and seven in Sydney and Canberra, meeting MPs. The Leader of the Lords had a rougher time of it, flying out to a meeting in Ouagadougou, attending the funeral of President Garrang in the Sudan, and sitting through a Gender Justice Conference in Stockholm. The Minister without Portfolio just visited MEPs, presumably (as Chief Whip) in order to browbeat the Labour ones to follow the Party line.

✈ Our Northern Ireland Secretary attended an event in Sligo to support a bid for a round of the world rally championships, and went to Dublin for an official lunch with the British Ambassador and to attend an Ireland/Wales rugby match.

As for the ex-PM, he was a very busy chappy. Tony Blair attended the funeral of the Pope in Rome; held bilateral talks with everyone of consequence, including the Prime Minister of Luxembourg; flew out to Singapore to back the Olympics bid (at a cost of half a million pounds, including a slight detour to drop in en route on the Crown Prince of Saudi Arabia); and attended the Commonwealth Games in Melbourne, presumably because just sending Tessa Jowell wasn't enough. A dozen or two officials tagged along every step of the way. Mrs Blair, meanwhile, in her own right did a joint visit with Mrs Bush to Kenya, and promoted children's literacy with other leaders' wives in Moscow.

Eighty five of these visits by ministers were on planes run by 32 Squadron – more familiarly known as the Queen's Flight. And some of these were for getting to Brussels and Paris, which have a regular Eurostar service.

The Cost of Living

These days, the government spends around £150 million on advertising. It is a massive sum. It dwarfs what even the biggest corporations in Britain spend. It's also a massive increase on past years. We think it's a cause for concern if the state spends such a large amount of money telling you what it's up to; it is, effectively, an advertisement for the government of the day.

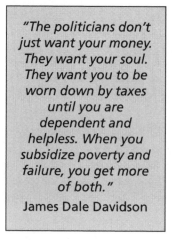

"The politicians don't just want your money. They want your soul. They want you to be worn down by taxes until you are dependent and helpless. When you subsidize poverty and failure, you get more of both."

James Dale Davidson

Imagine if, as of tomorrow, the government had a policy of handing out free bananas to schoolchildren whose parents fill out a form, and a million pound advertising campaign is put out there encouraging you to apply for the daily free banana for your kids. The subliminal message you walk away with is, "Thanks to this government and the party in power, I have benefited because of the banana policy". Never mind if your kids wanted or needed the banana, whether the bananas come from Guatemala rather than the Windward Islands and therefore unbalance the local economies, or how much the bananas cost you in taxes. You got your banana. Thank you, cartoon government spokesman.

If advertising didn't work as a tool, burger clowns, buffoonish secret agents, annoying bank managers, and cowboys who either smoke or eat white chocolate would be out of a job. If you can work out any of the adverts we've just referred to, we've proved our point.

But let's look at some individual aspects of advertising and see if it's money well spent. And let's be a little contentious to get you pondering.

The government's THINK road safety campaign cost £18 million last year. Its objective is to reduce road deaths and serious injuries by 40% by 2010, and 50% for children.

We do not include in that cost figure the hundreds of thousands of pounds spent on the Highways Agency driver education programmes such as *Pass Plus* and *Arrive Alive*, designed for new and young drivers. These are targeted packages designed for particularly weak drivers and clearly serve a benefit. Our concerns lie with the THINK programme.

We may not win friends saying this but anybody surely has a right to ask whether the THINK campaign as it stands is good value for money. We can remember the shocking adverts such as the pub table that crashes into a lass at the bar. We might even remember the one about using a phone while driving. But has it succeeded in altering driving patterns?

In part of course this can never be answered, because an averted accident is hard to spot as a non-statistic. But take the target rate set.

On the assessed level of spending, the campaign will cost £120 million. Almost certainly, the lion's share of this will be on advertising.

It is a bit tricky to work out the Department's maths from the figures they quote. But it looks like the government will spend that much money to stop 2,200 road deaths. This works out at around half a million pounds per death averted.

This may or may not be value for money. But that's a choice that ministers should make openly. What is clearly a concern, however, looking through the consultants' reviews is the way in which time is spent on assessing whether the government is being "seen" to do more on road safety, and whether it "appears" to do more on the issue.

The same principles apply to campaigns to prevent **fire deaths.** And the statistics suggest that advertising may not even work. In 2002, 262 people died in fires, at a time when the government was spending £4.8 million on fire safety media. The budget went up the following year to £6.3 million, but so did the number of deaths, to 302. The budget then dropped to £5.7 million, and so did the number of deaths to 230. In 2005, there was a further drop to 212 deaths, with a reduced budget of £4.3 million.

From this we make two observations:

- Firstly, in crude maths, the fire safety campaign is premised on an expenditure of around £20,000 per life attempted to be saved – or on the latest statistics £250,000 per actual casualty reduction, assuming with such small figures that the drop isn't just coincidental.

- Secondly, there is seemingly no evidence that spending more money does any good. Indeed, based on those statistics, a cynic would say: stop the fire safety campaigns altogether and the tally of fatalities will continue to drop.

Of course, this is nonsense. No doubt some lives have been saved by reminding people to check they have a working smoke detector. But as fans of *Friends* may recall, in New York they don't advertise: it's just the law.

The government has been challenged on this. Asked to produce evidence showing material benefit, the Minister pointed to questionnaires suggesting people *remembered* seeing the adverts, not whether they had changed their behaviour as a result, and only as an afterthought turned to the slight drop in the number of fire deaths. It is a sorry indicator.

These campaigns also hide some further regulatory costs. When the government came up with the Regulatory Reform Fire Safety Order covering England and Wales, it was required to run a cost-benefit analysis. It produced some shocking statistics on how much it costs when businesses and homes burn down every year – in 2001, it was £786 million, to be precise. It also showed that if one in every three detectors that went off due to some fault could be prevented, that would be 228,000 fewer false alarms. This all saves money, and, more importantly, lives.

Hence the Department came up with legislation that it assessed would cost businesses between £66 and £89 million to implement, excluding a £2 million advertising campaign. We assume the cost to the public sector was proportionate. But the Department failed to provide any rationale as to where the actual savings to business would come from, other than to assume that for some reason there would be between 5-15% fewer fires. It also assumed that businesses would be able to grapple with the detail of the new legislation, which involves a total rethink in the way fire risks are assessed, in two hours. This might not be a bad thing, but it should at least be properly costed as part of the debate. In short, the costs and benefits seemed based on optimism rather than science.

As a further case in point, the Department for Communities and Local Government spent £120,000 on fire safety messages specifically targeted at the South Asian communities during Diwali, Muslims during Eid, and the Chinese during the Chinese New Year.

A different issue concerns the effectiveness of the campaigning style. Some disquiet has been expressed by the Health Department's anti-smoking advertising, which shows people with fish hooks through their mouths. This might be great for a subliminal message to do with nicotine addiction, but this offensive and shocking imagery also makes smokers and non-smokers alike queasy. Perhaps it would be worth commissioning a private study to see how many people have been made ill by it. Compare this to the £188,500 known to have been spent on firework safety advertising in 2004-05. This means perhaps £150 of advertising per accident, or £450 per avoidable accident involving someone mucking around.

Other campaigns that the DTI have run have included one on carbon monoxide (£37,520), and on 'slips, trips and broken hips' (£249,164).

The Home Office has budgets that are targeted at criminals. It spent £94,000 last year encouraging us not to misuse alcohol or face a fine; £1,550,000 on three years of campaigns about domestic violence, warning (in the minister's words) "that they risk putting themselves and/or others at risk of personal harm"; £4 million on adverts over five years warning of bad people on the internet; and £350,000 this year telling rapists they will go to prison. Grim stuff, but does it work?

Alas, even regional government gets in on the act. But then, there's nothing like a branded public safety warning to get your name on the telly and show people that you're 'doing something'. Consider the Mayor of London. It's a new position, so the incumbent needs to persuade the public that the job is worthwhile. The solution? Buy air time. And you do that with public service announcements. Some involve adverts telling viewers not to crash their bike – a bit obvious really. Others tell them to buy into the Oyster travel system, as if they have a choice when the prices for those who don't are hiked. Here is a list of campaigns from the last five years:

Mayor's advertising campaigns

2002	£765,000: Congestion Charging
2003	£2.3 million: Congestion Charging (£1.2 million), London Underground (£820,000) and road safety (£280,000)
2004	£2.66 million: safer travel at night (£200,000), London Buses (£660,000) and road safety (£1.8 million)
2005	£3.57 million: safer travel at night (£100,000), road safety (£1.9 million), cycling (£935,000) and London Buses (£630,000)
2006	£2.47 million: Oyster (£560,000), public transport (£745,000), cycling (£635,000) and road safety (£525,000)

And for the cinema audience:

2002	£170,000: motorbike safety
2003	£857,000: motorbike road safety (£407,000) and teen road safety (£450,000)
2004	£1.66 million: London Underground (£610,000), motorbike safety (£230,000) and teen road safety (£410,000), London Buses (£410,000)
2005	£2.23 million: safer travel at night (£190,000), motorbike road safety (£630,000), teen road safety (£895,000), London Buses (£513,000)
2006	£2.03 million: public transport (£1.1 million), safer travel at night (£145,000), motorbike road safety (£670,000) and teen road safety (£113,000)

There's also the money that gets spent on TfL's own billboard adverts convincing us that a bus is a form of transport:

2002	£4.7 million
2003	£3.3 million
2004	£900,000
2005	£2.8 million
2006	£6 million

Just so you know, the Mayor's publicity and information budget last year included £78 million spent on advertising, £14 million more than it intended to.

Some of this went into tidying up bus shelters, but a heck of a lot didn't. £40 million was spent on advertising, customer information and research. £13 million was spent on "equality and inclusion", annual reports, stakeholder consultation, communications and customer magazines, £15 million on "activities not traditionally associated with marketing and communications, including . . . direct communications such as phone rental, call charges and purchase".

At least the £155,000 spent by the Maritime and Coastal Agency on advertising revived some favourite themes. The older fogies among us were delighted to see the thin man wearing the handkerchief on his head trying to make out why the yachtsman in distress was waving to him.

Buy British

Despite the government's manifest incompetence in negotiating PFI projects, we are obviously not opposed to the private sector helping share the burden of public expenditure. One way of doing this – as the government has lately realised – is to allow private companies and individuals to make use of public assets, and to make them pay for the privilege.

The 'Wider Markets Initiative' is the government's attempt to encourage revenue generation in a systematic way. It can work well. In the past, the MoD hired or loaned out warships to make James Bond movies, and Lynx helicopters for Britpop videos, thus defraying costs or planting subliminal messages about how cool it is to join the Forces.

The RAF was less successful in one aspect of its commercial side. RAF planes carry the red, white and blue concentric circles known as the roundel. The RAF tried to copyright it. But the Arcadia fashion group successfully argued in court that the design had been allowed to be used in popular culture since *Quadrophenia* in the Sixties. In short, the MoD was beaten by the Mods. So the courts allowed copyright to the RAF for everything but clothing, and you can still buy your roundel jacket at Bhs or Burtons. Just don't try it on the Parade Ground.

Even our law courts can make money. There are 48 of them on the books, plus another five parole boards, bringing in around £40,000 a year from being hired out to film units. A further half a million pounds comes from hosting events on court grounds. The Royal Courts of Justice has a shop, bringing in another £25,000 of hopefully tasteful tea mugs and aprons, plus a gym run on business lines. We are also intrigued, and possibly troubled, to find that the Lord Chancellor has been making over £60,000 a year from charging Smee and Ford for using these premises, a company which advises charities how to get the most out of legacy donations.

Perhaps a little more proactive is the Department of Health, which seeks to recoup costs voluntarily from the private sector. Over 2005-06 it ran a series of public information campaigns that cost a chunky £42.5 million. Some of this spending was offset by help from the businesses listed below:

ʊ Ann Summers provided £197,000 worth of support for a sexual health campaign.

ʊ Several companies, including Club 18-30, provided thousands of pounds of free condoms to their clients as part of a government drive.

ʊ Superdrug supplied promotion worth £55,000 in support of a tobacco control campaign.

ʊ BT supplied £300,000 worth of sponsorship for drugs prevention and NHS Live.

ʊ Wrigleys Oral Healthcare Programme sponsored £20,000 of the EU Presidency Dental Programme events.

ʊ AstraZeneca, Boots, Oracle, Olympus, GE Healthcare and BT between them provided £800,000 for NHS Live.

ʊ Equator Media and Livity Communications Consultancy provided £34,000 and £79,000 of support for the FRANK drugs prevention campaign. One of these organisations was directed by someone who once stood for Labour in a General Election against former Tory leader Iain Duncan Smith, but this is a coincidence.

Similar assistance was provided by elements of the private sector to the FCO. Over 2005-06, in no small part as a publicity booster for businesses during the G8 summit, the FCO raised a helpful £987,200 worth of private sponsorship for its activities. Two thirds of this went into Gleneagles, but there was also a Rolls Royce importer who sponsored the Queen's Birthday Party bash in Riyadh, Jaguar in Jordan, and Virgin Atlantic flying the flag all over the place.

We are pleased to give them extra publicity here, as they have saved you a few pence.

Ministerial Gifts

Last year, readers will recall we lifted the lid on one year's worth of the Donated Assets Reserve. This is the stockpile of goodies given to ministers. Those that are worth less than £140 the minister can keep, on the principle that your average Secretary of State isn't going to hand over missile secrets for a bag of chips. Anything over £140 and the minister can buy it for the actual value of the gift less £140.

Of course, a minister might not want to buy the garish porcelain jug of a sumo wrestler, because there might not be space on the mantelpiece at home. But it might be circumspect, like auntie's hand-knitted sweater, to have it on hand for display purposes if the donor comes visiting.

This is where the annual list comes in, showing which gifts have been kept by the department rather than been stored centrally, as in the closing sequence of *Raiders of the Lost Ark*. It also shows which gifts ministers have decided to keep for their personal use after all.

Last year, we revealed that Tony Blair had kept quite a few interesting items knocking around Number 10. Attempts by MPs to get to the bottom of why he needed them, however, have met with consistent stonewalling by the then Prime Minister. To what use had he put the jewelled ceremonial daggers, and had they been of use in any fighting with his neighbours? Had Blair family members been playing with the electric Ferrari? Was anyone insured to scoot around corridors on the Segway Transporter? Had he or his staff drunk the wine given to him? Precisely what was the 'Israeli archaeological artefact' that had been given him, and did it allow him to commune direct with the Almighty?

Then a source told us a more likely reason for Number 10's reluctance to answer Parliamentary questions about these holdings. It transpires that, during a trip to a Liverpool school, the Prime Minister's wife lost a bracelet that was a gift from President Berlusconi. Luckily, it was found by one of the schoolchildren and handed in. Sure enough, Italian jewellery features on the list of items that were being asked about by MPs.

Obviously, this was an embarrassing slip. But it also raised questions about to what extent the sundry items of jewellery, rings and expensive watches were being worn by the ex-PM's family which are in fact the property of the state. Add to that the incident in which John Prescott was caught out for not declaring a cowboy suit while ranching with a prospective buyer for the Millenium Dome and you have a whole area that government would prefer to draw a veil over.

Opening the section below, we lift that veil to reveal what else has been given to ministers over the past couple of years and which they've decided to keep their mitts on.

In 2003…

- The Culture Secretary borrowed a digital radio for a year then returned it. Her deputy also returned a UGC cinema card when he realised it was over the limit.

- The Defence Secretary was offered an Albanian silver eagle, a Kenyan tie and walking sticks, and a Mont Blanc pen by a US defence firm.

- The Foreign Secretary declined to buy a nativity scene given by Yasser Arafat, but a deputy bought another one. A minister also bought a Ghanese pendant and a Guyanan necklace. The Department held on to a ring gifted by the British Red Cross.

- The Home Office kept a genuine Afghan rug and a Belgian attaché case for its own use. The DTI kept a pair of tankards.

- The Attorney General's people held on to a Chinese watch and candlestick holders, though we are unsure of their need for the rabbit ornament and the necklace. The Lord Chancellor's people also had to figure out what to do with an engraved trowel.

- The Northern Ireland Secretary bought a newspaper magnate's pen.

- For some reason, the Deputy Prime Minister declined to buy two brooches, a camera, a model ship, a necklace, cufflinks and a tie stud, but his department kept hold of them.

- The PM bought a camera given by the Japanese government and a costly fountain pen from Jacques Chirac, a Pakistani wooden screen, a Bangladeshi 12 piece dinner service, Philippine menu holders, an 8 piece canteen of Thai cutlery, a Chinese painting, an Italian clock, two tennis rackets, a ring from an anonymous member of the public, Mr Putin's 12 piece tea/coffee set, and a swanky photo frame.

- The PM's department kept the following items for use at Number 10 by its residents:

For the well dressed man about town: a staggering 14 watches (almost all from the Italian government), 3 necklaces, a set of cufflinks, a pin, 2 bracelets, a ring, a dressing gown, an Italian coat, 2 holdalls, 2 daggers.

For the hard-working desk warrior: 2 boxes, a lamp, 5 pens, a ruler, an inkwell.

For the socialite: a tea set, a coffee pot, 2 half cases of French wine.

For that urbane homely look: 6 rugs, 3 paintings, a picture, 5 vases, 3 bowls, a dish, 4 sculptures, a carving, a statue, 2 religious scenes, a map and 5 books of maps, 2 books, an unspecified Christmas gift, 3 guitars and another one from Bryan Adams.

What is Downing Street? The Tardis?

Three hampers went to charity, which we do applaud. But we are puzzled as to why every time Mr Blair met an Italian, they seem to have presented him with an expensive new watch. Was he perpetually turning up late, was this some obscure Roman tradition, or is it a future bazaar-related career move we can expect to hear about shortly?

In 2004...

The government were still at it when the 2003-04 statistics were released. Here are some of the things departments kept which you, the public, own.

- The Foreign Office kept a number of rugs (two from the Libyans), an Arabian onyx statue, and a stylish 'Bottega Veneta Pyramid Nero'. The Home Office kept two Afghan rugs. The Leader of the Lords has a Michael Echekoba portrait hanging nearby. The Economic Secretary for the Treasury bought a bracelet that had been given, but presumably not made, by some shipyards.

- The PM bought some Australian clothes (and creditably, more were distributed to charity). In fact the PM and his advisors seem to have cottoned on to something here, because that's as far as the purchase list goes. It was the range of goodies kept by the PM's office that now begins to astound us.

- There were four sets of wine from the French (fast becoming a predictable gift), and two gifts of wine from other sources. We don't know if these have been drunk by officials yet. His offices were jazzed up with a picture, two vases, a clock, a statue, a piece of crystal, a soapstone figure, a silver dove, two sets of glassware, silver beakers from George Bush, three rugs, some coins, two pens, yet another Palestinian nativity scene, a flask, and (perhaps the old ones were losing their edge after all the reshuffles) a new dagger. There was additionally another unidentified Christmas gift.

- Of course, there were also more items for the Blairs to look good in. We see three Italian watches, two Italian necklaces, a bracelet, two sets of earrings, a ring, and a dress ornament.

- Plus there was Bono's guitar (there's that six string fetish again).

- The PM also got given a selection of Simpsons Merchandise, presumably from the time he appeared on the show with Homer. This was given to charity, as were some hampers. If only this were the norm.

Since we covered **2005** last year, this takes us to...

In 2006 ...

- The Saudis gifted the Secretary of State for Defence a gold ornate dagger and a ceremonial sword, which the MoD has kept (presumably for Defence cuts). The Home Office kept a Motorola RAZR V3, though this should come well under the limit so perhaps the minister didn't like the colour. The Law Officers Department retained a handmade glass bowl with inscribed images of Newcastle (we leave that one to your imagination).

- Presents which hit the news included a toy which Gordon Brown bought for his son, and the Deputy PM's embarrassing gift (held by the department) of a stetson, boots, spurs, belt, buckle and leather bound notebook. Attempts to find out if anything had been written in the notebook have currently come to naught.

- Once again, Downing Street's share of the loot exceeds all expectation. The PM bought a crystal vase, a set of five commemorative Russian coins, and a contemporary print of London from the 2012 Olympics people. His office kept on his behalf a commemorative plaque from Azerbaijan, four sets of French wine, four rugs, and a bronze Ukrainian sculpture. But no watches – the jewellery this year came from the Saudis. But then, President Berlusconi was busy running an election campaign.

We will try to find out for the next *Bumper Book* how many of these gifts were bought by the Blairs when they left Downing Street.

"What is the difference between a taxidermist and a tax collector? The taxidermist takes only your skin."

Mark Twain

SECTION 4

The Burdens for Our Children

Waste can be comic. Failure can have its amusing side. Incompetence can bring a wry smile to our lips, as we view the flailing and flannelling of people well out of their depth.

But as they sink into the yawning fathoms they are taking our gold with them – the taxes for which we have laboured long months out of every year, and which we deserve to see spent wisely on our behalf and for the true betterment of society and the economy.

Let's turn, therefore, away from the incompetence of the moment, and consider now the greater costs, the shackles that poor financial management today will attach to the current working population in old age, and to the generations that come after. It is no use enjoying a summer of idleness if the debt has to be paid later and with interest. Consider La Fontaine's fable, where the cricket sang all summer long, and found itself in dire circumstances when winter bit. It was only in Disney versions that the toiling ants took pity and helped the lazy songster out.

In this section, we'll look at the way that government, often without our knowing, has been turning us into that doomed fabled cricket.

Public Sector vs. Private Sector

The chart overleaf shows the proportion of the population employed by the state in 1999 and in 2005. It also shows how many people were being employed in the private sector. The right hand columns shows the percentage change over the years.

Remember that these figures don't include those who are on various forms of benefits and therefore also supported by the taxpayer – or to be precise, supported by the people working in the private sector jobs. Roughly speaking, a third of the population is effectively writing the cheques which support everyone else.

Public sector employment as a percentage of resident population by region, 1999 and 2005

	1999 Public	1999 Private	2005 Public	2005 Private	Change Public	Change Private
North East	9.3	30.7	10.2	32.8	+0.9	+1.9
North West	8.8	36.0	10.0	36.6	+1.2	+0.6
Yorkshire & the Humber	8.9	35.9	9.7	37.2	+0.8	1.3
East Mids	7.7	37.6	8.4	38.3	+0.7	0.7
West Mids	8.2	37.8	9.2	37.5	+1.0	-0.3
East	7.7	37.5	8.5	37.8	+0.8	0.3
London	9.9	43.5	10.0	42.4	+0.1	-1.1
South East	7.9	40.0	8.6	40.7	+0.7	+0.7
South West	8.7	39.4	10.3	39.2	+1.6	-0.2
Wales	9.9	31.5	10.3	33.9	+0.4	+2.4
Scotland	10.4	34.7	11.4	37.0	+1.0	+2.3
N. Ireland	11.7	29.2	12.7	30.5	+1.0	1.3
UK	8.9	37.4	9.7	38.0	+0.8	+0.6

Sources: Labour Force Survey, returns from public sector organisations (ONS, Scottish Executive and Department of Enterprise, Trade and Investment for Northern Ireland); PQ 108090; PQ 115920.

According to the government's own statistics, the public sector has grown across the UK at a rate higher than the number of jobs created by the private sector. In the North East, for instance, one job in four is paid for by the state. And remember, that excluding the people supported by the state on benefits.

Why is this important? Because state jobs do not as a rule of thumb generate wealth. They absorb wealth from the private sector. So the more people you have working for the government, the more taxes you need to take in order to pay for them, and the fewer people you actually have available to do the work in the industries that create wealth.

Bearing in mind that it's the private sector that pays for extra state jobs, it's disingenuous to cite high overall employment figures as proof of a healthy economy. Another false indicator is to cite high rates of private sector growth in areas on the periphery of the UK where there were low starting rates and where the public sector has grown quickly too. Growth in regional government means, of course, additional cost to business and the stifling of enterprise through higher taxation.

Using official data, the TaxPayers' Alliance has produced a 'League Table of Fiscal Dependency' which shows how some regions are receiving vastly more in government spending than they are paying in tax. These deficit regions are living well beyond their means, and have become heavily dependent on fiscal transfers from the rest of the country to support high levels of public spending.

The key findings are:

- Northern Ireland is the most dependent region, with a deficit equivalent to 29% of its GDP. It receives £9 billion more in public spending than it collects in tax revenues.

- Wales and North East England both have deficits of about 20%.

- Only three regions – East of England, London, and the South East – are paying their own way. In effect, these three regions are funding the rest of the country.

- Broken down to a cost per household, these figures show that the average household in the South East pays over £5,000 per year in subsidy to other regions.

The Fiscal Dependency League (2006-07)

	Govt spend £bn	Tax in £bn	Deficit /surplus £bn reg. GDP	Deficit /surplus % of (m)	No. of house- holds	Deficit /surplus per household
N. Ireland	19	11	-9	-29	0.67	-£13,473
Wales	29	19	-10	-21	1.24	-£8,064
North East	25	17	-8	-19	1.12	-£7,142
North West	66	50	-15	-12	2.93	-£5,119
Scotland	53	41	-12	-11	2.31	-£5,194
Yorks/Humber	46	37	-9	-9	2.20	-£4,090
West Mids	47	40	-7	-7	2.24	-£3,125
South West	43	40	-3	-3	2.21	-£1,357
East Mids	36	34	-2	-2	1.83	-£1,092
East of Engl.	44	52	+8	+6	2.39	+£3,347
London	77	92	+15	+7	3.25	+£4,615
South East	66	84	+18	+9	3.57	+£5,042

Note: Deficits/surpluses may not add exactly due to rounding. They also do not sum to zero. This is because the UK as a whole ran a fiscal deficit of around 3% of GDP last year.

Feel free to simulate this at home. We suggest the following components to make a working model of the failing system: one bottle of washing up liquid, three gallons of engine oil, one pin for creating leaks, a plug hole, a sump, and some sticky-back plastic. Once you've assembled it, buy a red briefcase, put on a suit, and now jump up and down on it.

The PFI and PPP Scandal

"Value for money in procurement should not be assumed to mean the lowest cost option."

Treasury paper on PFIs

This is a hard bit. Put a brew on, then come back. We did.

Now and again, as we peruse our papers over cornflakes and coffee, we come across references to PPPs and PFIs. But what are they?

Well, it's a way of semi-privatising parts of the state. It carries with it the advantages and disadvantages of both the state and the private sector.

A **Public Private Partnership** is where a government asset is run by a private company or a consortium of businesses, typically for a fixed number of years at a set rate. It might, for example, be a school that is built and looked after by a company. The state fills the school with teachers and pupils, and contracts to buy it back off the company over a couple of decades, paying in instalments. Obviously, the company makes a profit over the long term, while the state gets to pay off the cost of building the school over more years than it would if it was shouldering the entire capital cost itself (though at greater cost). It's a sort of mortgage.

A **Private Finance Initiative** is a type of PPP. The contractor receives an annual payment from the state provided that they fulfil agreed targets, say changing light bulbs in the school within 24 hours of them being reported as broken.

On one level, this way of doing things has been around for many years. Take the Romans. You might say that their way of defending their Empire during their last 100 years was a form of PPP, with barbarians being recruited into the system and paid in wages and donatives to keep them on side. Of course, sacking in those days was something that only happened to cities when the Treasury ran out of money.

A clearer parallel comes earlier in ancient history. Rome had a

PFI arrangement that it set up when it started to acquire its empire. It allowed its merchant class to bid for tax contracts in the provinces. An individual or a tax farming company would win a given contract, stump up the bidded sum, then go out to recoup it and make a profit by leaning on the poor provincials. This suited the government, as it secured a guaranteed tax intake at a given date. It suited the contractor, because he could make quite a tidy sum if he didn't have any scruples. Of course, if you were the poor provincial, it didn't suit you, because you were then subject to the heavies that the tax farmer – or *publicanus* – sent round to collect on his PFI profit margin.

A couple of examples show how this sort of scheme hits the locals hard. When Mithridates the Great, King of Pontus, went to war in the first century BC, he made a point of butchering every Roman citizen he got his hands upon. Perhaps 80,000 people were killed. Tax farmers he caught were made to drink molten gold. That was how popular they were locally. The victorious Roman general twenty years later secured stability by slashing back the tax farmers' profit margins, which also ended his political career.

Roman magistrates could also abuse their positions for personal gain. Closer to home, people tend to forget why Boudicca rode around the countryside in that legendary chariot resembling a prototype lawnmower. You could say it was the fall-out from Britain's first ever PPP. Her family were badly done over by rough soldiers calling in massive loans. They were the local royalty at that, so imagine how your average peasant was treated. The resulting fury saw 70,000 slaughtered as Colchester, St Albans and London were burnt to the ground, and barbaric horrors inflicted upon captives that fell into the mob's hands. The scale of it all puts the poll tax riot into context. The worst part of it was that the loans seem to have been forced on the locals for no discernable public need. They didn't even get an AD 0 Dome out of it.

This was a revolt against a system in which even great philosophers were implicated. Seneca, the leading thinker of his generation, was a massive beneficiary. It just goes to show

how defenders of PFI or large-scale borrowing in any age don't have a monopoly of wisdom, even if they had been given a monopoly on revenue.

Let's face it, collecting state taxes or engaging in ancient PFI was not a popular activity. So when Jesus was seen eating with the "publicans and sinners", he really must have been gunning for men's souls. Nor is it surprising if observers should have questioned his choice of companions, given the nature of the system at work.

An early PFI contract under review

Luke 19

1. Jesus entered Jericho and made his way through the town.

2. There was a man there named Zacchaeus. He was the chief tax collector in the region, and he had become very rich.

3. He tried to get a look at Jesus, but he was too short to see over the crowd.

4. So he ran ahead and climbed a sycamore-fig tree beside the road, for Jesus was going to pass that way.

5. When Jesus came by, he looked up at Zacchaeus and called him by name. "Zacchaeus!" he said. "Quick, come down! I must be a guest in your home today."

6. Zacchaeus quickly climbed down and took Jesus to his house in great excitement and joy.

7. But the people were displeased. "He has gone to be the guest of a notorious sinner," they grumbled.

8. Meanwhile, Zacchaeus stood before the Lord and said, "I will give half my wealth to the poor, Lord, and if I have cheated people on their taxes, I will give them back four times as much!"

9. Jesus responded, "Salvation has come to this home today, for this man has shown himself to be a true son of Abraham."

10. "For the Son of Man came to seek and save those who are lost."

The mechanics of modern PFIs these days are not as easy to grasp, even for the experts. One official survey showed that 45% of users found the payment mechanisms either quite difficult or very difficult to use. Another 45% found the whole process less or much less flexible, with only 5% finding an improvement. And that's the Treasury's own figures. So pity us poor taxpayers trying to grapple with it.

Over the page is a chart taken from a Treasury tome. Although it may look like a landslide at Bertie Basset's, in fact it shows how public expenditure has gone up over the last few years, and how PFIs and PPPs make up a small proportion of this, at around 10%. However, the key point is that they obviously accumulate debt over time in a way that one-off purchases do not.

Billions spent by the state on public services

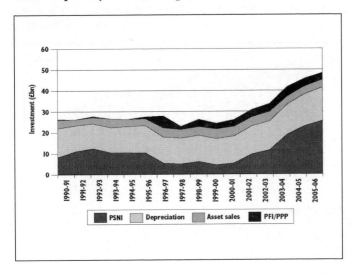

Basically, the issue that concerns economists covers the payments that take place off-balance sheet – the Treasury admits that this is about half of them (already an increase of several percent on three years back).

The chart on the next page reveals what the Treasury was estimating we would be forking out in the future, paying only for the 451 PFIs that were signed three years ago. It looks like a cross section of a nice rambling bit of Derbyshire.

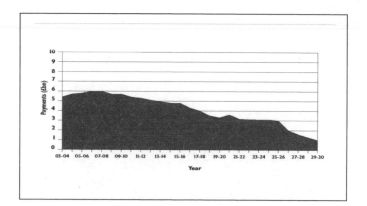

But this is the latest chart:

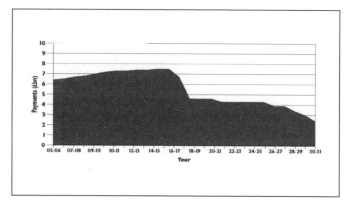

You can see the change. It's like a tectonic shift. A spending continent has rammed into the budget and the cost has risen. Moreover, it's continuing to rise every year.

No-one has any clear idea of what the total sum of these deals has been so far, and what the total end bill will be by the time all the debts are paid. An MP asking that question once gave an estimate of £1 trillion as a fishing exercise. This is quite likely to prove a wild exaggeration. But ministers refused to rebut the figure, probably through utter ignorance, which is always a bad sign. So too is their tendency to tell MPs that any attempt to tot up the various contracts, even on a departmental basis, is just too much hard work. So who can say for certainty what the final sum will be? Let's be optimistic and project a mere third of a trillion.

One of the key reasons given for involving the private sector is to shunt a large proportion of the risk onto them. This is a tacit admission by government that it thinks the state sector, managed by ministers, is congenitally incapable of spending money wisely and managing risk.

At the same time, departments like the Department for Transport have a distrust of straightforward debt management. Take the London Underground. The Department was told in an audit of its PPP contract that it might have been better for it to have simply borrowed the money it required in the form of bonds. The Department acknowledged that this would have saved money, but said that it believed it would save even more money by letting a private sector company run the Underground rather than itself. The examples civil servants gave were of the Central Line project – which cost taxpayers an extra £200 million in overrun – and the Jubilee Line – which cost taxpayers an extra £1.4 billion.

In essence, the Department for Transport was admitting that it was incapable of decent management, and couldn't run a whelk stall without getting into debt. So while it might have saved money by borrowing the money needed to improve the Tube, it didn't feel capable of spending it efficiently. Far better in its eyes to borrow the money at a higher rate by bringing in outsiders on a thirty year contract to do it instead.

If you are a householder and you hire an expensive electrician to change a light bulb, do you justify that decision by saying, "Ah yes, but if I had changed the light bulb myself and fallen off the ladder, clinging to the bookshelf and crashed through the patio doors, think of the cost of the French windows?" We think not. But that is the logic used by Whitehall to excuse expensive PPP agreements.

For a politician, and especially for someone who runs the Treasury, these schemes have a massive advantage. It's like the difference between buying a washing machine in one go and buying one on credit. In one go it hurts your bank balance overnight but after that it's yours to keep. An instalment payment plan shields your finances from an immediate hit, but also means that you pay more for the washing machine over time, and commits a chunk of your salary to repayment so that you can't spend it on anything else. For a politician this is ideal – it means you don't have to pay for the projects you initiate when you are in office, so you can spend money elsewhere and get credit from the voter for that spending too. Then when you are no longer in the job, someone else is getting the blame for the ongoing bill that's cutting the available budget over future years, or for something going wrong when they're stuck with the contract.

It is a policy of myopia. Let's apply the specs.

The Department for Education and Skills even has a dedicated quango set up to keep tabs on the PPP projects on its own books. Partnership for Schools (PfS) plays a key role in Building Schools for the Future (BSF), a 15 year programme designed to roll out over 3,500 state secondary schools, and involving capital of £45 billion. This body by itself costs £13 million to run, employs 81 full time staff, and hires two consultants.

Strikingly, the headmaster of one of the first secondary schools set up under PFI attacked the system, saying that it meant building shoddy schools that were poorly maintained. Simple requests to replace door handles got lost in bureaucracy, while the annual budget was eaten up before it could be spent on teaching. Work on the staff room was priced by the PFI firm at twice the quotation of a local contractor.

Separately, the Department had a £109 million PPP contract with Capita for its Connexions Card project, which it decided to terminate two years early. This scheme was a loyalty points system for youngsters which could earn them state-bought CDs, clothes, and tickets for events in return for attending school. Ministers were warned of failure in 2003, and by 2004 it was clear that only one in twenty five of the intended users were actually using it. Meanwhile, the rate of people who left school at 16 actually increased.

The MoD is also into PPP and PFI projects, but seems to prefer using consultants to negotiate them rather than handling the negotiation itself. Over the last five years of known figures, it appears to have spent £270 million on "consultancy to support teams seeking to engage industry in the delivery of Public Private Partnerships". This is in the context of £6 billion of PFI contracts. It seems that the MoD only trusts its managers to deliver if it gets consultants in to look after them.

The Department for Constitutional Affairs has five PFI deals for court buildings. The Home Office lists 11 PFI prisons with a value of £678 million. Like the MoD, it too uses consultants on PFIs, bringing in six firms last year alone. This bizarre mishmash of the unmentionable and the unquantifiable included £18,500 on "quantum issues in relation to a claim submitted by a contractor" (which presumably the Rutherford Laboratory helped with), £9,000 for insurance advice on all PFI prisons, and a whopping £450,000 for management advice on the PFI contract for the Home Office's new head office on Marsham Street.

The Department of Health, on the other hand, has what it styles the NHS Plan – a plan to build 100 hospitals, mostly under PFI schemes, by 2010. To give you some idea of the finances (and state debt) involved, in 2005, six PFI schemes became operational. Their value ran to £650 million.

Those are dwarves in comparison with what has been happening elsewhere. The biggest departmental PFI to date is St Barts and the London NHS Trust, worth £1 billion. The deal lasts 32 years. The PFI partner then gets £96.4 million a year (plus inflation).

Channel 4's excellent *Dispatches* programme recently found some shocking examples in specific hospitals. One Kent PFI contractor was being allowed to charge £420 for changing a light switch, while hanging a mirror cost £200. Did they have to bus the workmen in from Cornwall? No wonder that one report looking at the money pumped into the NHS has calculated that while spending has doubled, it is providing poor value for money and improvements have been disproportionately small to the sums spent. Indeed, in some areas such as CT scanners, number of practising doctors, coronary procedures, cancer care, radiotherapy training, public obesity, or number of surgical procedures, we are falling back down the international league table.

Where is this PPP splurge leading? Our eye was caught by a line on the departmental annual report which said that there would be a 16.4% real term growth in 'PFI Investment' next year to £1.327 billion. According to the minister, these are costs that will be incurred by the private sector in building new hospitals under PFI contracts that year. As with all other PFI contracts, "the figures do not represent liabilities because the schemes are regarded under accounting standards as being 'off balance sheet'".

This was part of the initial attraction of the scheme. Government can dodge having many of these schemes on the books, and can pretend not to be in debt.

When Health Minister Andy Burnham MP was asked to explain why he can't say how much extra it costs to build a hospital through the PFI system, this was his answer:

> "In working up their preferred option in the business case process, which is developed into the eventual PFI solution, trusts re-assess fundamentally their service configuration and patient pathways, taking on board the provision of new IT, equipment, new construction methods and innovations. It is therefore not possible to directly compare like for like annual expenditure before and after a PFI contract is signed."

The NHS is also running a PFI scheme that covers 'investment in personal social services'. Over 2006-07, £115 million of 'PFI Credits' have been earmarked to support other funding in this area, which basically covers residential and social work. It is not altogether clear from the public accounts what has been bought with this, and indeed whether it will leave any assets behind after the contract ends.

The Health Department has not had plain sailing all the way. It transpires that it had to spend £32,000 on a barrister to resolve a dispute on the Dudley Trust's PFI scheme. It's also emerged that the NHS supremos backed an orthopaedic clinic in Banbury without considering the knock-on effect on the Nuffield Orthopaedic Trust in nearby Headington. The latter is a £42 million PFI investment that local charity campaigners had fought tooth and nail to open, by raising financial support and leaping through PFI hoops. With the opening of the Banbury orthopaedic centre, the future of the one in Headington is in doubt, and with it the whole hospital.

Communities and Local Government has a PFI programme for fire and rescue authorities which will cost £487 million in remaining payments to contractors. It seems that the Department itself will pick up less than half of the tab, however.

The Department for Work and Pensions has been conducting a number of changes to over 1,000 of its property holdings through its estates PFI Contract. In part, these appear to have been forced on it by government regulations on disability access. The cost of compliance is some £4 million.

The main contract itself is codenamed PRIME, and covers the broader management of the Department's serviced accommodation as well as the former Employment Service estate. The contract runs to 2018, and the total repayments including rates and utilities are calculated officially to come to £11.5 billion. £1.8 billion of this is accounted for by 'rates and utility pass through costs'. But the actual capital value of the contracts is only £455 million. It starts to put the whole PFI and PPP scheme into scale and perspective.

The Home Office meanwhile has a £400 million PPP for the

Criminal Records Bureau, and £650 million in three prison PFIs that we know of.

The Solicitor-General's department has a ten year PFI running for the Crown Prosecution Service, which started in 2001. It covers all the CPS computers. The Department chose the PFI option over the alternative known as a 'Public Sector Comparator' approach (PSC), which would have broken down the procurement into separate sets of contractors. Costing them, the Department saw the two sets of costs as standing at £327 million for the PSC as opposed to £359 million for the PFI. But then the Department took off £31 million from the PFI because it was a contingency cost, which might never get spent, and added to the balance the detail that the PFI contract involved the transfer of £21 million of departmental assets, which somehow was supposed to be a benefit. In the end, the PSC gave a risk-adjusted possible cost of £400 million, which was higher.

What is not clear from all this barrage of detail supplied by the Solicitor-General's department is why a prime contractor for consultancy services was required; whether it would be cheaper to have in-house IT specialists covering the whole of government; how much profit the contractors are set to make from their bid; why the contractors believe that the total service cost of the contract will run at £250 million, and why it would cost £85.3 million if the government decided to back out of it.

The DWP has agreed a massive deal with a land consortium, transferring £455 million of assets in the process (albeit a majority of this was leasehold). The forecast cost to the taxpayer of the twenty year programme is £11.5 billion, including rates and utilities – or the cost of the assets themselves every year. This is quite probably Britain's single biggest property transaction ever. One thing it did have going for it at the time was that it made efficiency savings by simplifying the 160 existing contracts. Whether it is value for money over the long term is a different question.

The Department for Transport has awarded £600 million of

PFI credits to local government after a bidding round in late 2005. To judge by the Department's bumf, this was designed as a massive philanthropic gesture to "lead to brighter streets, help to reduce crime and road accidents, and ensure that street lighting across the country is not only renewed, but also improved". In turn, this was followed by a second tranche of a further £600 million of PFI borrowing in February 2006 for motorway maintenance. The total long-term liability for street lighting schemes presently runs at £1.9 billion. Blame for failures here must fall on the local authorities who carry out the value-for-money assessment.

We have totted up what we know of the Department's liabilities for all its contracts, which mostly cover builds for a number of relatively small bits of A roads. We calculate that the ministry has £4,836,000,000 (or getting on for £5 billion) it currently owes through PPP/PFI total debts that it will have to pay back. Naturally, this will come off budgets in future years. But if it had been spent up front instead of by PPP arrangements, we calculate it would have paid for the equivalent of 162 miles of motorway. It seems that someone in the private sector, and probably the shareholders of their bank, must be doing rather nicely out of this.

And we haven't even started discussing the expansion of the M25 to eight lanes. The cost of this project has been estimated at £1.6 billion, but the end price to the taxpayer through PFI is reported to come in at £5 billion.

The self-same department is also negotiating an 'EU PPP', which seems to be a first. This covers the operation of the Galileo project. It is ostensibly a sat nav system designed to ensure that the chauffeurs of government ministers can still read their TomToms when the Americans switch off their satellites because of some global rumpus, but in fact is mainly a vanity exercise for the French, and an opportunity for the Chinese shareholders to park their nukes on Washington DC. Two thirds of the commercial and operational phase will be offered out on a twenty year concession, thus excluding any share of the research costs of putting the things up there in the first place. When you consider the cost overrun ran at €200 million, because the system was easily hacked into by bored off-duty American boffins, this already seems like a bad deal for the taxpayer. They don't even know yet which legal regime will govern the contract, or which courts will have jurisdiction. It is set to cost the public €8 billion – and that's on the doubtful assumption that the private sector chips in. If it does, it'll only be because road pricing is on the way. More taxes. Just dandy.

We have also spotted reports of a PPP summit civil servants have organised for their EU counterparts. Given the traditional French approach of throwing state subsidy at *les fast trains* rather than namby-pambying around with the private sector, and our track record of sending Lancasters to the ball-bearing plants vital to their car manufacturing industry, we suspect the Department got short shrift.

If you take a more generous view of our partners' interventionist credentials, we refer you to the decision by the European Commission which said that the shareholder loan granted by France to France Télécom in 2002 was illegal, that it constituted state aid, that it ran to a whopping €9 billion, and that despite all that, the French government still didn't have to pay it back.

And then, incidentally, there was the little-known move by the French to provide up to €60 million annual tax relief for their video games industry. You qualify for state support if you either deal with a French cultural classic (like, say, a Balzac novel), or contribute to expressing Europe's cultural diversity. "This criterion will be assessed," the validation goes, "by examining the quality and originality of the content, plot, playability, navigation, interactivity and visual, sound and graphic elements." Think *Donkey Kong meets Quasimodo*, where the bonus round is played in a bar on the Rive Gauche smoking a pipe. *Et le tout pour préserver la langue.*

For the record, we give about half as much state aid as the French and Italians, a third as much as the Germans, and a fifth of what the Poles give. But our rate is leaping up in bounds:

£5.44 billion in 2004, up from £4.27 billion the year before. So we're catching up.

Back to PFIs. For its part, the Department for Communities and Local Government has awarded PFI credits of £65 million a year "to support private sector investment in the Joint Service Centre programme" which is described as "multi-agency and multi service centres to improve access to information and front line services". Its current long-term costs and liabilities are assessed at £426 million over the duration of its projects. The Department also appears to be spending £60 million on two projects to outsource its IT. Then there's the consultancy brought in as the National Change Agent for Capital Works in Social Housing, which costs us £2.4 million in advice to Social Housing Managers, on top of the £4 million for the Social Housing Efficiency Challenge Fund. A shocking £25.1 million is going to academics under the National Evaluation of the New Deal for Communities, which given the nature of the work threatens to be little more than a party political football.

DEFRA has several financial agreements. It has a PFI for its core department offices in Cambridge. Intriguingly, through its agencies, it also has a PFI for a flood alleviation project, a PPP for a British Waterways Pub Partnership, an IT contract, and two PPPs to develop a London wharf and a canal site, which include £112 million of land that will be sold off. Strangest of all, the Environment Agency has also entered into a PFI for Pevensey Bay Sea Defences.

Only two of these contracts have express early termination clauses. We are also troubled that the Department has difficulty in working out how much money they've possibly saved for all but one of these contracts.

The Ministry of Defence has gone PFI mad. It has signed up to 33 projects, plus another 25 that exclude IT or cost less than £20 million. The 33 add up to a staggering £26.964 billion in contracts set up to last an average of 25 years. The actual value of the capital these contracts cover, however, is £5.452 billion. A lot of them are related to property, like accommodation or colleges. What the Minister might have mentioned, when asked about these deals by an MP, was that this list refers only to PFI contracts, and excludes any other PPP contracts placed by the Department. So we have no idea of the true total.

Perhaps his choice of wording was used to help hide the ministerial incompetence behind the PPP deal with QinetiQ. QinetiQ is the privatised military research agency, reportedly owing its spelling to gadget man Q from James Bond. The government shunted most of the assets of the Defence Evaluation and Research Agency (DERA) into QinetiQ as part of a PPP deal. But the deal was arranged in such a way that the initial privatisation left the taxpayer with millions in liabilities and forced job cuts, while the PPP phase gave the new shareholders a windfall. One senior employee was said to have made £20 million from the arrangement through shares. The company's value has doubled since it was privatised – a triumph for the free market, but a gap in the taxpayer's wallet. Someone in the Ministry clearly didn't know the value of what he was holding. And we thought SCANDAL stood for the Scattered Nucleon Detection Assembly.

And just in case you thought it couldn't get weirder: the Treasury has a joint venture with a business called Partnerships UK, or PUK. It is a PPP costing the taxpayer £2.5 million a year. Its job is to develop the government's policies on ... PPPs.

Information Technology

To date, none of the *Terminator* films have been set in Britain. There is a good reason for this – the government's evil master computer would never work.

The government's record in IT makes us laugh and cry. So often, departmental heads try to be cutting edge, but fall flat on their faces when it comes to implementation.

Massive IT costs are perhaps inevitable. Technology dates rapidly. But do sums have to be spent so rapidly and why do requirements change so fast? Does anyone in government know how long, for example, the £850 million IT system DEFRA bought two years ago will last?

Of all government IT procurement, it is the NHS's which offers the most egregious examples of short-sightedness, incompetence, and profligacy. According to the Department of Health's annual report, some suppliers and their subcontractors have run up delays on IT projects because of difficulties interfacing their software with the Department's. Only the fact that the whole IT package is running on a ten year schedule has muffled the problem to date.

Government gave doctors autonomy in order to allow them to better manage their affairs. But now it expects them to voluntarily opt in to 'Connecting for Health', a massive and controversial IT system, which may not even be compatible with the systems they have themselves already installed.

One leaked document even suggested that the NHS would have been better off sticking with the old system. Following the biggest crash in NHS IT history, which took systems offline for four days, the document appeared in the post of an MP who scrutinises public spending. It apparently came from the office of one of the senior executives behind the IT changes. Worse, the whistleblower pointed out that even the official audit of the IT is misleading, because instead of measuring performance according to what was originally *supposed* to have been delivered, it looked at the less demanding revised brief.

Other documents indicate that once the 'Connecting for Health' scheme is finally implemented, the costs will outweigh the benefits by a factor of two to one. When you translate that into a cost of £12 billion in return for advantages of £6 billion, you begin to see the problem. Perhaps it will go the same way as the 'Benefits Reprocessing Payments Programme'. That was reportedly binned at a cost of £141 million. It was supposed to *save* £60 million.

Things have got so bad that one of the three lead partners on NHS IT has actually walked away from the deal. Despite the lure of contracts worth a billion a year, the company decided its glitches just meant losses. The Department of Health could have sued the company for around a quarter of a billion for failing to stick with the contract, but has apparently decided not to. This makes a mockery of the principle of contractual accountability – one of the main reasons for involving the private sector in these sorts of deals in the first place.

The extent of waste on the 'Curriculum Online' and 'eLearning' projects has barely dented the public consciousness. Yet they have cost £430 million since 2002 to set up, including one handout of £350,000 for "independent product evaluations", meaning a review by a non-departmental public body.

We've seen one of these evaluations. Among the failings listed, it identified a low level of awareness of the website, a lack of user friendliness, a bad search engine, and problems with using the IT hardware. One school that was part of the 'Laptops For Teachers' programme had also just had 60 of its laptops stolen.

Then there was an IT support team for the programme that seems to have come straight out of an East German holiday camp, criticism of a lack of time to do the necessary training, dullness, political correctness, a tendency to use buzzwords, teachers being bombarded with advertising literature which went straight in the bin, digital cameras that were still in the boxes because teachers didn't know how to use them, unused computers that had been bought for prestige purposes, and a majority of pupils who had already learnt IT skills at home.

The Clinger-Cohen Act

Fear not. This is not an out-take from M*A*S*H. In 1996, the US Congress adopted the Information Technology Management Reform Act. The Administration had been bitten by a number of scandals where projects had vastly overrun, or the technology simply hadn't done the job the civil service required of it, while the consultants had found a nice little earner.

Clinger-Cohen (as it became) required government departments to stop their impulse buying, conduct a cost/benefit assessment of every IT project mooted, figure out what the estimated lifespan of the thing was, and work out if it could be used by anyone else in government as well.

It's nice that the States has had a system in place for over a decade. So why are we still splurging on IT behemoths?

We applaud ministers who attempt to use existing technologies to inject democracy and accountability. Sometimes, however, their innovative spirit gets the better of common sense. David Miliband is a case in point. He had a blog. Nothing wrong with that, except that it turns out he got someone else in the civil service to run it for him, at a cost to the taxpayer of £40,000 a year. This is blog-cheating, and costing you in the process.

But other web warriors got their own back on this pseudo-blogger. Mr Miliband went that innovative stage too far. He put up a draft proposal for an 'environmental contract' in Wiki format, in other words inviting readers to modify the text in the expectation that the law of the cyber-jungle would create a perfect end product. However, the techo-Darwinism went horribly wrong. Hordes of people, encouraged by blogmeister Guido Fawkes, leapt onto the site and posted hundreds of helpful changes. Mr Miliband was seen exhorting people to look at "my face, my beautiful faaace". "Who are the parties to the environmental contract?" became "Where is the party for the environmental contract? Can I come? Will there be cake?" Taxpayers were now encouraged to "Pay a higher proportion of their income to the government, and see little tangible improvement in their standard of living". And a list of items needed to make policy work now included a Tony Blair mask, a big stick, and an owl magnet.

Incidentally, just to put you at ease: the chap who used to be in charge of the government's lead IT project was reported to be on £280,000. He apparently failed his computer studies course, and was originally a geologist.

The Pensions Crisis

Terrifying as government IT projects are, they pale beside the real horror of pensions.

The problems exist at various levels. First you have public sector pensions. Every person hired by the state to do work will have to be paid a final salary pension when they retire. The more people are employed, the bigger the bill will be. But the public sector workforce pays far less of its salary into the pensions pot than private sector workers. Critics point out that the rate at which they are awarded is generous to the employee, but calculated at a massively exaggerated rate of return – perhaps 16% above the going value.

No wonder unions don't want change. The generous pension package that public sector workers get used to be a perk that compensated for low pay, but that has changed with the tax bonanza that went into boosting pay packets. Coupled with early civil service retirement and increased numbers of state employees, it is an anachronism which means that one of the parts of this equation absolutely has to give.

Add that to the pension that most people get when they retire – the state pension, which is the state paying a benefit in return for taxing you throughout your life – and you have one massive unfunded liability. Some estimates put it at £1 trillion.

On a national level, the scale of the problem is well illustrated by looking at the pension scheme of just the NHS. It costs £22 million in annual administration costs alone. It employs 335 managers, excluding outside contractors. It's a large business in its own right, with projected liabilities of £165.4 billion.

Should we be so surprised, when we look at the track record of the department that is supposed to manage pensions? That department's auditors have qualified its accounts for sixteen years in succession, basically signing off the books but with a string of caveats and warnings. The Comptroller and Auditor General in so doing drew attention to "those aspects of complexity in the benefit system which I have long maintained are the main cause of the repeated qualification". Staff in the

Northern Ireland office administering their own finances were similarly found to be making frequent mistakes due to their complexity. In other words, if the system wasn't so darned complex, there wouldn't be so much fraud. Simple is best. The same management failures carry across to the way they have planned for pensions.

Even without the waste, the annual cost is a massive drain on the Treasury, because of the way it has been organised. The Teachers' Pension Scheme for England and Wales has liabilities of £143 billion. The Armed Forces Pension Scheme has liabilities of £76.4 billion.

As at March 2005, we know that the total state liability for pensions, just counting the liability to that date, ran to an unfounded £530 billion. NHS, teachers and the civil service scheme members comprised 70% of that sum.

Nor will the problem go away. In fact, it's getting worse with every passing day. In one year, the pensions bill of funding the public payroll has jumped by £50 billion. And that excludes the NHS increases.

Funnily enough, the top civil servants will be living off cream. According to statistics uncovered by the Liberal Democrats, the top 300 bowler hats have pension pots totalling more than £250 million. Twenty top mandarins have taxpayer-funded savings worth a total of £35 million.

Frank Field was brought into government as Pensions Minister when Tony Blair came to power. He came up with some radical solutions. Unfortunately, in politics, it takes a serious politician to carry out radical work, even if radicalism is what is needed. So Mr Field was dumped. You might say that we are going to pay the price for that decision for years to come.

The time bomb is not just looming; it is everywhere. The problem runs across government, as well as up and down the tiers of government.

Local government in England and Wales had 89 pension schemes with assets (as at 2004) of £80 billion. However, total liabilities stood at £107 billion – a difference of about twice their total annual budget.

Across the public sector, pension liabilities have reached £1 trillion, or about 80% of national income, according to the latest estimate by former Bank of England economist Neil Record. Expect taxes to rocket when someone figures this out.

Hot Air?

This year, DEFRA will spend £15.7 million on research into global warming. This includes funds for the Hadley Centre (part of the Meteorological Office), and the UK Climate Impacts Programme. At the same time, an awful lot more money is being spent trying to cut the nation's carbon footprint.

The new carbon trading rules, for example, have imposed costs on hospitals of several million pounds, a detail civil servants have conspired to hide. This scheme, you may be fascinated to note, has actually left leading petrol companies with a surplus of allowance and therefore allowed them to make hundreds of millions of pounds from carbon trading.

Britain is at a stage of near-obsession with green politics. Wouldn't it be a good thing if policy makers and leaders of industry were more aware of the consequences of their actions? Undoubtedly, and particularly where their actions affect the developing world. There were businesses in every country and every community, indeed many governments, that for years showed a willingness to put profit before local well-being, whether it was asbestos, silicosis, dodgy oil pipes or chemical factories with a tendency to leak. But what we are witnessing now is something more than this. We are on the edge of an obsession, which pretends to form a scientific hegemony. Combine the two and we might have a problem.

The Stern Report has been accepted by the British media almost without challenge. Ordinary Joe Soaps now assume that there is an unshakeable rock solid report stating that everything government does based on that report is justifiable. But that simply isn't the case. Professor Richard Tol is quoted by the

Stern Report 63 times, and he has since gone on record saying that he would grade it F for a series of what he calls "very basic economics mistakes that somebody who claims to be Professor of Economics simply should not make". Critics say that costs are double-counted and worst case scenarios placed in a time frame different from the consensus of scientific thought.

Science thrives through debate and openness. Where there is a 'received wisdom' and critics of it are shut out, science falls back. Even when scientists agree (which is not the case on global warming), that does not mean to say that they are right. At the time of the 1854 cholera outbreak in London, scientists universally believed the illness was caused by airborne 'miasmas'. Dr John Snow was going against the received wisdom of the day when he removed the handle from the water pump which he identified as the source of the problem.

We are not saying that one side is right or wrong. The point we are making is simply this: humanity clearly has made and is making some impact upon the environment in general, and on global temperatures specifically. But scientists who in future years question the costs and the benefits arising from particular courses of action should not be rubbished as eco-terrorists, and they should be allowed to present their evidence in a rational environment. Let's not be corralled by a television shot of an iceberg.

We support the reduction of pollution being pumped into the biosphere, just as we endorse campaigns to save rainforests and habitats across the globe. But we are not up for being panicked into a mass splurge of taxpayers' money on any unilateral spending spree that doesn't include other industrial countries, and especially if it doesn't involve the emerging carbon giants. China, you may remember, is the country that a few years ago switched off its factories for a day when the Olympic judges visited Peking, so that they wouldn't see so much smog. Meanwhile, most EU countries smilingly sign up to commitments they shamefully have no intention of keeping.

So let's develop those alternate sources of energy, before the oil runs out. Build those nuclear power stations. Develop low sulphur coal plants. Create an industry of renewables and micro-generators that people can put on their homes. Let's do it because it's going to save the state energy difficulties in the long term, especially with the Russians and Iran, and also since we can export the products and build a thriving national business as a world leader in the new technology.

As Tony Lodge, an expert on clean coal, explains:

> *"If we are to succeed in the campaign to get fuel bills down and eliminate fuel poverty, guarantee security of energy supply and tackle carbon emissions, the UK must embrace new nuclear power stations alongside new clean coal power stations. Clean coal allows Britain to utilise its substantial coal reserves in new power stations which gasify the coal and remove over 90% of emissions. Clean coal can plug Britain's energy gap; after all, a megawatt hour of coal fired electricity is now cheaper than nuclear and gas. A commitment to clean coal and nuclear will also significantly reduce our perilous overdependence on imported gas."*

But don't treat it as something to throw billions at overnight without a plan, and cripple businesses when our competitors are ignoring their own carbon targets.

Remember too the discrepancies that show us that the environment is a naturally fickle beast even without man's help. Reflect that in the fourth century AD, the sea level dropped and Roman ports in the East of England became landlocked. Recall how in AD 250, excessive rainfall caused a dam to burst in Yemen, creating a forced exodus of the local tribes (one branch created the Ghassanid Kingdom around Syria).

Consider the various mass extinctions throughout history – 488 million years ago, 444 million, 360 million, 251 million, 200 million, 65 million, often associated with massive volcanic eruptions (and by massive, we mean BBC drama documentary scale). Or land masses doing things that were generally unhelpful towards life. Try counting the ice ages that the Earth has seen throughout time. Or if you really want to scare yourself about how fragile life is even without factory chimneys getting in the way, reflect upon the discovery that human DNA marks us all back 70,000 years to a tiny number of scattered ancestors, suggesting everyone else who was alive at the time got wiped out.

Recall how 300 years ago we were in a Little Ice Age, with winter fairs held on the frozen Thames. Or before then, the halcyon days of the Mediaeval Warm Period. Reflect upon the changing lots of the colonists of Greenland, driven to wintry extinction, or reflect on the Roman vineyards in the North of England. Remember how scientists in the 1970s warned of the dire consequences of global cooling. Or ponder on the alternative scientific theories out there, such as the possibility that global temperature is affected more by solar activity impacting upon cloud formation, and then consider how we are going to stop that with our billions – giant orbital sunglasses?

Save the planet. But cost it rationally first. And while you're at it, keep a close eye on Lakes Taupo, Taal and Toba, Mount Baker, Yellowstone and La Garita, don't go swimming near La Palma, learn the lessons from Tunguska, and move Naples away from Mount Vesuvius. We forget the world is a dangerous environment, even without King Coal.

The National Debt

Debt comes from the Latin *debitum*, or that which is owed. National Debt is not like borrowing a fiver from your mate to get supper from the chippy. It's like getting money from your bank manager. You have to pay it back with interest – which means you and your children are paying off more for the National Debt than you got from it.

There are a couple of economic reasons why we might choose

as a country to get into debt. If we have high inflation, then borrowing money now may make some sort of sense because when we pay it back it is worth less. But it also means we are less likely to get a further loan when we need it, and having high inflation causes its own problems. Think of Germany in the 1920s.

Again, you might borrow money in order to invest it and make your economy grow, so that you pay the loan off from the profits over a few years. If you are a developing country, building a road from your farms to the port means you are able to export more and employ more people. Of course, that assumes that President Katanga doesn't spend the loan on shiny new tanks for the People's Popular Army, a top of the range Mercedes, and a nice palace complete with champagne-piped jacuzzi. And for a developed country like our own, the rates of return may not be as high as the rates of interest.

Which leaves us with borrowing in order to temporarily balance the books, and borrowing in order to pay for a war. As a nation, we have only just finished repaying the Americans for the loans they made to see us through the spat in 1939-45. On the plus side we will presumably get some of our ports back from the bits of Empire we used to run when the 99 year destroyer-for-bases leases finally run out.

One set of people keep a beady eye on levels of national debt. Thanks to the Maastricht Treaty, all EU countries are supposed to aspire to one day join the Euro. This means that certain EU institutions keep tabs on the levels of sovereign debt, to see if governments stay within the supposed limit: 40% of the national economy, or GDP.

This is how we know what has been happening of late with the UK economy. Back in his first budget, Gordon Brown proudly boasted that the UK had kept within that limit. In fact, the amount owed had stayed the same, but the economy itself had grown, so debt as a share of GDP actually dropped. Last year, however, the proportion and the sum both increased. This appears to be part of a general trend. As one EU document explains:

"The UK general government balance moved from a comfortable surplus in the late 1990s to a deficit of 3.2% of GDP in 2003/04."

This meant a drop in the balance sheet of 4%. Over the same period, government spending rose from under 40% to 43% of GDP. Meanwhile, money spent on what is called 'government gross fixed capital formation', or state investment in concrete, silicon and steel, has gone up from 1.2% of GDP to 1.6%. This might not sound like a lot, but as a share of an economy of a trillion and a half pounds, that is a lot of money that's coming from somewhere.

That 'somewhere' is taxation and debt.

According to the EU's assessment, in 2004-05 the government's general deficit was 3.2% of GDP, a level that was entirely of the making of the government. It was, however, matched by the growth rate in the economy. So the debt was increasing but the economy was increasing at a rate to pay for it. However, it was also clear that the debt increase was a permanent fixture and not a one-off set of payments. The capital formation was going up to 1.8%, and is set to go up to 2.3% under government statistics by next year. This was going to bump up the country's national debt levels even more. The European Commission therefore came to the striking and inescapable conclusion that Gordon Brown was breaking the Maastricht criteria, and that the UK was running an "excessive deficit".

The latest figures show us paying over £28.3 billion pounds in standard debt interest. Yes, that's *interest*. It's more than the entire budget of some government departments, and it comes straight out of the government coffers in exchange for absolutely nothing. As a comparative sum, it's not much less than the entire budget of the Ministry of Defence. You could build another three Channel Tunnels for that.

Health and Safety

"DO NOT place fingers in the automatic stapler."

Sign on House of Commons photocopier

Ah yes. H&S. The art of telling people not to do the obvious, like stick their head in a mincing machine, because it might have deleterious consequences.

This is a sad and growing trend. One that threatens to wrap us in red tape in order to cushion us from the world.

We are not opposed to basic principles of the duty of care. We believe, at the TaxPayers' Alliance, that state-run businesses just like those in the private sector have a responsibility to ensure, say, that the fire exit isn't just painted on to a brick wall. Or that the practice of stuffing orphans up chimneys to clean them should not be reintroduced as part of the Gershon savings. But there are limits, and we have passed them. Why oh why does Trafalgar Square have fountains with 'no entry' signs, telling people that it's dangerous to jump in them (and yet, strangely, no signs at all about clambering on the back of a gigantic lion)?

Safety awareness is a good thing. Safety obsessiveness is not. Look at the following historical examples to see what we mean.

c. 3000 BC   Tower of Babel built. Hard hats not worn.

456 BC   Playwright Aeschylus killed when an eagle mistakes his head for a rock and drops a tortoise on it. The father of tragedy dies tragically.

26 BC   Lightning grazes the litter holding Octavian (later Augustus). His torch bearer is frazzled. Octavian dedicates a temple to the God of storms and becomes astraphobic.

c. AD 30   Claudius's son tries to catch a pear in his mouth. He chokes to death. *Moral:* never play with your food.

c. 59   Nero tries to kill his mother with a collapsible ceiling. It fails, so then he tries a collapsible boat. She swims to safety. So he has her stabbed.

64   Nero at it again. Great Fire of Rome. Christians take up smoking.

79   Eruption of Vesuvius. *Timewatch* viewers two millennia later are introduced to pyroclastic flows and instant statuary.

c. 1010   Eilmer launches himself and his flying machine from the top of his Abbey to become the Flying Monk of Malmesbury. He flies a furlong, and breaks both his legs.

1100   William Rufus dies after being hit in the chest during a hunting accident. Suspicion mounts as the arrow was allegedly 'deflected by a deer'. A ninja deer.

1120   White Ship disaster. Party-going heir of Henry I and other relatives drown. Nobles send a child to tell the King, fearing to be the bearer of such bad news themselves.

1216   King John loses his crown jewels when his baggage train takes a short cut across the Wash near Wisbech. These days it's cars that go missing.

1628   The top-heavy Swedish warship Wasa sinks in Stockholm harbour. Ikea learn from the mistakes.

1666   Great Fire of London. Hot cakes lead to a rebuild of the capital.

1702   Death of William III after he is thrown from his horse when it trips over a mole burrow. Jacobites toast "the little gentleman in the black velvet waistcoat".

1752   Benjamin Franklin flies a kite in a storm, taking appropriate precautions, unlike several others who read his essay and trip the light fantastic.

1786	West side of Hereford Cathedral collapses. This puts it in the same league as other Health and Safety disasters: Beauvais (1284), Ely (1322), and very nearly Lincoln and Winchester (rescued by architects at the XIth hour).
1830	Statesman William Huskisson run over by Stephenson's Rocket, which then becomes the first motorised ambulance in a vain attempt to rush him to a doctor.
1846	Possible first mention of Sweeney Todd, putting council food hygiene inspectors in a good light.
1883	Eruption of Krakatoa. Charlton Heston points out that matchsticks float. Everyone else dies.
1912	Loss of the Titanic. The band plays on, as H&S flaws about the lifeboats are discovered.
1917	K13 – a submarine with a funnel – sinks on trials.
Also	Halifax explosion. Nova Scotia subject to the largest pre-nuclear man-made blast as an ammunition ship explodes. Witnesses at the extreme edge of the radius see shards of glass in mid-flight, coming across the room at them, suddenly sucked back away.
1926	Celebrated Catalan architect Antoni Gaudi is run over by a tram. Work on the Sagrada Familia in Barcelona is set back 80 years.
1935	Marie Curie discovers the perils of polonium a few decades ahead of the Russians.
Also	T.E. Lawrence clips a bicycle while breaking the Highway Code on his Brough Superior, and becomes a legend.
WW2	Air travel proved to be less than 100% safe for Glenn Miller, General Sikorski, Amy Johnson, Antoine de Saint-Exupéry, Admiral Ramsay, Air Chief Marshal Leigh-Mallory, and Orde Wingate.

But Otto Skorzeny breaks the rules to fly Mussolini from a mountain top prison, and lives.

1970   "Houston, we have a problem." Apollo 13 introduces scientists to the art of understatement.

1973   Fellow astronaut Steve Austin has a bigger problem and has to be rebuilt, at a cost to the taxpayer of $6,000,000.

1976   *Omen I* first shown at the cinemas as a cautionary tale to double glaziers and steeplejacks everywhere.

1982   Darwin Awards begin to list incidents in which a lack of forward planning has strengthened the gene pool.

1991   Faulty railing on board a yacht off the Canaries opens questions about pension funds.

1998   Paragliding MP Lembit Opik crunches horribly into the ground. He is nowhere near Malmesbury at the time.

The world is, indeed, a dangerous place. Worse, there are daft people in it. But at the end of the day we are kidding ourselves if modern Health and Safety is really about protecting people from themselves. It's about protecting managers against being sued by creating a society of obsessives, and that's where the problem lies.

So with H&S high on the agenda, it is a delight to look at how the swamis of Health and Safety obsession have themselves come a cropper.

The Health and Safety Executive is the organisation that has run initiatives on back pain, slips and trips, and work related stress. Its 'Better Backs' marketing campaign cost £2.5 million. Its 'Watch Your Step' campaign cost another £1.7 million. The current series of 'Healthy Workplace Solutions' workshops has a predicted final cost of £627,000.

The Health and Safety Executive also spent £5,000 in October 2005 on its 'Fit Out' campaign. This involved sending inspectors out specifically to target the possibility of 'low falls' and general housekeeping at construction projects that were nearing completion.

So it is intriguing to learn how safe the home of the watchdogs is itself. In 2003-04, there were 10 accidents that were serious enough to have to be reported by law; there were 17 the following year, 13 the next, and 6 for the financial year up to last December. All these took place on the actual premises of the Health and Safety Executive. It appears that most of these accidents involved HSE personnel, with only a couple accounted for by visitors.

Oh, to be able to see the staff notice board the following day.

Health and Safety also haunts the heart of democracy itself. Portcullis House is the £230 million building on the Parliamentary Estates that houses spill-over from the Commons. Its prestige position overlooking Parliament Square and Westminster Bridge affords staff in the first room bar a fantastic vantage point. So it is a surprise to learn that this expensive showpiece of modern architecture has a flag pole from which the Union Flag could never fly – on Health and Safety grounds.

It transpired that a recent H&S report noted that access to the flag pole was by ladder but that there was no safe means of passing the flag up the ladder; the flag raiser needs to climb over a ventilation duct; lighting is poor and there is no emergency lighting. In addition there are heavy hatch doors with no means of preventing closure and no harness anchorage points.

Consequently, the flagpole was only used once, in September 2000. Means of rectifying the health and safety risks were being looked into, and a decision made on a costs basis. So a flag eventually flew from this new building on the Parliamentary estate seven years after it was built.

Safety can be a genuine concern. In Portcullis House itself, one elderly baroness was, for instance, involved in an horrific accident involving a wonky escalator. Yet even months on it continues to shudder and shake like a Sopwith in a dogfight. It does seem like a strange mix of priorities. Perhaps the fact that a new set of lifts at 1 Parliament Street (installed to comply with the Disability Discrimination Act) is costing £337,000 might have something to do with budget constraints.

On the next few pages we share with you correspondence between one of the authors of this book and the House of Commons health & safety officers. It relates to a marvellous part of the Palace, a rooftop vista that was the perfect location for a sandwich lunch on a summer's day. Some readers and fans of political drama might even remember it as the place where Francis Urquhart pushed journalist Mattie Storin to her doom. Is that an unrealistic prospect to visitors today? You might think so, but we couldn't possibly comment.

From: Parliamentary Notices
Sent: 28 September 2006, 16:12
Subject: Access to Roofs and The Commons Roof Terrace

A risk assessment is currently being carried out to assess the safety of the roofs of the Palace. Initial assessments reveal that there are a great number of hazards giving rise to unacceptable risks to people who may be on the roof areas either for work or social reasons. As a result it has been decided, for the time being, to put all areas of the roofs out of bounds, including access to the Roof Terrace above the Commons Chamber.

The only exceptions are the areas where safe access has already been agreed as part of this summers works programme and for those requiring access to the portacabins on the Roof Terrace.

The fire escape routes may still be used but only if directed to do so during an emergency. A programme to allow staff access to the roof areas is being developed. Managers should ensure that all staff, contractors and consultants are briefed about the content of this notice.

Serjeant At Arms
Black Rod

From: Rotherham, Lee
To: H&S
Sent: 30 September 2006, 15:33
Subject: RE Access to Roofs and The Commons Roof Terrace

Hello,

Out of professional interest, what was the mechanism whereby this decision was made? How much paperwork was involved? And how many incidents have been reported (excepting *House of Cards*)?

Best wishes,

Dr Lee Rotherham

From: H&S
To: Rotherham, Lee
Sent: 02 October 2006, 13.00
Subject: FW Access to Roofs and The Commons Roof Terrace

Dr Rotherham,

Further to your recent e-mail, the decision to restrict access to the roofs was made by Myself, PWSD Group Safety Coordinator, The Director of Works Services, and both the Serjeant's and Lords Offices, as well as an independent Health and Safety Consultant. The decision was not made lightly but is based on the immediate findings of a series of detailed risk assessments for each of the 140 or so roof areas on the Palace itself, which is ongoing. As you can imagine, a considerable amount of paperwork is involved, as at least 1000 photographs, plans and detailed risk assessments are being produced which fully support our decision.

It was also brought to our attention that a number of Parliamentary, Lords and MP's staff were abusing the roof terrace facility and the restricted access to several of the adjoining roof areas, and were putting themselves and others in considerable danger.

To date we have had some minor injuries on the roofs, but in order to prevent any potential major or fatal injuries, we have closed access to the roof for the time being until a more suitable means of allowing access can be found.

I appreciate this is an unpopular decision with some people but I would be neglecting my role as a Health and Safety Professional if I was to ignore the evidence that the roofs require considerable remedial measures before a satisfactory means of safe access can be achieved.

We will be making every effort to open the roof terrace area as soon as possible.

Kind regards,

PWSD Group Safety Coordinator, House of Commons

We understand why Parliament's administrators might not want to allow lawyer sharks an opportunity to swarm in a megabucks killing frenzy. We feel genuine sympathy for the administrators of a policy which we know many of them actually loathe. But if people even in that building won't stand up against the compensation culture, what hope is there for the rest of us?

Legal Aid

To find the answer to that, here might be a good place to start.

Over the last ten years, the legal aid fund has increased from £1.5 billion to £2 billion. Costs are rising exponentially and the budget is overspent – and that's just the government's view.

According to a senior judge quoted by a government minister, the UK legal aid system has the highest level of state support in the world. In countries with a justice system described as "good", legal aid cost taxpayers between €1 and €5 per person – the higher part of the range in France and Germany, for instance. In "countries with civil liberties we admire" e.g. Scandinavia, it runs at between €10 and €30 per head. In the UK and only the UK, it runs at €60 per taxpayer.

But aside from the costs, there's no sense of fair play. Animal rights activists, for instance, have been given legal aid to fight an injunction that bars them from harassing staff, students and builders at Oxford University.

Or take the sheer lunacy in the case involving one female prison officer. She was awarded £145,000 for the 'humiliation' of having to frisk male prisoners. The real rub is that it was female wardens who some years before had demanded the right to search male prisoners, because they claimed that not being able to search them was hurting their careers. Male prison officers, meanwhile, are still not allowed to frisk female prisoners.

Or again, the drug-addict thief who was shot by a policeman diving out of the way of his speeding car. He won legal aid to sue the police, despite removing the bullet himself rather than going to hospital, and being well enough to carry on burgling a few days later.

How about the crook that got legal aid to sue the police, accusing them of undue force when he was nicked trying to ram-raid a jewellers.

Or the prisoners granted aid to sue for stress caused when other prisoners went on a £3 million riot, in a row about sandwiches. Just as well, then, for the compensation budget that David Blunkett was ignored when he wanted the army to machine gun the rioters.

We believe that some lawyers are playing the system to its limit. They should be named and shamed, as a prelude to action to stop them living a gold-plated lifestyle thanks to our taxes.

Compensation culture

Some months ago, we were sent an unsolicited email. It came from a claims company, and had a helpful link to a compensation calculator. So we experimented with it. As they promised, it did take less than a minute. We ticked the boxes they asked for.

Were you injured in the last three years?
No. Let's imagine we weren't planning on suing until you asked us, and we had completely forgotten about it. It happened four or five years back and we've recovered.

Did you receive medical attention for your injuries?
No. Let's say it wasn't serious enough.

Was the accident your fault?
Let's say yes, I was stupid. Totally stupid.

Where was the injury?
My back. An easy choice, and a common injury. I did it while moving a hat stand in a government building. Foolish me, I forgot it had many, many hats on it and was likely to weigh a lot. And umbrellas. By the way, the injury might have been caused by something else as well. I moved house the week before and had lots of cast iron furniture which … oh, you're not interested.

Insert a name and contact details so we can contact you.
You get to choose your title too. Alright, Reverend Jonah Lumbago we are then. Claim submitted and the response is:

> Back Injuries: Strains, sprains, disc prolapses, soft tissue injuries up to £6,500. Severe injuries, e.g. permanent disability, up to £14,000.

Excellent. Free money. I'm up for that. So I am now incentivised to launch a legal action for an 'injury' about which I had forgotten, and for which I was entirely to blame. Thank you, Accident Advice Helpline. Someone reading this, please make sure that their CEO never gets a CBE.

But who are the big culprits in all this? Surprise, surprise: the Home Office. Over the past two years, it transpires that compensation has been awarded to a number of prisoners on surprising grounds. Three claims were awarded for abuse or harassment; 15 involved the state paying after an assault by another prisoner; 15 involved claims of assault by staff; 55 cases of suing for slips, trips and falls; 2 for sports injuries; 63 miscellaneous injuries; 18 cases of supposed medical negligence; and 80 cases involving personal property. Shamefully, almost none of these went to court – it was decided it would be cheaper to settle and cough up, which hardly discourages spurious litigants.

Over the past three years the sums paid out by the Home Office total over £8.8 million, not including £2.8 million paid to a prisoner for injuries sustained in a botched suicide attempt, which by definition you might think was his own doing. The total included hundreds of pounds paid to inmates to compensate them for the confiscation of their DVD players, which warders found were used to store pornography. Two hundred other inmates were awarded £750,000 when they weren't given enough drugs and were forced to go cold turkey, and three illegal immigrants were awarded £80,000 because they weren't deported quickly enough.

The DTI over 2005-06 was lumbered with a payments bill of nearly £52,000, a tenth of which related to staff property. £15,629 was paid out to one individual who seems to have been sacked for being inefficient.

Some of the most shocking examples come from the NHS, however. The Department has accepted that it will be the target of court claims, and has even broken up its compensation department to cover the different types. Here are the ten largest claims made under the new systems up to the end of 2006:

Ten largest settled liabilities under third party scheme up to end of 2006	
Cause of the complaint	*Damages paid*
Tripped over telephone wire	£200,000
Pulled bed away from wall and experienced a sharp pain in her lower back	£200,000
Stepped back onto a board covering cable duct, board shifted as not secured and leg fell down duct	£201,624
Contracted Legionella. Subsequently died	£210,000
Injured while closing a vehicle entrance to the ambulance station	£212,975
Caught leg on spike protruding from bed	£250,000

THE BURDENS FOR OUR CHILDREN

Scanning numerous maternity patients and suffered repetitive strain injury	£250,000
Slipped on wet and soapy floor	£258,771
Hit by radiography lead screen	£310,000
Swivel chair fell backwards causing fall to the floor	£400,000

Ten largest settled liabilities under the property expenses scheme up to end of 2006

Cause of the complaint	Damages paid
Fire possibly caused by a patient smoking	£358,377
Fire	£468,437
Fire in/adjacent to A&E department	£480,000
Fire	£480,000
Fire – cause unknown	£486,341
Refrigerator malfunction leading to ruined blood products	£488,279
Fire in main kitchen	£525,046
Fire – suspected arson	£632,171
Fire in/adjacent to A&E department	£1,000,000
Fire possibly caused by a patient smoking	£1,000,000

It is not known if any of the patients who were smoking in hospital were themselves sued, or if they were in hospital in the first place for smoking-related diseases and therefore deserve to be clubbed with an irony stick.

Again, we don't know how much of this was money handed by the taxpayer to a PFI firm, or how much came from hospitals in deficit that could have done with the money themselves.

Ten largest settled liabilities under the clinical negligence scheme up to end of 2006

Cause of complaint	Damages paid
Failure/delay in responding to an abnormal foetal heart rate	£5,555,000
Delay in diagnosis of foetal distress	£5,620,290
Informed consent not correctly obtained	£5,624,976
Failure/delay in diagnosis	£5,749,111
Failure to respond to birth complications	£5,793,782
Failure/delay in responding to an abnormal foetal heart rate	£5,800,000
Failure/delay in diagnosis	£6,248,845
Failure to monitor second stage labour	£6,635,000
Failure to perform tests	£8,300,000
Fail to diagnose pre-eclampsia	£12,400,000

These are obviously awful situations for some of these patients to be in. But the sums being handed out are astronomical, given that lawyers are expecting perfection from the uncertainties and complexities of medical science. We are also always suspicious about damages based on failure to obtain consent, which often hide a doctor's dilemma acted upon in good faith.

Work and Pensions is just one of a number of other departments that run a compensation scheme (as does the MoD, but the latter seems to have stopped publishing a glossy annual report since last year's *Bumper Book*). In 2005-06, the DWP paid out significant sums in compensation. Over £2 million was handed over for "loss of statutory entitlement" where an allowance was incorrectly not given; £3.4 million went out to cover maladministration; £8.1 million was compensation for delay in payments; and £822,000 were "consolatory" payments in cases where "individuals have suffered gross inconvenience, gross embarrassment, or severe distress in consequence of maladministration". No doubt some of these would make interesting reading as well.

We've also been able to uncover the latest compensation list for the Department for Education and Skills. It reads like a Mr Bean movie script.

Reason for payment	Payment amount
Damage to personal property – clothing damaged by contaminated water flooding from pipes in ceiling.	£77
Damage to personal property – motorcycle helmet damaged when car park barrier came down on staff member's head.	£269
Personal injury – injury to neck when car park barrier came down on staff member's head. Physiotherapy treatment required.	£210
Road traffic accident – DfES driver collided with external third party in road traffic accident. Third party claim for repair of damages to vehicle and hire car costs.	£7,144
Damage to personal property – clothing damaged on sharp edge of desk	£23
Damage to personal property – watch damaged by premature closing of lift doors.	£40
Damage to personal property – clothing damaged	£16
Road traffic accident – DfES driver collided with external third party in road traffic accident. Third party claim for repair of damages to vehicle.	£5,596

Personal injury – DfES driver collided with external third party in road traffic accident. Personal injury claim from passenger in third party's vehicle. Compensation and medical costs sought.	£4,483
Road traffic accident – DfES driver collided with external third party in road traffic accident. Third party claim for repair of damages to vehicle.	£364
Personal injury – injury to head and shoulders when whiteboard fell off wall and hit staff member. Compensation and medical costs sought.	£3,200
Compensation for loss of interest due to delay in making an ex-gratia payment for loss of employment.	£412
Compensation for unfair dismissal of a temporary employee following a ruling by the Civil Service Appeal Board.	£13,504
Ex-gratia payment for loss of employment as part of a compromise agreement to settle a dispute and avoid subsequent litigation.	£13,400

The government has at least recognised that there is a problem. Quite what good will come from its Compensation Act remains a mystery. We were hopeful that the £20,000 ceiling on legal fees would have some effect. But it transpires that the Department believes it will see as much as 43% more claims taking place as a result of any changes, so any savings in legal bills will be eaten up by an increased number of cases. Apparently, ministers are "working with stakeholders to encourage organisations to resist bad claims". We saw this work in the Wild West, but with less effect in a vampire movie.

Par for the Course

Government likes its workforce to be well trained. So why, you might ask, send them on so many useless courses? Because it's PC for one thing. Because it shows an employment tribunal that your bosses did care for you, despite what you might claim. And because the management might get some daft certificate that pretends to demonstrate that they run an establishment which looks after its workforce. It is in one sense a symptom of a litigous society.

DEFRA, for example, spent £10,000 of taxpayers' money on sending staff to a Buddhist retreat, as part of a bonding session after a departmental shake-up reportedly caused friction. Actors led role-playing exercises creating ludicrous situations in order to establish a sense of togetherness. Sounds like a regular day in the office, then.

£340,000 was reportedly spent by departments on a variety of 'life courses', intended to help civil servants deal with stress. None is on offer to help readers of this book cope with the stress that these same departments cause. One firm apparently uses concert piano recitals, and cookery, to encourage the little grey cells. Psychiatrists have also ministered at £250 an hour.

The Health people have a selection of courses for their civil servants. These include:

- *Time Management*
- *Handling Difficult Situations*
- *Promoting a Participative Team Environment*
- *Develop-Inspire-Achieve*
- *Self Awareness and Managing Relationships*
- *Working and Developing in a Changing Environment*
- *Communicating With Confidence*
- *Influencing Skills*
- *The European Computer Driving Licence*
- *Equality Issues and Responsibility Sessions*
- *Policy Skills*

If you've been on one of these courses, do drop us a line. We would love to know if you had to hug shrubbery or express your inner self. We are particularly interested in the physical ins and outs of the course called *Presenting With Impact*.

SECTION 5

Going European

> *"It is not government practice to publish exact forecasts of the [EU] contributions and receipts of other member states, as this could prejudice the UK's relations with these states."*

Government minister

We can't escape the fact that an awful lot of taxpayers' money is being spent via Brussels, just as an awful lot of the decisions about how this country is run are being made through EU institutions.

This means that it is inevitable that any book about government waste in the UK will cover what is happening with the spondoolees that trickle and leak in Euro format.

There's a lot of material out there. We will share with you a bare minimum, covering some of the horror stories that make up the big budget spending sprees, the tales of woe that have reached our ears from insiders, and the lessons that can be learnt by studious perusal of the reports of the EU's very own auditors.

For starters, you may not be aware that according to the government's own figures, the administative burden alone that flows from EU's laws and regulations – a burden that is borne by business, charities and the voluntary sector – costs £6.3 billion a year. That excludes the costs on the City, and the costs on government. One of the EU Commissioners, Gunther Verheugen – actually the one in charge of the Enterprise portfolio – said that he believed that the overall burden of regulation was costing the EU a mind-boggling €600 billion a year.

Funnily enough, shortly after attacking the way the EU was piling on costs, Mr Verheugen's staff reportedly froze him out of policy-making; a staff union demanded he apologise or resign; and within days a German magazine leaked stories about a relationship the Commissioner was alleged to have had with a member of staff. Meanwhile, even the uninspiring objective of simplifying 54 laws in a year seemed to have been stalled by bureaucratic obstructionism.

EU regulation imposes astronomic costs on UK business. According to research undertaken by the British Chambers of Commerce, over the last ten years there has been £55.66 billion in red tape costs piled on to British businesses. They calculate that 72.5% of this, or around £40 billion, is due to EU red tape. These are costs which reduce the ability of our businesses to make profits and expand, or simply to compete on the world stage. The official response appears to be not to fix the problem, but to change the way the cost of red tape is counted.

It's not clear if the UK's way of running things helps much. There seems to be a tendency to hide the origins of EU legislation. Attempts in the House of Commons to print EU-origin material on different coloured paper, so MPs can check the laws haven't been added to by zealous civil servants, have been repeatedly rejected. The government says it cannot accurately work out which of the hundred UK agencies are simply replicating work done by the European Community's own 18 (and growing) agencies. One example is the European Food Safety Authority, set up in 2002, and the UK's own Food Standards Agency, set up in 2000. Another is the UK's Health and Safety Executive, which is even described as the 'UK Focal Point' for the European Agency for Safety and Health at Work.

That's before you even get within a mile of the really contentious material that the TaxPayers' Alliance was the first to uncover, like the EU plan to create a combined list of national terror targets (which will obviously in time need an EU force for protection), and a Gas Coordination Group for joint policy on energy supply (while remembering we have the North Sea reserves and they don't).

On rare occasions the sloth of bureaucracy is capable of

speeding up – but only when it suits its purposes. Take the example of a document dated 26 October 2006 last year. It warned of a business merger, and gave readers ten days from publication of the text to submit any observations. The document arrived in the Commons on 6th November, i.e. nine days after publication, which is quite quick for the normal rate of things. It went through the internal mail, arrived in the in-tray and was read by Mr N. Onymous in the House of Commons at precisely 2.34 pm on the following day. Allowing for a one hour time difference with Belgium, there was just 86 minutes left for a potential comment to be officially submitted.

The EU bureaucracy's contempt for member state individuals and companies will come as no surprise to businesses that supply it. Officially, businesses owed money by the Commission have to be paid within a set time. This used to be 60 days, which is a long time, so the Commission changed it to 45. However, its bureaucrats developed a tactic to get round the rule: on Day 44, an official would send a letter to the supplier querying one point in the invoice. When the frustrated businessman replied, the deadline clock would start from zero again. It's been suggested to us that the problem is that the Commission is full of bright people who have been put into an administrative role without the proper training, and simply don't understand how small businesses work.

There's also a bit of a 'them and us' attitude to the way the Commission is run. Take the Working Time Directive, which set limits on how long workers are allowed to be in the office, and which had knock-on effects on small businesses. Funnily enough, senior civil servants were allowed to "volunteer" to avoid the ban. As for the Prime Minister, in Tony Blair's words:

> *"Holders of political offices in the UK are not defined as 'workers' under the terms of European working time legislation, and are therefore not subject to the working time limits: as such, they do not need to opt out."*

So it's official – government ministers don't do any "work".

Before we accelerate down this speed-bumped housing estate of financial pain, here are some of our favourite documents and policy decisions to have emerged of late from the brotherhood of European cooperation that is the European Union:

• *Council Regulation No 881/2002* was enacted in May 2002, and has been updated 73 times since. It was a response to the 9/11 attacks on the World Trade Centre and the Pentagon. It bans named Al-Qaeda members from travelling in planes.

• *Commission Regulation (EEC) No 3149/92* allows governments to take food from the various mountains and lakes of scoff and drink and hand it over to the poor and needy. The UK stopped doing this a few years back when it was pointed out to them that among the recipients were the families of convicted IRA terrorists.

• *Commission Regulation (EC) No 1737/2006* on monitoring of forests. This requires civil servants to log data on individual trees, including categories for 'actual latitude and longitude coordinates', 'humus type', 'orientation', 'mean age of dominant storey', 'crown shading', and 'social class'. There is also a section for 'visibility', allowing for all sorts of puns on being able to see the wood for the trees.

• *Commission Regulation (EC) 1739/2005* creates passports for circus animals.

• *Commission Recommendation 2005/491/EC* says that Eurozone countries have to forward their coin designs to each other. This is because they might object to a national hero being put on them, like Wellington on the old fiver.

• *Article 4.7 of the Forces Agreement with Gabon* allows Brussels to bring EU-flagged submarines into the African country. This is to help in peacekeeping operations during a general election in the Congo – a vast, mostly landlocked, country with just 20 miles of coastline. This was in keeping, however, with the decision to send a Rear Admiral to run peacekeeping in Bosnia (12 miles of coastline and no ports).

• *Directive 2006/60/EC* as part of the fight against third world fraud allows for snooping on ministers, MPs, judges, ambassadors, soldiers, civil servants and those running state bodies like public broadcasting or quangos. It also covers their wives and immediate family. The UK government astonishingly looks set to introduce it to the UK too. Let's hope the PM doesn't have any offshore accounts in the Channel Islands.

• *Joint Action 2005/797/CFSP* sets up an EU police monitoring mission for the Palestine Territories. Its official name is EUPOL COPPS.

• *Commission Regulation (EC) 105/2007* puts down a common set of shorthand codes for counties and regions for statistical purposes. It's called NUTS.

• *An aid scheme allowing Bavarian farmers to share machinery*, like tractors, was meant to help with the cost of seasonal agricultural equipment. The farmers were found to be using the equipment to build roads, create waste water treatment plants, run garden and landscape maintenance businesses, and build golf courses and other sports facilities.

• *Two EU officials attended a WMD non-proliferation conference for Caribbean countries*. Because, as we all know, Trinidad is on the edge of becoming a nuclear power.

• *A major cigarette company was nobbled to fork out €1.25 billion* as part of an international agreement to fund a clampdown on counterfeit and smuggled cigarettes that were dodging the tax man, over which as a company it obviously has no control.

• *The EU's celebrated Ladders Directive was aimed to prevent ladder-based accidents*. Ladders must 'be so positioned as to ensure their stability during use'. Portable ladders 'must rest on a stable, strong, suitably-sized, immobile footing so that the rungs remain horizontal' and their feet must be prevented from slipping. Ladders should always provide a 'secure handhold and secure support' especially 'if a load has to be carried by hand on a ladder.' Snakes are excluded from the directive.

• *Com (2006) 0004* as codified, authorises state aid to silk worms (at €86 for every 100 eggs).

• *Regulation (EC) 1462/2006* sets out that a 10cm ceramic sheep with a glued-on fleece does not count as a toy, but counts as a household ornament. There is a handy little mugshot attached to this official document (see right).

We apologise in advance to journalists and editors, who will now be getting phone calls from the press officers at both the Commission and European Parliament UK offices, saying how important bundles of paperwork on tree spotting is to fight acid rain, and how tax officials must be able to understand which excise rate to apply to Flossy. There is a way to halt such tedium in its tracks. We recommend that before you let them speak, they have to tell you how much their media outlets and literature cost the taxpayer every year, and what pay grade they are on.

You can then tackle the spokesmen for the European Parliament with this one:

> **The Strasbourg-Brussels Shuffle**
>
> *Le Monde* recently investigated the costs of maintaining two assemblies for MEPs in Strasbourg and Brussels. It transpires that just the cost of renting removal lorries to transport 200 tonnes of material is €9000 every week. Each time 3,200 boxes of papers are transported, as well as video material and reportedly even hospital equipment in case anyone has a heart attack.

The Parliament recently spent €830,000 replacing the filing cabinets, because the old ones tended to fall over and injure the removal men. So much needs to be carted around on the seven hour drive, because MEPs and officials are never sure if the agenda will change at the last minute.

On top of that, every Monday when there is a session in

Strasbourg, 500 European Parliament civil servants based in Luxembourg come to Strasbourg to join 1,200 of their colleagues from Brussels.

In addition to the expenses of the civil servants, MEPs, their staff, and the staff of the political groups, around 60 journalists get paid as well. So much for journalistic integrity. The extra costs associated with all this are estimated at €205 million in 2006, not forgetting of course the size twelve carbon footprint that goes with it.

And all that is without even considering the democratic issue of how the institutions work on a daily basis. The way, for example, that MEPs spend entire days pushing *yes/no/abstain* buttons every few seconds. The chairman sometimes has to be retranslated into a third language before it gets to the MEP's ears, so he might even be voting on the last motion while a new one is being proposed. And he quite probably is pushing his little button on votes where he himself hasn't read the draft, or where the draft may well not have been translated into his native language so he couldn't understand it even if he had seen it.

The French lately developed a wheeze to get round all this. Leading politicians got together and held a press conference to say that the authoritative language of the EU should go back to being French. Their credibility was blown when the fellow from the *Académie Française* had to be corrected halfway through his speech for using the English word "understatement" to explain himself.

How much does it cost Britain to be a member of the EU? Some think tanks calculate that thanks to recent botched negotiations and EU enlargement, Britain's net payments will now go up to £10 billion a year. To be honest, nobody in government knows, because every time someone in the Treasury has started to do the sums, totting up what we pay out and what we get back in grants, and adding the burdens and costs to boot, officials have been told in no uncertain terms to stop working it out.

The true cost of EU membership might be just too unpalatable.

An Insight on the Wires from EUObserver.com

"I'd better burn all those papers."

A conversation overheard in the back seats of Wednesday's conference gives a humorous insight into the European Commission's internal attitude to transparency and consultation, with consultation usually handled by putting a notice on the Commission's website asking people to send in ideas.

When the head of a film music writers' guild stood up to say that the Commission had not consulted him on its recommendations, one Commission official in a grey striped suit turned to another one in a grey striped suit and joked "What, did he expect us to call him personally?"

And when Danish Eurosceptic MEP Jens-Peter Bonde complained on the podium that he could not get access to key documents on how the Commission prepares its recommendations, the striped suit quipped "I'd better burn all those papers I've got at home."

On Mountains and Deserts

Two big destinations for EU money are the Common Fisheries Policy (CFP) and the Common Agricultural Policy (CAP).

Indeed, these two projects could be regarded as modern parables. They are just like the miracle of the loaves and fishes. Only in reverse.

We could write an essay on what's gone wrong, but we'll just highlight the salient details to show where your tax money goes. Let's begin with the CAP.

The Common Agricultural Policy

This is a policy, to be frank, which was designed in the 1950s to support French rural society, in a culture that had historically and traditionally relied on its rural manpower, that was psychologically as attached to the bucolic idyll as the UK had been to, say, its coal miners, and in an age where the rulers in

Paris were painfully aware that their country, once Europe's most populous, had been overtaken by the titan east of the Rhine. So Germany paid a form of latter-day reparation to support agricultural France, in return for rehabilitation on the international stage and new markets for its industries.

That was the philosophy fifty years ago. The net result today is taxpayer support (especially for certain major land owners, and by a couple of countries in particular), at a colossal price. One payer is the developing world, whose growers often have to stump up at the border in order to access European markets in which local producers are subsidised. Of course, that pushes up prices at the till, so families are paying twice – once for subsidies, and again in the shopping basket.

Last year, the EU paid out €920 million to subsidise mainly Greek and Italian tobacco growers in Flavour Country. This year, it will be €317 million. At long last, the EU is phasing out its subsidy, mostly to small mountain farmers, to grow a product whose quality even as a noxious weed is questionable, and whose sole benefit is to decorate upper stretches of the Apennines for the benefit of poor farmers. But this reduction will take until 2010 to complete, and we are still faced with a quota of 350,600 tonnes. This, incidentally, doesn't limit the amount grown – it's just the limit that gets subsidised. It also shows how long reforms can take. The tobacco regime was first introduced in 1970. It bodes ill for fixing any of the other EU problems in a hurry.

Just over half of the tobacco crop gets exported. Lucky Africans. Literally.

Meanwhile, the New Zealanders have started to get seriously whacked with their butter exports. Part of the arrangement when we joined the EEC was that we didn't harm our Commonwealth trading partners. Hours of parliamentary debating time were spent guaranteeing that very point. But the Commission has rejected the old deal, and import tax has leaped from just under £2 million in 2004 to around £25 million today. Last year, we imported about 42.5 thousand tonnes of kiwi butter. To put it into shopping trolley talk, every pound of the creamy yellow stuff you bought at the supermarket cost an extra 25p in customs tax.

Tot all these up, and even the government itself says the CAP costs us. Shared out evenly between absolutely every EU national (though of course many of these countries aren't paying), it costs everyone £210 each in payments alone. That, of course, ignores the higher food bills, and the fact that the subsidies go mostly to a group of people who ban our beef and set up roadblocks when we are trying to go on holiday through their ports. It's not even as if we've got rid of the food mountains yet. In this country we still have 13,500 tonnes of cereal, rice, sugar and milk sitting in silos and warehouses, plus 3,500 hectolitres of alcohol including wine. Last year, the UK spent £1.38 million buying up some more or storing its current stock, though we also sold some off. But this was a tiny proportion of the whole EU budget for 'intervention buying', which ran at over €1 billion last year. Who are the main beneficiaries, we wonder?

The Common Fisheries Policy

And then there is the CFP – the system that has allowed Spanish fishermen to upgrade their massive fleet and spruce up their ports, while our fleet suffers a disproportionate share of the cutbacks. While modern, foreign-owned trawlers ply our waters supported by grants totalling countless millions over the years, attempts to revitalise the Shetland fishermen with rare grants of a few thousand pounds have lately been taken to the European Court by the Commission, in no less than four separate court cases.

Between 1976-80 in Britain, 707 under-10 metre fishing boats were built, and 140 larger deep sea vessels. In 1996-2000 the figures were 486 and 102 respectively. The numbers continue to drop, the average age of the surviving boats increases, and the proportion of smaller boats rises. From 1997 to 2005, the number of under-10 metres boats dropped from 5,474 to 4,833, and the larger ones from 2,338 to 1,508. Such reductions might be good for conservation if the competition was also shrinking the size of its fleets. But it hasn't worked like that. Our coastal communities have borne the brunt, to conserve stocks on their very own doorstep, with science that is contested.

Whereas in 1997 there were 18,600 working fishermen, by 2005 there were 12,600. British fishermen, to abuse an expression, have been kippered.

Meanwhile, the system continues crazily to require fish caught in excess of the quota to be dumped back overboard, sinking to the bottom to pollute the seabed. The latest government figures confirm that Scottish fishermen have to dump 15% of caught cod, 15% of haddock, and 49% of whiting overboard.

Tot up the major species and you are looking at 152,000 tonnes of fish north of Brittany going straight back into the sea. A disproportionate number of these will be fry, small fish that will never grow to adulthood, but could still be used as a protein source if landed.

It is an unfathomable amount that is descending into the fathoms. The public is unaware of the issue because the dumping is distant and out of sight. But imagine the outrage if it were done in full view of a cross channel ferry. We are looking at the equivalent in simple weight of 12,300 sperm whales being killed and left floating out at sea. Or 6.08 billion fish fingers bobbing around the Channel.

It is an ecological slaughterhouse of pure waste, being forced upon fishermen against their will. But we haven't told you the worst. Those figures only cover British boats in British waters. The Fisheries Commissioner, Joe Borg, is on record as estimating that total discards under the CFP run to an annual dumping of roughly 880,000 tonnes. The average rate of discards is about 8% in the rest of the world. In some waters off Scotland and Ireland the figure is believed to be more like 90%. By a harsh statistical coincidence, 880,000 tonnes is also the target for the amount of biodegradable landfill for Scotland by 2013. This total is also more than the entire weight of fish both landed and farmed by the whole of Egypt.

It is an outrage. We in the TaxPayers' Alliance object to tax money being used to support one set of fishermen, while more tax money is used to wind up the businesses of another. We particularly object when it is UK tax money that is doing both, and predominantly non-UK fishermen who are reaping the benefits.

We also note with shame that the government could have invoked the Hague Preference on numerous occasions to reserve a bigger share of the allowed catch, but has only ever done so when the Irish have taken the lead, because they have been afraid of annoying other governments. But not, it seems, of annoying our own fishermen and putting them out of work.

El Mundo Audito

We could spend forever on fraud and waste. But that would be like accountancy prison. Or running Belgium. So let's just focus on what the official auditors have found out over the last year or so.

Let's start with the main blast. Every year, the European Court of Auditors carries out a general review. By long-established tradition it exposes lots of dodgy bookkeeping and refuses to sign off 97% of the accounts (one good year they actually only objected to 91%, but that was an aberration). Here are some of the key features from their critique of last year – the latest available – which in fact covered the accounts for 2005.

Report of the Court of Auditors

✗ The auditors note that the Commission amended its provisional accounts several times after they were submitted, because its data management system was so poor that the maths was out by some €200 million.

✗ DG Education and Culture is such a bad bookkeeper that the auditors cannot be sure what its assets and liabilities actually are.

✗ On funding activity outside the EU, the auditors note a

"lack of a comprehensive approach to the supervision, control and audit of these organizations".

✗ The auditors hint that senior management stalled internal reforms by delaying the annual audit itself.

✗ In a random sample of 141 invoices, there was a "material level of error", i.e. where the figures were wrong or recipients were being paid twice. In some cases, the paper trail was so complicated it was impossible to follow.

✗ Over half of the declarations made by senior staff about their budgets contained reservations – i.e. the department leaders themselves had found their budgetary control to be flawed.

✗ Neither member states nor the Commission are convinced about how much money should be being handed over under VAT rules.

✗ In the case of the UK, Customs and Excise may have allowed dues on temporarily stored goods to slip. Indeed, assessments have been taking so long that time barring may kick in, so that EU taxes might be completely avoided.

✗ Audits of pre-selected CAP projects in certain member states were once again found to have had a lower error rate than those chosen randomly. In other words, there is suspicion of state cover-up.

✗ 40% of CAP payments tested by the auditors showed claimed fields were larger than the real fields.

✗ Particular attention is paid to the CAP in Greece – especially:

    (a) the quality of inspections is low and findings are poorly or not at all documented, reporting of results is unreliable and is not always based on genuine inspections;

    (b) in certain local authorities in Greece, the techniques used when measuring parcels lead to a higher technical tolerance than the maximum allowed (5%). The financial impact of this practice cannot be quantified;

(c) farmers' unions control the input of all data into the computer system. None of the data in the system is secure and they can be and are modified by the farmers' unions at any time before payment. The computer system does not record when and why changes to the original data are made. Many of these changes are irregular but cannot be precisely quantified.

In plain speak, this means that there is official collusion and the farmers unions change the records for their member's benefit.

✗ In Hungary and Slovakia, farmers may have been punished as their neighbours' imaginary fields were deducted from their own.

✗ Hungary paid one set of aid twice instead of once.

✗ One in four tested Single Area Payment Scheme grants was overpaid.

✗ 11.4% of Italian suckler cows either didn't exist or weren't suckler cows. The equivalent figure in Slovenia was, astonishingly, nearly 50%. Meanwhile, over one in ten special beef premium cows in Malta didn't exist or weren't premium, one in five in Italy, and over half in Slovenia.

✗ Phantom sheep and goats also appeared – one in ten in Italy, and one in four in Slovenia. Maltese aid was "systematically calculated incorrectly".

✗ Olive oil grants are worth €2 billion. All cases tested found errors or overpayments, and also revealed two cases of suggested fraud.

✗ The auditors hint that as the reforms have not been implemented, with the new system about to come on line, existing fraud will be regularized for the future.

✗ On aid to poorer/weaker farming communities worth over €6 billion, there was a high incidence of error as no one checked properly whether claimants were eligible.

✗ A tenth of the Polish farmers receiving grants for good farming practices (worth €225m) were using bad ones.

✗ A range of problems is caused by customs officials themselves. The UK has been one of several countries tipping off businesses about paperwork checks; jobsworths have been checking on material of small value; two countries have allowed exporters to put their own customs seals on; and the UK systematically (thanks to computerization) fails to check whether seals have been broken.

✗ In five of the Commission's own audits it didn't use audit procedures.

✗ For one transport scheme, the Commission failed to spot that it could only finance 10% and not 50% of the project, resulting in an overspend of €146 million. Meanwhile, the funding of €78m towards the controversial Galileo project had no legal basis.

✗ Damningly, "The Commission does not have a clear approach or strategy on the coordination of key control procedures, such as the use of audit certificates, desk reviews of cost claims (basic checks or in-depth desk audits) and on-the-spot audits, to reduce the over-declaration of cost claims, and does not compare the costs of controls with the benefits they provide."

✗ Local administration of a project in Albania was so bad that the Commission had to go back in and take control. No one had thought to properly assess whether the local team was up to the task required.

✗ The Committee of the Regions failed to reclaim money from several Members who had fiddled their claims.

✗ There remains a backlog of untaken leave by employees across the institution, which can be swapped for cash. This previously identified liability (which runs into many millions) remains on the books.

✗   MEPs' second pensions continue to be illegal, and remain an unfunded liability.

We've also discovered a little more about one fraud mentioned in the 2003 annual report. It seems that several EU countries have been instructed to recover funds for grants that were given for illegal exports of meat to Iraq in the 1990s. An official investigation appears to be ongoing, but don't hold your breath waiting to see someone in court over it.

You might think all that was bad enough, which it is. But the auditors also report on individual budget lines.

Individual budget lines

There was, for example, a report on how the Commission responded to the Indonesian Tsunami. It revealed that too many charities rocked up and did their own thing, hampering attempts to coordinate. This meant that some communities in Aceh were "overwhelmed with aid while others were neglected". There was too much health assistance in Indonesia, for example, and too many boats in Sri Lanka – so many in fact that the UN warned that local fisheries wouldn't cope. Fishing boats were given but no fishing nets were available. One year on, 67,000 people were still living in tents. One water treatment plant couldn't function for four months due to a lack of chlorine. A million and a half bottles of chlorine, meanwhile, couldn't be distributed because of a lack of transport.

Then there was the special report the Court of Auditors produced to look into pre-accession aid for Bulgaria and Romania. These two countries, you may recall, have since joined the EU. Heaven help the taxpayer. In half of the projects that were looked at, money was being spent only partly or not at all on what it was supposed to be spent on. The report criticised the Commission for its blind over-optimism and for not checking that matched money was actually being stumped up by the locals. The result was inevitable. €1.9 billion was up for grabs.

Software intended to help the Public Prosecutor's Office in Bulgaria was only being used in one of eight places visited. The software was incompatible with the system already in place. Hardly surprising, then, that in one location the investigators found 37 brand new computers locked, unused, in a storeroom. A similar situation occurred in Romania, as the government simply hadn't come up with funds it had promised to make the system work. €400,000 spent on IT for agriculture has similarly been found to be faulty.

And what about the project intended to modernise and develop the tourist infrastructure in Pietra Neamt. The auditors found the place to be an untouristy dump. The money went into a bridge and a 2 mile street for local traffic. The 'tourist' area itself – euphemistically known as The Strand – was discovered to be a part of town the locals liked to hang around in during the summer, whose principal feature was an empty, degraded swimming pool.

Next there was the bridge linking Romania and Moldova over the River Prut, which cost €3.1 million. Unfortunately, it can't be used, as there is no road to it on the Moldovan side. Moreover, border checkpoints were missing on either side.

A hall for international fairs in Romania with a budget of €6.4 million was halted halfway through when the local council withdrew the permit, claiming technical discrepancies.

The fund to invest in Bulgarian privatised companies spent €4.5 million on management costs alone, and blew €4 million backing a company that went bust.

Money spent on building an asylum centre in Romania was discovered to have gone towards a building that was running at an 8% occupancy rate, and only reached that meagre level because people were shipped in from elsewhere in the country. The auditors found out that there had never been any asylum applications along the Eastern border at all. This left two floors of the building empty and supplies still in the packets.

The Bulgarian border police were obliged to buy a westernised vehicle, three times the price of the standard Russian model, and which has no local dealers when bits go wrong. EU rules prevented local companies getting the contract. Border patrol police also had to send back half of their night vision goggles because they didn't work.

Their Romanian counterparts had to buy 43 vehicles of a particular make. But these were out of service for a third of the time because they had to be serviced abroad. Two of the river patrol boats could not be used during the winter, despite this being a key part of the specification.

In comparison, the MEDA report on Euro-Mediterranean cooperation is a model of correct simplicity. It revealed that in Egypt, small local contractors had problems complying with the paperwork to apply for tenders because they were all in English. The requirement that all supplies had to be European or Mediterranean in origin also caused difficulties, especially with computer and electronic equipment.

Environmental concerns

What one might charitably call blips are a recurring feature of the audit report on environmental policy, an area which was supposed to be central to planning in delivering third world aid. A consultancy firm was contracted for a year in 1998 to come up with a manual, which it delivered only in 2001. However, it was so long and shoddy it was treated as a draft and locked away. Another consultancy firm was brought in to rewrite it in 2004, but 18 months later the text still hadn't been completed. Staff training was also dropped when it was made voluntary and only half the planned number of people turned up. Reports from consultants brought in to assess projects were just filed away.

Out of twenty developing countries that had received general budget support by 2005, for only one had the planners thought of including measures to support the environment as per the original plan. The Commission's Regional Delegation in Nicaragua, covering six countries and employing 140 staff, were found neither to use environmental guidelines nor even to have an environmental expert. In Tanzania, an €85 million road building project plan had one page on environmental impact. In Botswana, there was none on a €30 million plan for a copper and nickel mine with a shaky dam and a smelter that belched out sulphur dioxide. In Guatemala, no impact assessment was carried out on a major refugee resettlement programme. A Kiribati seaweed project failed to spot that wooden posts would be cut from crucial mangrove swamps and that protected turtles would be killed by the seaweed farmers.

In some cases, suggestions were made but never implemented, such as a project to replace a pipeline in Mauritius where no checks were made to see that promised measures were actually taken, the replanting of trees and monitoring of water pollution in a Mali rice programme, and ensuring that a Fijian bridge didn't pollute the water of a nearby fishery.

Fraud was found by the Commission in four projects in Brazil, Guatemala and Morocco. In three cases, projects were delayed so long that the original reason for undertaking them was no longer valid. In many others, projects were put together without involving the local community. In one subsidised nature reserve, locals turned to poachers when promised tourism failed to materialise because the gorillas were nervous and hid, and the news channels were full of stories of ebola. Disastrously, in Brazil measures to limit deforestation seem to have actually accelerated it, as the plans clearly identified areas which weren't to be protected.

The auditors' reports for the latest European Development Funds shows that there are concerns across many of the funds. It appears that there is a special provision under international accountancy law, IPSAS 19, that the Court has decided is rather appropriate. This covers what are euphemistically called 'doubtful debts', and allows the auditors to take for granted that for every year of an outstanding debt, the chances are 20% that it won't be repaid. It also allows them to look at a debt and just laugh at the reality of it being refunded. It looks like €6.4 million has been written off this way. But then, the IT system couldn't provide a full audit trail.

The auditors took the same view on an account in the Congo. Here at least, the taxpayer would witness a happier story. €2.75 million was sitting in a bank account in a country in which the Commission had no presence, in an account whose paper trail had simply vanished. But the bank account was found again. So at least this part of €15.5 million of doubtful debts might be redeemed.

The audit of the auditors' department itself reveals that they gave themselves an extra €4 million in employee benefits. Bearing in mind that staff didn't take leave due, worth €1.6 million, this might perhaps be understandable. Rather than bottle up the stress, open up a bottle for the stress. Still, it seems a lot even for a group that we would otherwise hold as unsung heroes.

Profligate EU agencies

The baffling array of EU agencies has also come under the auditors' scrutiny. Among the revelations:

- The European Aviation Safety Agency suffered from a lack of internal audit and a failure to use open competition, for instance simply awarding one contract worth €86,000 "by direct agreement and without justification", and another of a quarter of a million by straight barter.

- The European Medicines Agency deviated from best practice in awarding IT contracts and played fast and loose with the rules on evaluation committees.

- The European Agency for Reconstruction did not show a real control of its spending in Kosovo.

- The European Agency for Health and Safety at Work was signing off for public procurement expenditure without any supporting evidence on the quality of the bids, and without all the committee members' signatures.

- The European Maritime Agency had files covering payments and commitments which were often "incomplete or confused".

- The European Food Safety Authority was found to have key documents missing, and to have paid out for unjustified mission expenses of staff. It also seems to have failed to check that new employees weren't faking their own certificates, and was forking out €3.5 million a year for temporary accommodation because the move into its own buildings had been botched.

- The European Centre for Disease Prevention and Control had seen all its payments handed over without due authorisation.

- The European Centre for the Development of Vocational Training (CEDEFOP) had dodgy accounting software, ran 17 websites in a costly and higgledy-piggledy manner, and handed out allowances that weren't covered by the regulations. Two contracts worth a half million Euros broke competition rules. It was also discovered to have used inappropriate criteria in its recruitment, a graduate of philosophy, with barely enough professional experience for the job, being placed in a management position – somewhat embarassing given that its *raison d'être* is to promote vocational training.

- Eurojust has a badly drawn-up list of assets which means that no one can say where some of them are. This, to remind you, is the body that is meant to coordinate the fight against organised crime.

- The European Training Foundation's books had two items representing 10% of the budget missing from them.

- The European Foundation for the Improvement of Living and Working Conditions spent money on projects that were not quantifiably linked with its mission statement.

- The European Monitoring Centre for Drugs and Drug Addiction appeared to lack an inventory of its assets, and used questionable recruitment practices, such as recruiting someone who did not get the best assessment in the selection procedure. Furthermore, in the auditors' words:

"At the end of 2004, a member of staff was sent on a long-term (two year) mission to Brussels. It has not been possible to ascertain the purpose of this mission, which had cost around 70,000 euro (in pay and allowances) by the end of 2005, and the person concerned did not have a heavy workload. When the mission was terminated, he was seconded to the Commission, yet the Centre continued to pay his salary."

Procurement contracts also were found to have serious flaws, like bids accepted before the start date and a clear underestimation of contract value that seems to have favoured one tenderer.

- The European Monitoring Centre on Racism and Xenophobia was found to have staff on recruitment panels selecting people who would be senior to them.

- The Community Plant Variety Office did not have a computer system that could handle the different account audits reliably.

- The Office for Harmonisation in the Internal Market had several hundred payments that had been signed for and signed off by one and the same employee. It also had unusual recruitment procedures, such as advertising for one post and recruiting two people, and some questionable contract awards.

Add to this a special report on rural development agencies, which found money being spent on areas "which are not predominantly rural", and with projects so designed that it was impossible to work out whether they were effective. Given that this covers a six year set of projects worth €24 billion, this is quite a concern.

Deadweight projects

What particularly struck us was the report's findings on "deadweight", which is funding to provide aid for projects that would have gone ahead and been self-funded anyway. One example the auditors found was that of two Italian farmers who quite happily told their visitors that they would have carried out the farm improvements anyway, and had in fact expanded on the EU-funded project using their own money. In one case, the farmer increased the scale of the project by a factor of five from his own bank account.

There were also some dubious investments. In Brandenburg, a 100" steel viewing tower has been built to provide scenic views over the Seftenberger See. The auditors liked the views, but didn't appreciate the fact that it made no difference to tourist figures. That was €380,000 spent with no discernible benefit.

Then there is the special report on support for fruit and vegetable growers. This found recipients ticking every box available in order to claim grants, or simply picking a funding line at random to justify buying a forklift truck. Mind you, you have to feel some pity for the farmer in his efforts to manipulate the paperwork. One irrigation project in Italy was funded in order to "improve quality", then in 1999 continued as "concentration of supply", and by 2002 was receiving money for "reducing cost". No doubt poor Luigi was trying to find a box for "delivering water".

Farmers seeking grants to buy pallet boxes faced the same challenge when giving reasons for their application. Some said the pallet boxes would "stabilise producer prizes" because a box of fruit is easier to sell in bulk; others reasons that the boxes would "increase product quality" no doubt because the fruit wouldn't get trodden on, "boost the product's commercial value" because it wouldn't get bruised, "reduce production costs" because farm labourers wouldn't have to chase rolling fruit, "improve environmental practices" because the lost veg wouldn't spoil, and "reduce withdrawals" because it helped management. All this, to convince conniving bureaucrats that they should spend money on projects that the auditors found to have negligible long-term development benefit, like vehicles, crates and salaries of existing staff.

It turns out that only the UK set targets for farmers that could be measured. Our civil servants apparently just never bother to measure them. They know a bureaucratic trap when they see one.

The long and the short of this system was that money got misspent. A €3 million programme in Spain was supposed to go to things like greenhouses and irrigation. But 98% was spent on cardboard boxes.

Perhaps something got lost in translation. There's no excuse for that, though...

Serving Babel

The Commission spent around €106 million in 2003 on interpreter services, and the European Parliament another €57 million. This was, mark you, before the recent round of expansions. It's not even as if the translation services on offer were well used: auditors found that permanent translators were spending on average 33 days on 'implicit stand-by duty' – i.e. physically present at the building but not actually needed for anything. A high proportion of these days – 130 interpreters a day, or a quarter of the staff interpreters – occur in the slow month of August. As a result, about 15,000 interpreter days, corresponding to about 15% of the workforce's working days, weren't used. Even the temporary staff, or ACIs, were sitting around unused for a total of 6,000 days. Since each day costs an average of €865, that meant a waste of €18 million on having interpreters drinking espressos. 6,300 half-days were lost when interpreters were booked but not told in time by MEPs or officials that they weren't needed – about 8% of total interpreter use, or €6 million in costs at the European Parliament alone.

Other findings

In another assessment we discovered how the Commission miscalculated the asset value of its buildings by €188 million, the total lease liabilities by €254 million, and the accumulated depreciation value by €23 million. With accounting sloppiness of this order, is it any wonder that the system has its problems?

The same report also details hidden liabilities. As at the close of 2004, the EU's pensions liabilities were estimated at an astounding €26 billion. That is a massive future burden that simply hasn't been prepared for. There are serious questions about their legality, and who is financially liable in future years.

That €26 billion (a figure already now massively out of date) was up €3 billion on the previous year. It was the estimate for 14,000 then-current pensions and all the pensions of the existing employees. It didn't include pensions liabilities for the influx of new staff from Eastern Europe.

But there is no real excuse for the sort of things we find emerging from another report on the Structural Funds. A discrepancy, for instance, in the bookkeeping for two countries comes to €11.5 billion. The UK's by comparison is a mere €842 million, or 18% gaffe. Management systems were deemed to be adequate in just under half of the eligible states. A high level of deadweight was deemed likely to have occurred. You can sense the palpable frustration of the auditors as they find that the money trail makes absolutely no sense at all.

Contrast this litany of incompetence, fraud and irresponsibility with another international institution. COSAC is the committee that brings together MPs from the national parliaments. It doesn't have a proper budget, as it's not an EU institution as such. It doesn't even have legal personality. It meets only four times a year, hosted by the parliament of the country that holds the EU Presidency, while its secretariat is made up of staff briefly on loan from those parliaments. So the opportunities for fraud are basically non-existent, its participants are directly elected on a national level, and its staff have got day jobs. It's also the nearest thing the system has got to a real connection with the public and democratic accountability, which is why it will never get given any real power.

Whistleblowers

It takes a special type of person to become a Brussels whistleblower. For starters, the pay and benefits packet for those who stay silent is superb, and no-one wants to throw away the trappings. More significantly, the type of person who is attracted to the bureaucratic environment in the first place tends to be something of a fellow traveller, someone who shares to some degree in the European dream and ideal. To speak out publicly against what is happening in the institution is seen as being synonymous with criticism of the project itself.

That's why we would like to pay due tribute to the handful of people who have tried to fix bust systems in the EU, but who were stonewalled, and were driven against their will to try to end fraud and corruption by the only means at their disposal – going public.

The Brussels machinery is not like the mechanisms of governance in governments and even local councils. It is skewed to suppress. That's why an entire Commission was sacked by MEPs. That's why Neil Kinnock pledged when he was a Commissioner that he would undertake radical root and branch reform. And that's why he basically failed, and the key faults in the system persist to this day.

It might help if the EU workforce weren't almost encouraged to bend rules. Take the following example. This is how staff are instructed to claim for expenses by the European Parliament Selection Office.

Procedure for reclaiming expenses

1. Ask your department to issue you with a mission order, using the MISS system and entering code 874; sign it and attach a copy of the notice of the meeting to it.

2. Have your mission order approved by your direct superior in accordance with the practice followed in your Directorate-General.

3. At least three days before this mission, fax the mission order and a copy of the invitation to attend to:

EPSO – Mr ▮▮▮▮▮▮
C80 Building, Room 4/27
B-1049 BRUSSELS
Fax: 0032 ▮▮▮▮▮ (tel: 0032 2 ▮▮▮▮▮)

4. You will receive an EPSO mission order by fax. Sign it, have it approved by your direct superior and fax it back to Mr ███████.

5. If you need to purchase a ticket for the mission, you can obtain this as follows:

   - For officials or other staff working in Luxembourg, from CWT's Luxembourg Agency in the Jean Monnet Building, ground floor, Room ███████ (tel.: ███████) on the basis of a copy of the EPSO mission order.

   - For staff in Brussels, Mr ███████ will make the necessary reservations (███████@ec.europa.eu); alternatively CWT's Brussels Agency, rue Joseph 11 79 (tel.: ███████) will be able to make reservations;

   - In emergencies you are authorised, exceptionally, to purchase tickets directly, in which case you must pay for them directly (by cash or credit card) and submit them for reimbursement.

6. Where the statement of mission expenses is concerned, you should send Mr ███████ confirmation that the mission has taken place as detailed in the mission order, and notify him of any change. Accordingly, you should complete the second part of the European Parliament mission order, sign it (your direct superior soes not need to sign it) and send it to Mr ███████ through the internal mail, together with the supporting documents (originals of the ticket and hotel bill). You are strongly advised to retain copies of all documents.

7. You will receive the final EPSO settlement statement from Mr ███████ by fax. You must sign to indicate your agreement and fax back to Mr ███████.

8. The Commission's PMO Office (Brussels or Luxembourg, depending on where you work) will settle your mission expenses as soon as possible.

9. Following the reimbursement of mission expenses by EPSO you are entitled to request supplementary reimbursement from the Missions Unit (KAD 03███). To do so, you must summit the mission declaration form generated by the MISS program (code 874) to the Head of the Competitions and Selection Procedures Unit (KAD 03███) for signature; this must be accompanied by the

> declaration made following the mission using the EPSO form, together with the settlement statement from the PMO Office, as supporting documents. The Competitions Unit will forward the full file to the Missions Unit.

No wonder the EU picks the brightest to work for it, if they have to spend all day deciphering that gibberish. You will further note the text refers to a credit card. This is because officials who regularly go on business trips are given a Mastercard. As the in-house reminder informs staff, "This card is totally free and may also be used for private purposes."

No annual charge is paid; cash withdrawals outside of the EU are paid for by the European Parliament; and there is accompanying Travel Accident Insurance of up to €260,000 on tickets paid with the card.

The card limit is a mere €5,000 a month, but reassuringly those limits can be reviewed.

If that wasn't enough of an incentive to put your private bills on the European slate, the memo staggeringly underlines: "As the MasterCard Corporate card may also be used for private purposes, the EU Parliament is of course never allowed to have a look at all card transactions being made."

So buy the Bollinger at once, and we'll never know. Or, as one European Parliament official privately acknowledged to us, "I always wondered how I could afford that extension on my house in Uccle".

The overall scale of the fraud is mind-boggling. In 2005, the EU's own anti-fraud unit (which has itself been heavily criticised) indicated that there were 12,000 reported cases of "irregularities", involving over €1 billion in grants. Only 5 of the 511 cases the unit was actively pursuing in 2004 involved whistleblowers. But that belies their importance in revealing institutionalised cover-up.

So what examples of fraud and waste have been revealed by these unsung heroes? Well, they range from revelations about key personnel breaking the treaty rules to get deals done, through petty larceny, to mafia-related fraud. Here are some recent revelations, modified only to hide their sources:

- An official was accused by his boss of committing a crime in saying that fraud is rife within one of the institutions.

- One woman employee allegedly received invalidity benefit after spending time regularly asleep on her office floor, though was fit enough to work on an election campaign team.

- An employee got caught stealing. He then had a seizure and was kept on the books.

- A staff member decided "to start acting like the majority of fonctionnaires" by coming in late, leaving early and taking long lunches, because his salary was reduced when he was found to be overpaid.

- One of the institutions uses a temping agency which is reportedly run by the daughter of the head of the typing pool.

- An ex-boyfriend of an employee is said to be regularly flown in to be employed as a permanent member of staff in his own right. One official was overheard complaining that the regular staff never get sent to Strasbourg because of all the fake officials working there. So he and others just hang around cafés back in Brussels and Luxembourg.

- There are reports of individuals being ostracised for refusing to sign off doctored accounts.

- Instances of petty fraud in the offices of the most senior personnel are rife.

- Car rental procedures are routinely abused.

- Staff pull 'sickies' by regularly using up the full regulation 16 days uncertified sick leave allowed every year.

- Building contracts have been awarded to the husband of someone working in the team of a very senior official.

- Senior staff have planted false allegations about whistleblowers' private lives in the press in order to discredit them.

- Where a whistleblower has been identified, management has failed to use the correct disciplinary procedure.

- Hard evidence of fraud handed over by whistleblowers has been suppressed, and incriminating evidence has mysteriously "gone missing" or been stolen.

- A senior official took a job transfer and bought a house, but then was given his old job back with a pay hike – which he took while still collecting an allowance for accommodation in the house he was now renting out.

But this is just the tip of the iceberg. The Commission, for instance, has been accused of trying to get troublesome staff declared mentally ill in order to provide a pretext for their removal. Typically, cruddy or dodgy staff are said to be bought off by expensive early-retirement packages. But at least three cases have emerged of an attempt to get rid of a potential fraud critic this way, and we ourselves have come across a similar instance.

> "They fail because they are isolated. Few people can afford to have their lives closely scrutinised. Few people can risk losing their job and an adequate income to feed the family. Few people have nerves that are strong enough to withstand the constant battering by those who believe that the best form of defence is attack and these people usually work as a team against a solitary soul."

But whistleblowing in Brussels is not about causing problems for bosses. It's about breaking free of attempts to cover up. And it's about coming up with solutions.

The Dr Bunsen Honeydew Award for Complex Science 2007

The TPA is delighted to be able to award a bag of gobstoppers to the EU bean counters for a truly mind-bending piece of official literature.

Calculation of the uniform call rate for VAT own resources
Article 2(4) of Decision 2000/597/EC, Euratom):

Uniform rate (%) = maximum call rate - frozen rate

A, The maximum call rate is set at 0.50 % for 2006,

B. Determination of the rate frozen by the correction of budgetary imbalances granted to the United Kingdom (Article 2 (4) (b) of Decision 2000/597/EC, Euratom):

(1) calculation of the theoretical share of the countries with a restricted financial burden:

In accordance with Article 5(1) 01 Decision 2000{597jEC, Euratom, thc financial contribution of Germany (DE), the Netherlands (NL), Austria (AT) and Sweden (SE) is restricted to a quarter of their normal contribution

Formula for a country with a restricted financial burden, e.g. Germany:

Germany's theoretical VAT contribution = [Germany's capped VAT base / (EU capped VAT base - UK capped VAT base)] x _ x United Kingdom correction

Example *Germany*

Germany's theoretical VAT contribution = 9 768 554 000 / (51 058 678 000 – 9 373 896 000) x _ x 4 838 879 797 = 283 489 899

(2) calculation of the frozen rate:

Frozen rate = [UK correction - theoretical VAT contributions (D + NL + A + S)] / [EU capped VAT base - capped VAT base (UK + D +NL+A +S)]

Frozen rate = 4 838 879 797 - (283 489 899) + 72 011 957 + 31 891 153 + 36 976 995)] / [51 058 678 000 - (9 373 896 000 + 9 768 554 000 + 2 481 403 000 + 1 098 912 000 + 1 274 161 000)]

Frozen rate = 0,163127272501441 %

Uniform rate: 0,5% - 0,163127272501441% = 0,336872727498559 %

We hope this instils in you a greater appreciation of the trials your average auditor goes through. Oh, and by the way, we found a mistake in the formula. Lunch with the authors for the first reader to spot it.

"The avoidance of taxes is the only intellectual pursuit that carries any reward."

Mark Twain

SECTION 6

Taxes Past and Future

Words are fascinating things, with a history of their own. Did you know, for instance, that the word 'toilet' comes from the French word for a piece of cloth that was used in the shaving process, which by euphemism came to refer to the room and the throne itself?

> *"This tax was so extremely oppressive, either in itself or in the mode of collecting it that, whilst the revenue was increased by extortion, it was diminished by despair."*
>
> Edward Gibbon, Decline and Fall of the Roman Empire

The word 'salary' comes from the Latin *salarium*, which is connected to the Latin word for salt. The arguments over the exact source for this drive etymologists into drunken bar room brawls. Some believe it was because in olden times soldiers got paid in the briney stuff. Other linguists consider this heresy, and club them with the snooker cue, because they hold that the salary was pay for those who guarded the *via salaria*, the salt road on which Rome rather handily sat.

Taxation, on the other hand, is agreed to come from the Latin *tangere*, to touch. These days, however, it should be called carpeting, from *carpere*, to pluck or snatch. Taxes are as old as your income. On the next two pages is an historical overview.

AD 50   Romans subdue the Frisians (modern Northern Netherlands). In return for autonomy, the proto-cloggies supply a tax in hides and tough mercenaries.

500 onwards – Frankish monarchs exact a Nature Tax – on land, water, air and old Roman roads. Public amenities without the upkeep costs.

1215   Magna Carta requires that fish traps, a lucrative monopoly but a hindrance to river trade, are restricted.

1275   Edward I imposes an export tax on wool. Hence Baa Baa Black Sheep.

1286   First appearance in France of the *gabelle*. Not only was it a state monopoly, but the tax varied on where the salt was extracted, and people were forced to buy a regular amount. Smugglers were condemned to the galleys. Ironic, really, because then they'd be surrounded by the stuff.

c. 1380s   The devshirmeh. Christian youths begin to be seized as human taxation, converted by the Ottomans, and trained as bodyguards to the Sultan. Recalcitrants are strung up from their lintel. So Customs and Excise has improved after all.

1476   Russians end payment of tribute to the Golden Horde, a Stop-the-Mongols-Pillaging-You tax.

1543   Spanish explorers arrive at the Micronesian island of Yap. They find 12' large stone wheels, so heavy that they are traded like modern bullion, with ownership travelling rather than the rockery. The Spanish tax men are disgusted at this ballast and sail off.

1568   Spanish arrive at the Solomons. The Malaita islanders use money made out of shells; in Santa Cruz they use red feathers. The sorely disappointed Spanish tax men strike out again, and the islands are forgotten for two centuries.

1628   Charles I first stamps playing cards (an early form of gambling tax). The Ace of Spades remains marked until the tax is abolished in 1960.

1662 The continental Hearth Tax, aka Chimney Money, is introduced onto England's fireplaces to help pay for the expenses of the Court, what with all that Restoration comedy, frills, stitchwork, and floppy hats.

1696 William III introduces the Window Tax to pay for wars. It affects buildings with more than six windows. George and Zippy from *Rainbow* are therefore exempt.

1795 British tax wig powder introduced at one guinea a year. The powder, and the wigs, go out of fashion. In France, the guillotine had done the same.

c. 1818 Baron Karl von Drais invents the Velocipede, a boneshaker bicycle, to collect rents from his tenants. A success for private enterprise.

1850s High taxes on mutton, pork and fuel (which hit the poorest worse) are scrapped by Johan Thorbecke in the Netherlands as revenue grows from the East Indies trade.

1852 Soap Tax abolished in England and France. The soap industry flourishes, and hygiene takes a giant leap forward.

1937 The state of Maine introduces a Potato Tax, which is used to support the blueberry industry. But then, so is its Blueberry Tax (established 1945).

c. 1992 Turkmenistan introduces a Carpet Tax. Apply at the Carpet Museum at Central Ashgabat for the export permit. Note, it'll probably be closed on National Carpet Day (last Sunday of May).

2005 Milton Keynes introduces an informal Roof Tax on developers that could rake in £18,000 per new home built. You get your new school a couple of years early but the housing market goes even further through the roof, excuse the pun.

The Flat Tax

No, this is not an impost on Norfolk.

The concept of a flat tax is quite straightforward. Indeed, it's because it's straightforward that a number of people don't like it.

In a nutshell, it means having an extremely simple taxation rate. This leads to a higher overall tax take as people who can afford to pay have both less reason and no mechanism for dodging taxes through avoidance schemes.

Some critics say that a major disadvantage of a simple tax system is that it does not allow governments to use tax for social engineering. It's claimed that simplifying taxes means the government can't, for instance, encourage healthy eating over unhealthy eating, marriage over single parent lifestyles, or environmental fuel over fossil fuels, by using tax incentives and penalties.

Regardless of the pros and cons, we disagree with this analysis. If you have a straightforward system of tax revenue, any targeted taxes that follow will command greater public support (if they are just) and people will be more aware of the fact that they are paying them. It's also, crucially, a massive incentive for politicians to get their targeted taxes right. On the environmental example, look at the tax rate on bio-diesel as it stands under the current system in many countries. It's treated pretty much like a fossil fuel, and you might as well buy sunflower oil from the supermarket, paying the lower tax rate for food.

Other critics say that the British tax code is too "mature" for it to be replaced by such a basic system. By that they mean one of two things. Either, they fear they will lose their jobs as a civil servant or accountant. Or, they have some unnatural attachment to a system which they have spent the best part of thirty years trying to grapple with and on their death bed don't want to look back on their lives with regret. Of course the tax system in the UK is mature. So is dodgy cheese. What they mean is "complicated", or "too hard to reform so let's not bother".

One or two critics also espouse the lazy notion that a flat tax system is immoral because the same rate is applied to everyone in society. That it is not "progressive". This ignores two key details. Firstly, even with a flat tax system you can have tax exemption for the poor (a 'flat tax plus' system); and secondly, the richer may pay the same rate, but they obviously pay more of it. As there is less incentive to hide their wealth offshore, the nation's tax take benefits, so the poorer in society are better off over the long term from the increased state revenue being directed at them.

Having a simpler tax system also means having smaller government, and less time wasted by businesses and families when they fill out a postcard-sized form instead of the current paper pile.

We support a simpler tax system. We also support having an open and frank debate about adopting a flat tax system in the UK. It seems that politicians are running scared of yet another subject that they have allowed to become taboo because of a small number of vocal critics.

Strangely, it is the post-Communist states of Eastern Europe that have seized the initiative. Politicians there realised that their countries' dire economic situation called for a total overhaul and went to work. As a result, Western European leaders are now beginning to see real evidence of what is possible.

Here's what Mart Laar has to say. Mr Laar was Prime Minister of Estonia after that country's independence, and after the fall of Communism introduced a flat tax system there, so he should know.

Flat Tax – It works!

by Mart Laar, MEP

Freedom of people is connected with fair taxes. The progressive income tax system used in most countries of the world today is not fair. The idea behind such a system is simple: the more you earn, the more you have to pay in taxes. Such an attitude however brings down the motivation of the people to work more and plan for their own future. It makes them rely more heavily on the public welfare system.

Although this is known all over the world, there are not many countries which have been able to take any real steps towards the re-introduction of proportional income tax - progressive income tax was namely actually first introduced only in the 19th century. In their "Communist Manifesto", first published in 1848, Karl Marx and Friedrich Engels demanded "a heavy progressive or graduated income tax". For the founders of Marxism, progressive taxation was so important that in their demands it was listed as second in importance only after the "abolition of property in land". While the destructive nature of the first demand is largely recognized, the next main pillar of Marxist thinking is still used in most Western countries. In the long run, the results of this can be very destructive too. It takes from human beings one of his most valuable abilities: to make his own decisions, use his talents, to be creative and innovative; his human dignity is strongly endangered.

This is a reason why many scholars such as Milton Friedman have advocated flat rate proportional income tax. But for a long time the only country which really introduced it was Hong Kong, which in 1947 introduced a proportional 15% personal income tax. This has been highly succesful and supported Hong Kong's fast development. After the collapse of the Soviet Union, nations in Central and Eastern Europe had to find ways to get out of post-communist chaos and build up modern societies and economies. Some of them tried to move immediately to the Western Welfare State and failed. Others tried to learn from the German economic "miracle" after World War II and other similar "miracles", and introduced radical market orientated reforms. Among the latter was a small country called Estonia.

On 8th December 1993, the Estonian ruling coalition - overcoming massive protests from "economic experts" and left-wing populist parties - pressed through in the Estonian Parliament a reform of personal income tax on a flat 26% level. The impacts of reform were very positive. After the decrease in the level of taxation, budget revenues did not fall but increased significantly. Very fast was the growth in personal income tax, where revenues actually doubled with two years. The introduction of a flat rate proportional income tax helped to boost economic activity and create new working places, helping Estonia to avoid massive unemployment. The success of Estonian tax reform encouraged Estonian neighbours to follow its example. In 1995 Latvia introduced a flat rate personal income tax, and in 1996 Lithuania followed.

But comparing the growth rate of economies in Central Eastern Europe with a flat rate personal income tax, with growth rates of same-region economies with progressive income taxation, we can see that countries with a flat rate grow significantly faster.

Percentile increases of economy by economic model

Year	Flat rate countries	Progressive rate countries
1995	4.3	3.0
1996	4.0	0.3
1997	8.0	1.4
1998	4.1	3.3

The difference in growth rates has become even bigger at the beginning of the new millennium. When we compare how fast Central and Eastern European countries are growing and getting nearer to the European average GDP per capita level in Purchasing Power Parity, then we see that countries with a flat tax have done two times faster as countries without a flat tax. The same is true on revenues. Countries with a flat tax are not producing the sort of budgets with deficits as we see in progressively-taxed Central and Eastern European (CEE) countries. It is often declared that flat taxes create social inequality and are not socially fair. This is not true. After the introduction of the flat tax, the GINI index has not grown, but fallen; social inequality and poverty have decreased in all flat tax countries.

The success of Baltic tax reforms encouraged Russia to start their own tax reform. On 1 January 2001, a 13% flat rate tax on personal income took effect in Russia. Russia's flat tax has been remarkably successful. In the three years since the top rate of personal income tax was reduced from 30% to 13%, real flat tax revenue has risen by 79.7%. Russia's budget is relatively healthy. Tax compliance has improved, so that actually for first time in the history of Russia people are really paying taxes.

Russian reform encouraged other countries to move to flat rate personal income tax. In 2003 Serbia introduced something similar to it and from 2004 Ukraine moved to the flat rate 13% personal income tax. In all those countries flat rate taxes have stimulated faster growth and more revenues. The lowest flat tax – on 12% – in the World was in 2004 introduced in Georgia, helping it to get out from its disastrous situation. As in other countries, economical growth has gone up and the budget rose fivefold within three years.

The most challenging tax reform in Europe was from 1st January 2004 introduced in Slovakia where VAT, corporate income tax and personal income tax were all moved to a flat rate 19% level. The results of reform were impressive – more money was gathered from income tax to the budget as planned and economical activity has sped up. From 1st January 2005 Romania has introduced the flat rate tax – and it is a great success there. There is now evidence from 12 countries what happens after flat tax is introduced. In some countries the flat tax will soon have been working more than ten years. And this evidence shows that the results of flat tax are everywhere the same: more growth and more revenues to the budget and less social inequality.

As a result of these examples more and more countries are planning to introduce the flat rate personal income tax. The latest country to do this is Macedonia. It is possible to predict that with five years all Central and Eastern Europe will move to a flat rate personal income tax – because flat tax works.

The Taxpayers' Axioms

1. It's not the government's money – it's *your* money.

2. Big government projects always take longer, and cost more, than anticipated.

3. Throwing money at a problem is rarely the solution.

4. It is possible to cut taxes and improve services at the same time.

5. If it isn't broke, the civil service will try to mend it.

6. Less regulation means lower costs for businesses and more jobs.

7. Managers should manage. Government shouldn't waste money on armies of consultants.

8. An ambulance-chasing legal system is a threat to good government.

9. An obsession with lists, targets and quotas distorts priorities and diverts resources away from those who need them.

10. Small gaffes and political correctness add up.

11. The bigger the system gets, the more money it soaks up.

12. Lower taxation creates wealth, which creates more tax revenue, which better supports the needy over the longer term. High taxation does the opposite.

The Tax on Death

The TaxPayers' Alliance continues to speak out against the most immoral tax around. Inheritance tax is, quite frankly, designed so that the state can grab your money before you manage to pass on the family silver. Except, of course, that it works so that the bill arrives at a stressful moment, and after the will has been read.

There was a time when it applied to relatively few families. It ruined them. That's why so many great estates fell into rack and ruin. Large chunks of the inheritance had to be handed over to the taxman when the head of the family died. It even became a tool for vengeful class warfare. The bills became absolutely preposterous during the World Wars, when families who had lost several family members in the service of the realm were ruined by a greedy Exchequer.

Nothing new there. Admiral Nelson's heirs were awarded an annual grant by a grateful Parliament in perpetuity. Until, that is, 150 years later when some MPs caught sight of it on the books and swiped it back. Gratitude has little memory, especially amongst your political enemies.

That was then, this is now. Where once the few were mugged, now the many are. With the explosion in house prices, millions are being caught in the inheritance trap. The market value of a home is pushing the inheritance value over the limit, meaning that thousands of people every year are being forced to sell off family homes simply to pay the taxman.

People who scrimp and save throughout their lives are being denied the opportunity to help provide their family with security, at a time when it is frankly impossible for many people to buy their own home. The Treasury might as well send round some thugs with condolence cards to press gang your possessions.

At least one newspaper has picked up on this. We support the *Daily Express's* campaign to end this wretched tax.

Conclusion: Gold in the Balance

We started off this book by welcoming you as a fellow traveller to the fabled El Dorado of public spending. By now, you might have figured out why. It transpires that not all of the people running the public sector have their terrestrial passport properly stamped.

Or perhaps we're not giving due credit. The mere fact that money is being thrown around seems to be enough for some people. So long as the money is going to the right people.

Some critics are quick to point out that of 105 hospitals threatened with closure in England, only 18 are in constituencies which have Labour MPs. That of the 123 hospitals being built, 83 are in areas represented by the Labour party. That twice as much lottery funding is going towards the constituencies of the Cabinet than those of the Shadow Cabinet, and that of 23 railway stations that are closing, 20 of them are in seats held by opposition parties.

This may be unduly unfair. Bring your stool to the fireside and prepare for an anecdote. Students of Canadian history will recall that for the better part of two decades, Quebec was run by Maurice Duplessis and his party, the Union Nationale. He won elections quite simply. He practised favouritism. Quite apart from his appetite for the good life (he had his own province-funded private plane), he ruthlessly exploited constituency concerns and needs. You could tell instantly when you crossed from a constituency held by his party to one held by the Opposition by the fact that myriads of potholes started appearing in the roads. Opposition politicians would wander the streets canvassing, to be told by the voters, "We're Liberal party through and through, but just this once we're voting Duplessis in order to get our new school".

So let's put it all into perspective. We are still, thank goodness, a long way from that scenario. No doubt government ministers will claim that they represent rundown inner city areas as opposed to rural expanses. Well, that is true. But poverty and social needs are not confined to a few square miles bearing a government rosette. As we pointed out in last year's *Bumper Book*, the choice of some of the constituencies chosen for road building projects over the last few years is a mite suspicious.

Let's be charitable and assume incompetence is the cause. The fact that departments keep getting caught wasting so much of our money may go some way to explaining why they employ so many spin doctors – estimated to cost us £300 million a year, three times as much as a decade ago. Whitehall and its offshoots are calculated to employ 3,200 staff in 'information management', selling ministries and their quangos.

The exact figure was only revealed when a copy of their telephone directory was released, and was found to run to 200 pages. The Ministry of Defence tops the league with 229 spin doctors (or the equivalent of two companies of soldiers), the Department for Work & Pensions has 181, the Home Office has 145, the Department of Health has 117, and DEFRA has 107 press officers. Then there are the quangos. The Health & Safety Executive has 58, HM Revenue & Customs 51, UK Trade & Investment 39, and Foods Standards Agency 38.

Government does, of course, need press officers in order to answer questions from journalists and act as middlemen for busy ministers, but the increase in numbers suggests that the priority is on selling an image rather than making information available. And when you think that the Home Office reportedly employs nearly 150 media handlers, and then you consider all the press disasters this department gets itself into, it looks like the taxpayer isn't getting value for money either.

The buck doesn't stop with money from ministries. When the National Lottery Fund was set up, it was designed to generate money for good causes through a sort of 'voluntary contribution by people who felt lucky'. In return for a person gambling, the state took most of the profits and handed them over to worthy campaigns and voluntary organisations. These were recipients which the taxpayer did not, in many cases, enjoy throwing billions of pounds at, but which were deemed to better society as a whole.

These were sports, arts, heritage, and celebration of the third millennium.

Unfortunately, in 1998 that cause was slightly sullied. Government decided to add a fifth cause of "health, education and the environment". In other words, it began to siphon off these funds in order to bolster its own spending plans.

37,000 grants have gone into this new bracket. As at September 2006, the balance of the fund was running at £477 million, as against £531 million of commitments, making it £54 million overcommitted. This is a clear pointer of Lottery priorities. So too is the reported shift towards political correctness in the funding.

It is perhaps not surprising that people need to continue to be sold the merits of where their money is heading. The National Lottery Promotions Unit has cost the Lottery distributors and license holder £9.4 million since it was established in 2003 to keep ticket sales going.

> *"Collecting more taxes than is absolutely necessary is legalized robbery."*
> Calvin Coolidge

There is waste and loss everywhere. The range varies massively. At the modest end of the scale, the House of Commons supplies newspapers for its denizens in designated reading areas, which have in some locations been unceremoniously swiped by selfish staff and MPs by lunchtime, at a cost to taxpayers of several hundred pounds a year. At the other end of the scale, Parliament's new Portcullis House building cost £235 million, a quarter more than planned.

Less well known, however, is that the link bridge between the new and the old Parliamentary estates on Whitehall is a ramshackle affair that has lots of small gaps that are open to the elements. Staff can thus be treated to the bizarre experience of walking down an enclosed link bridge and strolling through a flurry of snowflakes without even leaving the building.

Portcullis is also the location for a catering area. The chairs here kept suffering from "structural failure" and had to be replaced once under guarantee. But then the warranty ran out, so they have now been sent off for public auction and new ones brought in, at a cost of £57,800 plus VAT. Clearly, members of the public can afford to fall on their posteriors on discount furniture, but such falls are beneath the dignity of MPs.

Meanwhile, the Estate is also getting a new visitors centre. We have bad vibes about the likely final costs. The builders asked for a five week extension on the building time, which will mean an extra £100,000 (plus VAT) for the quantity surveyors and £230,000 for the builders. We assume that no bad publicity will arise from this, as four contracts from the £12 million project are classified as being to do with "public information", so we assume at least one of them is a PR company.

Now the political parties want to get in on the act. Aside from certain loons lobbying to push their own take-home pay beyond the stratosphere, some politicians are asking for the taxpayer to fund their parties to the tune of £28 million a year. Maybe if they didn't spend so much on ludicrous election expenses or on mega-expensive advisers and spin doctors, they wouldn't get into such dire financial straits in the first place. We believe that state funding of political parties will only encourage them in their bad ways. Far better for parties to be funded by lots of small donations, so why not let small ones be tax-deductible, as with donations to charity? It'll also keep the bigwigs listening to their grass roots.

Despite the laudable objections of some politicians, sitting MPs are also now being given £10,000 budgets to pump out propaganda. Ostensibly this is for producing leaflets to tell constituents what they are doing, but in reality it is a slush fund that will allow sitting members to campaign at state expense for years in between elections and churn out campaign material, selling the incumbent and reminding their voters why he is a good egg and deserves to be re-elected next time round. It is absolutely disgraceful, and we encourage our readers to send us the worst examples of these taxpayer-funded excesses so we can build up a Hall of Shame.

Having made such a mess of the Lords Reform, the government meanwhile continues to advance a variety of ludicrous schemes that will extend such gravy-ness to the red benches too. Attempts to create an elected House of Lords will only create a competing Chamber, whose members will by definition include a batch of second-raters roped in to make up the numbers in a hurry, and who are driven to establish their own power base and get their mugs on the telly. Of course, they'll need their own budgets to handle "constituents" (the same people represented by the MPs); they'll need their own staff; they'll demand all the perks that MPs get; and it will all be index-linked. A pointer we already have comes from the daft idea to create a Speaker of the Lords, whose job was already being done by the Lord Chancellor anyhow, in a Chamber which by tradition doesn't get rowdy enough to require a chairman, and who gets paid superstar wages (around £102,000 per year, plus £34,000 in allowances, and a state apartment).

It is yet another quango-style plum post that provides the taxpayer with no discernible benefit. And yes, if the current incumbent believes we have insulted the new post unfairly, send round the men in tights and drag us before the Chamber for an apology. But let's turn aside from these unwholesome innovations and summarise the nation's woes.

Over the last decade and a half, Government has seen fit to take ever more money from you in taxes and spend it on your behalf. But has it been value for money? Over the last ten years, according to the Government's own stats and definitions:

- School funding has gone up by 62% in real terms, but GCSE top grades have improved by 10.5%.

- Further Education colleges have seen funding go up by 48%, but average student success rates go up by 19%.

- Higher Education input went up by 11%, but the number of top degrees by 5%.

Remember too that this is against a background of grade inflation.

So simply throwing £18 billion a year extra into the system might make improvements, but they might not be the improvements you could have gotten if you had targeted the money more wisely. Or again, the same improvements could have been made with less cost and therefore less tax take.

Or look at it this way. Below is a table looking at five years when spending went up in the NHS. The number of patients in hospitals went up, but the number of beds went down. That's beds as in 'beds', not beds as in 'trolleys in corridors to keep waiting time statistics down'.

Year	Beds	Patients admitted
2001-02	197,833	25,138
2002-03	197,932	25,554
2003-04	198,433	26,202
2004-05	195,376	27,108
2005-06	189,816	28,252

Why is that? Well look at the figures of where the increase in the NHS budget went in 2005. Some of it makes it to the patient. But so much doesn't – depending on how you view it, as much as two thirds.

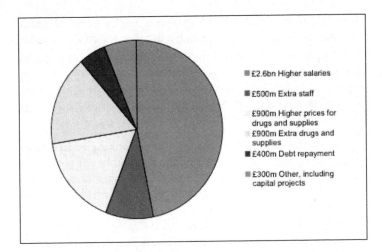

- ■ £2.6bn Higher salaries
- ■ £500m Extra staff
- □ £900m Higher prices for drugs and supplies
- □ £900m Extra drugs and supplies
- ■ £400m Debt repayment
- ▨ £300m Other, including capital projects

Of course, this simple chart can't even begin to take in the waste as well – the higher costs from PFIs that fall under debt repayment, or the £85 million a year the NHS should be saving by using cheaper versions of cholesterol-busting drugs, statins, that have been on the market for years and are as good as the new stuff.

Money spent by the state, even on good causes, has to come from somewhere. It comes, of course, from taxation in all its forms. It could be from taxing you directly; it could be from taxing something you do voluntarily or involuntarily; it could be from taxing you where you work. The end result is that the state is spending that money for you. The more it takes, the less you have left to spend, either to improve your family's lifestyle, or invest for an uncertain future. The more it takes, the less your business can expand; the fewer new jobs it can create; the more at risk it is should a recession strike.

It is not immoral to support lower taxes. Lower taxes over the long term actually mean more tax coming in, as low tax economies grow faster. This means that the government's share of the tax take might be smaller, but the pot is bigger from which that percentage comes.

So we shouldn't fall for the old guilt trip pushed by government tax thieves. It might at first seem harsh to keep state costs under control, but in fact over the longer term you are increasing individual wealth, developing a stronger economy, and building a bigger and more lasting share for public services. It is actually the confiscation of so much of people's wealth that is inhuman. Although it may be for decent motives, you are condemning society to penury rather than opening up a road for improvement. Excessive tax-and-spend is misguided and flawed benevolence.

Take the Irish example. Charlie McCreevy remembers the arguments well:

> "Back in the 1990s when, as Ireland's Minister of Finance, I started cutting taxes, many people feared that the loss of revenue to the exchequer would be massive and that the policy would have to be abandoned. But the opposite happened. Far from the policy causing an erosion of the Exchequer's revenue stream, reduced tax rates generated higher economic activity, greater tax compliance and a surge in the tax take for the exchequer... the policy was an essential part of Ireland's economic boom. Inward investment rose strongly, economic growth has been at levels more commonly associated with a Far East tiger economy than Europe and the overall tax-take – with much reduced rates on business, income and capital gains – has grown well ahead of expectations."

It is perhaps no surprise then to learn that the light-touch lower tax economy of the Irish Republic has outperformed the burdened economy of Scotland by a factor of approaching 5:1. Even if both received subsidy (Ireland from the EU, Scotland from the UK Exchequer), the comparison in growth rates is shocking – 61.2% versus 13.5% over six years. As Lord Forsyth, who chaired the independent Tax Reform

Commission, notes:

> *"Ireland is not alone. Australia, Austria, Belgium, Canada, the Czech Republic, Denmark, Estonia, Finland, France, Germany, Greece, Holland, Hong Kong, Hungary, Italy, Korea, Mexico, Poland, Portugal, Spain, Slovakia, New Zealand have all been simplifying, flattening or cutting rates with some dramatic results. In government, we cut the top rate of tax from 83% to 40% and the top 10% of earners contributed more, up from 32% to 45% of the total. Capital gains, dividend and income tax cuts in the US in 2003 were followed by a 14.6% increase in income tax receipts and a 42.3% increase in corporate tax take."*

That way of thinking is currently under threat. Some politicians have for years shouted out that any attempt to cut back on how much the state takes from our pockets is tantamount to closing down hospital wards with every announcement.

This is clearly nonsense. Even the present government found over £20 billion of waste in the system, and as it's the people who put it there who found it, you can bet your bottom dollar that there is a darned sight more.

Our calculations, supported by the European Central Bank, indicate that the government is only hitting one quarter of the potential target, and perhaps one eighth if you consider that so much of the 'savings' are in fact only juggling costs from one budget to another.

Meanwhile, the main opposition parties identify individual items, but fall shy of recognising the problem as a whole. Politicians are afraid of being targeted by their lazy opponents as reckless and feckless. These days, most politicians seem to imagine that the public will see them as some kind of latter-day French *tricoteuse* rampaging from building to building with lit torch and streaking hair, cackling maniacally as sundry peace loving citizens see their schools go up in flames.

We give more credit to the British people. Moreover, many journalists are also beginning to see through the charade.

Lower taxes, less waste, and responsible spending are all hallmarks of a successful and growing economy that generate more wealth and more money for our frontline services.

Taxes also have to be planned sensibly. That means realising that if you plan taxes to punish people, you may end up losing their skills as they go overseas, or close their businesses and open them up somewhere else.

Or again, if you plan taxes for headlines rather than for actual benefit, governments must acknowledge they too risk paying a price themselves. If, for example, as a minister you rush through a tax on flights without consideration for the travel companies who have to collect it retrospectively, you have to accept that the public isn't going to think that you are particularly competent when they are nobbled with a tax bucket at the airport check-in desk.

We should not expect our politicians and civil servants to be flawless. But we trust that, when confronted by the realities of unnecessary tax burdens and shocking waste, they should at least yield to the principles of good government and common sense.

About the TaxPayers' Alliance

The TaxPayers' Alliance, launched in 2004, is Britain's independent grassroots campaign for lower taxes. After years of being ignored by politicians of all parties, the TPA is committed to forcing politicians to listen to ordinary taxpayers. To achieve this it has offices in London and Birmingham with six full-time staff and over 15,000 supporters, including some of Britain's best-known businessmen and academics.

The TPA's mission is:

- To reverse the perception that big government is necessary and irreversible
- To explain the benefits of a low tax economy
- To give taxpayers a voice in the corridors of power

To this end, the TaxPayers' Alliance will:

- Oppose all tax rises
- Oppose EU tax harmonisation
- Seek the abolition of inheritance tax
- Criticise all examples of wasteful and unnecessary spending
- Champion opportunities for votes on tax and spend

We welcome people of all parties and of none who want to stand up to the way the state press-gangs our wallet. We support all democrats who highlight the shameful frittering away of our money, be they Liberal Democrats, Conservatives, or Labour.

Some campaign organisations are criticised as 'astroturf' – bodies with fake grassroots. The TPA is not one of them. We are the grassy knoll of the fight against tax and waste.

TPA Grassroots Campaigning

By Tim Aker, TPA Grassroots Co-ordinator

Many of you reading this edition of the *Bumper Book of Government Waste* will ask "what can we do about the mess we're in?" Frustrated, you'll want to take action but won't know exactly what to do.

Since the last edition of the *Bumper Book*, we have expanded our grassroots activism. It's my job to see things are done, that we can do something about high taxes and incompetent politicians.

The position we are in, as a country, has taken decades of encroachment by those in favour of waste and big government. Countering this will, similarly, take years of hard effort. But it is not impossible.

A number of our activists and supporters have emailed or called in asking precisely what can be done. Short of a pitchfork rebellion, I simply say that it's a matter of talking to one person at a time, house by house and street by street if necessary, and convincing them that big government is the cause of the problems and not the solution.

Just think how many years politicians have told us taxes need to rise. How long have we heard the mantra that to get better public services, we need to pay more to government? Just as the big government consensus didn't come overnight, nor will reversing it. It's up to all of us in favour of lower taxes to leaflet, convince, call local radio, write letters, campaign and get active in favour of lower taxes and better government.

If you want to get involved and make change happen instead of just hoping for it, email me at tim.aker@taxpayersalliance.com so we can get you involved in our campaign. Things can change if we do something about it!

Further Reading

Books

For essential statistics on all aspects of public life:

Britain in Numbers: The Essential Statistics, Simon Briscoe, Politico's, 2005

To see just what a mess the welfare system is, look no further than one of the guides to it:

Welfare Benefits and Tax Credits Handbook 2007-08, 9th edition, Child Poverty Action Group, 2007

For a *Bumper Book*-style analysis on the silly rules and regulations that are strangling Britain, see:

How to Label a Goat, Ross Clark, Harriman House, 2006

For an overview of the TPA's modus operandi:

Death by a Thousand Cuts: The Fight over Taxing Inherited Wealth, Michael J. Graetz and Ian Shapiro, Princeton, 2005

On how to reform the EU:

Plan B for Europe: Lost Opportunities in the EU Constitution Debate, edited by Lee Rotherham, EUbookshop.com, 2004

The big picture:

For Good and Evil: The Impact of Taxes on the Course of Civilisation, Charles Adams, Madison Books, 2001

Reports

For the best tax reform proposal to come from any party in recent years – pity the Conservative leadership has not pledged to adopt it in full:

Tax Matters: Reforming the Tax System, The Tax Reform Commission, October 2006

A mixed bag from the Liberal Democrats on tax:

Reducing the Burden, Policy Paper No.81, Liberal Democrat Party, July 2007

For a summary of the negative effects of recent government spending rises, see:

Public Spending 1999-00 to 2009-10, Corin Taylor, Reform, December 2005

For a description of a new public spending rule to put them right, see:

The Growth Rule, Corin Taylor, Reform, February 2005

For an up-to-date Growth Rule calculation, see:

UK Growth and Opportunity: the Need for a Fundamental Reassessment, Professor Nick Bosanquet, Andrew Haldenby et. al., Reform, March 2007

Websites

The department that puts up all our taxes:
www.hmt.gov.uk

The department that collects all our taxes:
www.hm-treasury.gov.uk

Tax Freedom Day
www.adamsmith.org/tax/

The TaxPayers' Alliance, leading the fightback from taxpayers:
www.taxpayersalliance.com

Appendix 1: Better Government

The following paper forms the basis of the TPA's Better Government campaign. As well as seeking to reduce our tax burden, we are also trying to find ways to improve the quality of public services, to give taxpayers value for money. This is a short summary of Better Government analysis.

Better Government

The current system of government is failing the nation

- Successive governments, under both the major parties, have increasingly taken responsibility away from civil society and local government. Compared with 1900, politicians have increased the share of national income they control from 12% to 45% and the number of people they employ from 6% to 35% of the workforce.

- But an objective appraisal shows that this centralisation of power into the hands of a few ministers has failed to provide even adequate public services or to serve the poor and disadvantaged. Below are just three examples.

The evidence of failure

Education is the means whereby individuals can raise themselves out of poverty and the country can compete in the global market. Yet after 11 years of schooling, at a cost of £75,000 per pupil, our state-managed education system:

- fails 4 out of 10 pupils, who leave school without the minimum standards in English and Maths that the QCA deems necessary for 'Life, Learning and Work';

- fails 6 out of 10 pupils who do not achieve a GCSE grade C or better in the three core subjects; and

- provides Britain with the second highest level of low-skilled workers out of the 30 OECD countries.

Healthcare provided by the National Health Service is ranked:

- as just about the worst of 19 peer countries by the British Medical Journal and the EU; and

- as having the highest rate of hospital-acquired infections, such as MRSA, by the National Audit Office.

Crime levels in England and Wales are the third highest of 39 peer countries.

It is, of course, the poor and disadvantaged who get the worst education, the worst healthcare, and suffer the highest rates of crime. With a large unskilled and uneducated workforce, the future prosperity of the country and the wellbeing of its citizens are bleak.

The reasons why politicians fail as managers

1. Politicians lack management experience

- Politicians do not have the management experience or the in-depth knowledge to become the chief executives of the largest, most complex and most diverse organisations in the country – the NHS employs 1.3 million staff, the Home Office 350,000 – and they change their roles too frequently to learn. In the last 10 years, John Reid has had 9 different Ministerial posts and the Department of Transport has had 7 separate Ministers.

- It is difficult to name a successful business, charity or football club where the three senior management positions (Secretary of State, Minister of State, Parliamentary Under-Secretary of State) are held by unqualified, inexperienced executives, who change after two years in office.

2. 'Public services' are monopolies

- The services that politicians manage are monopolies. Yet in every other area the government's Competition Commission protects the public by ensuring that organisations do not create monopolies. Government is right to prohibit monopolies as they:

- remove the basic tools of management;
- kill the need to innovate, improve and reduce costs; and
- focus on serving their own ends and not the customer.

How politicians can get themselves out of management and retain democratic control

The principles:

- Politicians should set high-level policy but they should never manage its execution.

- Execution should by done by people who have the management experience and the in-depth knowledge of each area.

- Monopolies should be broken up wherever possible.

The outcomes should be dramatic

- The organisations, listed below, doubled their output once monopoly status and political management were removed. BT, which was typical, not only increased its productivity by 2.8 times but it also increased the quality and choice of services while reducing prices by 40%.

Increase in output per person pre and post de-nationalisation 1979 to 1994	
British Coal	341%
BT	180%
Cable & Wireless	123%
BAA	115%
British Steel	104%
Electricity	100%
Rolls Royce	100%
British Gas	73%
British Airways	14%

- There is no reason to think that similar increases in quality, choice and cost reduction would not be achieved in today's 'Public Services'.

Appendix 2: Ending EU fraud

Earlier in the book, we referred to an important text showing how reform of the EU could in part be achieved. The background to this text is that a few years ago, around two hundred politicians from across the continent met to debate during the 'Convention on the Future of Europe'. Rather than fix the existing problems, they decided to add a whole range of new ones by drafting the EU Constitution.

But the debating process did come up with some solid observations and some concrete proposals, which could still be taken up. One paper submitted was 'Systems of Mismanagement' by David Heathcoat-Amory, MP. Reproduced on the following pages, it draws on the experiences of six whistleblowers who had emerged from anonymity when their attempts to stop fraud were blocked from within. In every case, their efforts to do some good were rewarded by the system crushing them for trying.

'Systems of Mismanagement' is an official, and unique, proposal. It's still on the table, because the EU Constitution got blocked when it failed to pass the Dutch and French referenda. Anyone with a desk in government who is reading this book could do worse than to mull over the lessons that it provides.

Systems of Mismanagement

A submission to the Convention on the Future of Europe by the Rt Hon David Heathcoat-Amory, MP

As the Convention turns to 'The Policies and Functioning of the Union' (Part III), it may be worth a moment's review of how elements of the Communities are presently being mismanaged; how attempts to correct these failings are being stonewalled; and what the Heads of Government could do to achieve reform and restore public confidence.

Certainly, the system needs to be fundamentally repaired before we contemplate adding even more powers and responsibilities to those who manage it.

I am referring to the issue of fraud, which is close to being institutionalised in key sectors of the Union.

After the scandals which led to the unprecedented resignation of the Santer Commission in 1999, there followed promise of major reform. A Commission Vice-President was charged with overseeing the task. However, the promised reform has failed to materialise. The European Court of Auditors continues its annual tradition of refusing discharge for the budget (a practice now in its eighth year). The last independent audit of the Commission Treasury took place ten years ago. No change to the Commission accounting system has yet taken place, despite three years of promises.

Faced with these management failures, a political solution has been suggested – the European Public Prosecutor. But this is the wrong answer to the wrong question. Quite aside from the political consequences that lie with the establishment of a supra-national agency, and on top of all the concerns over democratic accountability, it will be doomed to follow in the tracks of its predecessor. Just as the anti-fraud unit OLAF adopted its predecessor UCLAF's blinkers and flaws, the proposed new fraud investigative agency will carry over the current operational failings – except that it will have extra powers to ruin honest peoples' lives in the process.

Instead of more political institutions, we need a real reform of the system. To establish how this must be achieved, we have first to analyse something of the fraud and other failings which have come to light, which has only happened because of the determination and selflessness of whistleblowers.

The Price of Truth

Their lot is indeed not a "comfortable position", as one privately explained. The personal experiences of several confirm a general trend. Initial complaints are filed away in the system.

The real grief is reserved for the persistent, those who have witnessed too much corruption or nepotism and have had enough. Then, the administrative machine kicks in. The employee is hauled in before his or her senior grades, who try to determine precisely how much he knows before instructing him to keep silent. When the frustrated individual then sees ranks close around the fraud, he is driven outside the "usual channels" – typically to MEPs, MPs, or national authorities.

The price is a heavy one: suspension (perhaps on half pay); transfer to a department to 'count light bulbs'; legal proceedings; pay stoppage; internal isolation; depravation of support staff; and sometimes the sack, when the whistleblower hasn't been induced to quit. Health frequently suffers. The Sword of Damocles finally falls. Pension entitlements are lost; a promising career is finished.

And all for nothing. Because someone has spoken out, the institutions have an even greater need to cover over their failings. The fraud goes on regardless. To quote senior whistleblowing auditor Robert Watt, "My colleagues have learned how pointless it is to risk their careers for the public interest."

It doesn't end there. Beyond the competent authorities refusing to investigate even claims which are easily checkable (such as nepotism in an institution - a post being created to accommodate a relative, for instance), there have been several reports of attempts to intimidate witnesses. To quote another whistleblower, "Staff are simply too scared to speak out".

Across the Board

Not all Communities' whistleblowers are alike, and while they share a rare combination of propriety and public duty that goes (for them) dangerously beyond their own self-interest, their stories are different ones.

They are to be found across the institutions: the Commission, European Parliament, Committee of the Regions, and Court of Auditors have all faced them in different guises. They might be an *administrative* whistleblower (exposing the breaking of treaty law, for instance); they may be *structural* and expose organised and major fraud; or they might be from a lower staff grade and expose the *systematic* - "common fraud".

Amongst the latter types of fraud have been listed: overclaiming on airline tickets; the disappearance of keyboards; the siphoning off of thousands of six packs of typewriter ribbons and printer cartridges; and sick leave claims. It is fair to concede that cases of such 'petty larceny' are likely in any large and impersonalised institution, but not to the extent where such fraud has become an unofficially-sanctioned bonus that compensates for other elements of the work package. Such a climate engenders fraud higher up the chain. To quote Carol Thompson, a whistleblower at the European Parliament –

"People put on blinkers and see what they want to see. You will never change anything much unless everyone has a crisis of conscience."

There is certainly a great deal of scope for embezzlement at all levels. The annual Communities budget presently stands at some 100 billion Euros. Of this, 85% lies in the Structural and the Agricultural funds. These are run by the member states, but lie under the supervision of the Commission, which has a responsibility to ensure the money is properly accounted for and misspent money is reclaimed. The remaining 15% is managed directly, and was the cause of the fall of the Santer Commission. In any event, what is clear is that all this money should be properly accounted for, whether managed directly or indirectly by the Commission.

The proposal to create a European Public Prosecutor (EPP) as a solution is based on flawed premises. This is demonstrable through case history. In 1993, the Head of Division responsible for tobacco subsidies died suddenly in suspicious circumstances. Ten years on, the Communities authorities have yet to adequately follow this up, because the old operating practices and attitudes had been passed on to the new investigative body. There is an institutionalised omerta in the higher ranks of the administration - which has, incidentally, been linked to masonry. The failure of the investigating organisation to pursue the case despite the opportunities presented sets a poor precedent for the EPP – "a catalogue of material failures in the performance of the inter-related EU systems of administration, internal control, external control, fraud investigation and political oversight". The stakes are high: representatives of the tobacco industry are reported to have informed the Court of Auditors that the mafia makes 60 million Euros from the tobacco market in Southern Italy every year.

What can be done?

These faults may be serious, but with a new work atmosphere they are surmountable. The institutions need a radical management overhaul and fresh blood, to inject transparency and openness, with an increased role for national institutions (which are harder to subvert, and further removed from the institutions that encourage the political protection of particular Commission members).

The Heads of Government, as they reflect upon the Draft Constitution in its complete form, will have an ideal opportunity to discuss this. There may be opportunities to incorporate elements into the Constitution guaranteeing these changes.

External Input: There has to be an external review of the accounting system of the Communities funds. This could be by providing a formal role for budgetary control committees in national parliaments. Past experience has demonstrated that the European Parliament cannot be guaranteed to rise above party politics in respect to individual Commissioners. If the European Parliament cannot act the role of guarantor, that leaves national assemblies. This could be linked in with individual Commissioners being appointed by national parliaments, being responsible before them, and being sackable by them.

More national secondees should be appointed to replace, on a short-term, rolling basis, key officials of the European institutions. While this may slightly slow down proceedings as new staff come up to speed, this more than offsets the benefit of stopping 'fraud footholds' being created. A study could even be made on the practicality of replacing all European civil servants with nationally-delegated staff in this way, in order to end conflicting political loyalties.

Audit Reform: It should mean something that accounts have to be signed off by the Court of Auditors and the European Parliament. Where a budget is not endorsed in this way, non-essential funding under the budget line should be blocked until it is signed off. If this does not occur within two years, the line is clearly flawed and should fall.

However, the Court of Auditors itself is not above criticism. One option would be to ensure that it is comprised solely of professional national auditors on a short-term rolling basis, headed by an auditor of repute appointed by the national governments, and responsible before the European Parliament and the Council, either of which can fire him for mismanagement. (Presently fifteen 'Principle Auditors' posts operate by roulement, on a renewable two years basis, while the Members of the Court itself are appointed for a renewable six year period.)

To quote whistleblowing auditor Robert Watt –

"Financial accountability underpins political accountability; and when neither the accounts nor the audit are reliable, the financial and

the political legitimacy of the European endeavour is undermined."

Investigative Reform: The present status of OLAF is untenable. It should be granted operational independence under a respected figure subject to democratic scrutiny and appropriate disciplinary powers. All cases passed to it should be subject to an obligation to pursue, and its findings should be published. Consideration might even be given to providing for its headquarters to be physically at a remove from those of other European institutions. Evidence of malpractise shall be forwarded to national authorities to pursue in their own right; the investigative authority would continue to monitor such pursuit, however.

Transparency: Employees of the Communities should be required to declare membership of societies and organisations likely to affect their activities, particularly freemasonry. Communities officials should also be barred from attending closed meetings of 'bridging organisations' whose purpose (like the Bridge Forum Dialogue or similar 'sponsored' meetings) is to bring together senior officials in private discussion. The Commission for its part should be depoliticised, and its efforts put towards transparency of policy, rather than penning newspapers articles or appearing in campaigns or television programmes espousing partisan political views

EU Whistleblower Rights: In the light of the present lack of options open to employees of the Communities who seek redress against institutional failings, the Convention may care to consider including a Communities whistleblower clause setting out the principle of the right of free speech where normal avenues have been blocked. Perhaps this could include the establishment of a right of any employee to appeal directly to the EP Budgetary Control Committee; perhaps there is room for increasing the scope of the Ombudsman; perhaps again, a right of referral to a national parliament Public Accounts Committee by a national appointee. Dossiers presented should not be withheld from the public domain (subject solely to the principles of restrictive classification of national documents, and prejudicing ongoing and genuine investigations). Likewise, European Court of Auditors reports should be made public as a matter of course.

Countdown on fraud: There have been too many promises of reform, and instances of cover up, to expect serious reform without incentive. A fraud deadline should therefore be imposed; a six months period for the present Commission to report on how it has in that timeframe corrected the current abuses in the system. After this period, and failing this turnaround, a temporary Fraud Czar would be appointed to carry out real reform and the Commission would be sacked, and replaced by figures with a reputation for tackling organised crime, corruption, and gangsterism. This would be a simple extension of the reasoning behind the establishment of the Committee of Wise Men to look into the Santer Commission.

Conclusion

Patently, there are many employees of the Communities who carry out their tasks efficiently, fairly, and honourably. But their activities and the honour of their institutions – and with it, the respect of the European citizens for these institutions – are sullied by the failings around them.

Corruption is a human failing, and without entering into the religious debate in the Convention by an analysis of Original Sin, the fault of the individual. But the systematic cover up of these faults, not once but as a matter of course, is a failing of the system itself.

In one case, the authorities have been seen to have failed to act against fraud through fear of running into Trades Union action. But most employees are honest people, who do not down tools to support dishonest colleagues. There can be no excuse for inactivity.

Inaction suppresses reform, and drives the chance of reform away. "My actions have always been 'in the interest of the Service and the taxpayer'," explained one whistleblower. "I thought I could jump on the bandwagon and deny the existence of these problems but I cannot. However, I am sure that there is more to life than standing by watching the taxpayers' money flow out of control through loopholes in the Regulations."

To quote another whistleblower, "There is no incentive to reveal wrong-doing in the European institutions, other than the self-knowledge of having served the public interest."

But the cost of such public service interest is widely known at present to be prohibitively high.

How are we to have faith in the ability of the institutions to manage even more powers, when the suspicion lingers that they cannot even look after the ones they presently hold? The time has indeed come to flood the Augean stables.